PETRARCH'S GENIUS

PETRARCH'S GENIUS

PENTIMENTO AND PROPHECY

MARJORIE O'ROURKE BOYLE

University of California Press
Berkeley · Los Angeles · Oxford

University of California Press
Berkeley and Los Angeles, California

University of California Press, Ltd.
Oxford, England

©1991 by
The Regents of the University of California

Library of Congress Cataloging-in-Publication Data

Boyle, Marjorie O'Rourke, 1943–
   Petrarch's genius : pentimento and prophecy / Marjorie O'Rourke Boyle.
     p.   cm.
   Includes bibliographical references and index.
   ISBN 0-520-07293-6 (alk. paper)
   1. Petrarca, Francesco, 1304–1374—Criticism and interpretation.
2. Petrarca, Francesco, 1304–1374—Knowledge—Religion. I. Title.
PQ4543.B69   1991
851'.1—dc20   90-19877
                                                                                                         CIP

Printed in the United States of America
9 8 7 6 5 4 3 2 1

The paper used in this publication meets the minimum requirements of American National Standard for Information Sciences—Permanence of Paper for Printed Library Materials, ANSI Z39.48-1984. ♾

To Brendan

And, lo, you are to them like one who sings love songs with a beautiful voice and plays well on an instrument, for they hear what you say, but they will not do it. When this comes—and come it will!—then they will know that a prophet has been among them.

                              Ezekiel 33:32–33

Contents

Introduction	1
1. Hail, True Apollo!	11
2. The Sylvan Citizen	44
3. The Babylonian Captive	74
4. Wounded Lovers	113
Epilogue	153
Notes	159
Primary Sources	207
Index of Petrarch's Works	213
Index of Names	214

Introduction

Petrarch the plaintive lover is so familiar a figure that he has solidified into Petrarchism. His love, as he wrote in the initial poem of his *Rime sparse,* made him "the talk of the town." Yet this phrase echoes an ancient prophetic complaint about the contempt of the populace for oracles (Lam. 3:14; cf. Job 30:9, Ps. 69:12). If Petrarch personally courted a woman in verse, he also publicly criticized the Avignon papacy. The lyricist of love struck a political chord. In hearing the polysemy of his verse we may recognize that a prophet has indeed been among us (epigraph). This book is about Petrarch the poet as theologian.

As Petrarch has commonly been interpreted as oscillating, sometimes in torment, between sacred and secular values, some critics would consider his piety problematical. The issue is not whether Petrarch was a sinner, however, but whether he was a theologian. These are not mutually exclusive states; in the human condition they coexist. Theologians wrote prolifically about sin. If the reformers and the satirists are correct, they did so from much personal experience. In fourteenth-century spirituality penitence was the vogue, a penitence so exorbitant as to be erroneous.[1]

It is one opinion that Petrarch's poetry is about sin, quite another that it *is* sin. This has been identified as "the sin of idolatry," whether thematically or semiologically.[2] In the original interpretation, the meditation of Petrarch the lover (who is the poet) converts the phantasm of the beloved Laura into a beautiful idol, in archetypal violation of the first commandment. This idolatry that perverts the beatific vision of God is central to the *Rime sparse,* whose very theme is the unresolved conflict in Petrarch between love and religion.[3] In a development of this argument, the thematics of idolatry is stated as necessary to create a poetic presence that is autonomous. The poetry becomes "semiological idolatry."[4]

Petrarch the poet as irreligious, even idolatrous, is the legacy of an obsolete historiography that demarcated the Middle Ages and the Renaissance as sacred and secular cultures.[5] In consequence the piety of the medieval poet may be sincere, but the piety of the Renaissance poet must be ironic. As Petrarch is precariously positioned between those cultures as Janus-faced, his piety must be suspicious: ambivalent, or at least ambiguous. The historiographical probability may be that what the periodization has discerned is not a difference between the sacred and the secular, but rather two different ways of apprehending the sacred: the one by distinction, the other by diffusion; the one by antithesis, the other by analogy. This tension persists with varying emphasis throughout the history of theology and the practice of religion.

The status of Petrarch as *poeta-theologus* need not be denied because his aspiration and achievement of it may differ from that of Dante as *poeta-theologus*,[6] as if that medieval model were the only sacral model. Another figure adduced as historical proof of Petrarch's impiety is his brother Gherardo as the Carthusian monk. Yet Petrarch's writings to and about him are not historical record but epideictic rhetoric.[7] This literature requires for its interpretation a sophistication in its moral topicality, regressing to the fraternal paradigm of Cain and Abel, who offered different religious sacrifices, vegetable and animal.[8] The historical evidence is that Gherardo was not a monk at Montrieux but only a rendered cleric. In the hierarchy at that charterhouse, this juridical status was by civil contract not by religious vow.[9] Both Gherardo and Francesco seem to have been lowly ecclesiastics, the one at but not in a monastery, the other largely at large in the world.[10] It is instructive to compare the brothers, not in the theological categories of belief and unbelief, but in the sociological categories of the institutionalization or privatization of belief.

The dismissal of Petrarch's piety is also influenced by modernist literary criticism, which evaluates and values texts as ironic. His poetry is legitimated by its interpretation as the inversion and perversion of sacred into secular values. This subversion of literature has been contested by theorists and humanists who question the validity or utility of projecting modernism anachronistically. The case for irony has been roundly rejected for the meaning of another poetic masterpiece, the *Roman de la rose*.[11] In that case irony is adduced as a device to read the text as religious; in the case of the *Rime sparse,* to read it as irreligious. In both cases the imposition of irony is allied with historiographical assumptions about the relation of religion and culture and fabricated from a quasi- or pseudo-scholarship about theology. Petrarch's poetics is not modernist but humanist, an allegory of truth toward the purpose of virtue. Yet the criticism of his poetry as irreligious interprets the *Rime sparse* not in continuity with this poetics, or his other poetry, but in continuity with the *De secreto conflictu mearum curarum,* or *Secretum,* as if that were its prose version and hermeneutics.

Petrarch's poetics is a humanist ideal. It may have eluded him both poetically and personally. His lyrics lament its evanescence both thematically and imitatively. His charitable purpose toward the civic good may have been flawed by cupidinous ambition for personal fame. Politically, the ideal just failed. Truth and justice did not meet, nor righteousness and peace embrace; nor did the lion lie down with the lamb. There was no inauguration of a golden age, except perhaps as poetry. The tension in the *Rime sparse* is not essentially, however, a moral conflict of sin and grace. The crucial tension is not that of a divided self (warped will) but that of a frustrated self (feeble, failing, futile genius). The Petrarchan problem, as distinguished from the moral problem, is the poetical illusion and political impasse of language and reality.

The poetics of idolatry is most especially the invention of a theological naïveté. This confuses the fictional Augustinus of the *Secretum* with the historical Augustine and, more grievously, assumes that the anti-rhetoric of either is normative for Christian faith. The asceticism of Augustinus that demands Franciscus's renunciation of his poetic gift is spiritual pathology. The notion that human art contradicts, obstructs, or rivals the love of God is perverse. The authentic experience of God in the Judeo-Christian traditions is not the negation but the fulfillment of human nature. Although an antagonistic dualism between human and divine creations recurs in Christian culture, dualism has consistently been refuted, as in the ecclesiastical condemnation of the Manichaean and Albigensian heresies. It is intelligible that Petrarch, who survived in a century whose criterion of sanctity pitched otherworldliness to its zenith, may have been troubled in conscience by such fears. If so, he did well to banish them. There were also circulating in that century strong religious currents of *this*-worldliness, as in the laicized piety of the tertiary and confraternity movements. To cite but one example of piety that would have encouraged poetry, there was a shift in the practice of prayer from a contemplation that was transcendental, intellectual, and iconoclastic to a meditation that was incarnational, affective, and imaginative, as in Petrarch's own consideration of Christ crucified.

Petrarch's poetics and poetry argue that Augustinus is a devil's advocate, a straw man, into whose mouth Petrarch inserts a polemic against art as carnal and therefore unchristian. And although criticism has assumed that the counsel of Augustinus is the religious commandment, it is rather the conscience of Franciscus that is sound in mind and soul. While the argument of Franciscus that poetry does not impede but encourages the love of God contradicts that of the fictional Augustinus, it coincides with that of the historical Augustine. That theologian taught that every human act originates in love, whether as cupidity or charity, and intends the good. Augustine's validation of rhetoric was to convert its concupiscent nature, as he judged it, to a charitable end.[12] Although the enthusiastic promotion of rhetoric by humanists such as Petrarch exceeded its wary tolerance by "humanists" such as Augustine, it was not the sin of idolatry.

The authority of Augustine cannot be argued for a poetics of idolatry. It is the established premise of scholarship in religion that his thought is suffused (some would argue, invaded) with Greek and Oriental wisdoms; hence the necessity of discriminating the authentic in the development of Christian doctrine.[13] His theology is not divine verity but human concept, and as such is subjected to much discussion and disagreement. Even a devout scholar has rejected his aesthetics as transcendental rather than incarnational.[14] The semiotics of Augustine has been extensively documented as Stoic.[15] Petrarch's poetic displacement of this referentiality with autoreflexion or reification cannot constitute "the sin of idolatry," or "semiological idolatry."[16] To dissent from Augustine's semiotics is merely to be un-Stoic, not ungodly. The option is irrelevant to God, religion, and the first commandment.

The burden of proof—in an adequate theological argument for the concept—is on critics who wish to retain the thesis of a poetics of idolatry. The very notion is, to this theologian, irrational and irreligious. Scripture as the norm of Christian faith is rhetoric, including poetry, even some erotic poetry. Petrarch himself argued from this premise. If the first commandment is rhetoric, how can it be idolatrous to write rhetoric? The illicit love of a woman, moreover, is not idolatry but lust, in transgression of the sixth and not the first commandment. Petrarch's poetry might only be theoretically idolatrous in a universe of absolute dualism, the exemplar of which is not Augustine but Luther. The mature theology of Augustine rejected the doctrine of the radically fallen soul, with its implicit dualism, and established his magisterial speculation on the analogy, not the antithesis, of the human and the divine. The interpretation of Petrarch the poet as natural man limed on the laurel as the idolatrous manufacture of his own aesthetic grace is very Lutheran anthropology. Yet as Luther's anthropology is derived from premises that are philosophical—an absolutely necessitated metaphysical dualism and a logic of signification that excludes accidental attribution[17]—it does not represent a theological statement for the judgment of human art as idolatrous. It seems implausible for Petrarch's poetry to be any sort of sin, except in fundamentalism, which reads texts grammatically rather than rhetorically, and judges their "immorality" as in fundamentalist Christian censorship or fundamentalist Moslem persecution (the notorious case of Salman Rushdie's *The Satanic Verses*). If the concept of a literary persona is eliminated, so that the poet is recording his personal blasphemy or obscenity for which he is personally liable as sin, then the text is not poetry but history, not art but document.

These theoretical criticisms are supported by an alternative interpretation of Petrarch's poetics, as developed in this book. The argument for idolatry was developed from the *hapax legomenon* in *Rime sparse* 30 of *idolo,* read as "idol."[18] The noun *idolo* is derived from *eidolon* whose lexical meaning is: phantom, insubstantial form, image reflected in a mirror or water; image in the mind, idea. It has already been suggested that *idol* is a useful term only insofar as its meaning of "graven image" collapses repeatedly into the psychologistic meaning of "phantasm."[19] Yet it is unnecessary to retain the sense of *idol;* that of *image* suffices for the understanding of the poem. Its semantic referent is not Hebrew cult but Greek optics. This was a general science, which from antiquity through the Renaissance comprised a medical tradition of the anatomy and physiology of the eye and the treatment of ocular disease; a physical or philosophical tradition investigating questions of epistemology, psychology, and causation; and a mathematical tradition of geometrical explanation of the perception of space. The noun *eidolon* was a technical term in the intromissive theory of vision. As originated by the atomists and developed by the Aristotelians, intromission posited the eye as a passive organ that perceived through emanations from the external world. These emanations were corpuscular effluences that streamed from the surfaces of objects to impinge on the eye and cause the sensation of sight. An effluent particle or film in this process was an *eidolon*.[20] Although this hypothesis was disputed by the popular extromissive theory, it was entertained as late as Leonardo da Vinci's speculations on vision. That artist and scientist referred to visual impressions with the same word Petrarch employed, as *idoli*, equivalent in loose terminology to *simulacri, similitudini, species*, and *radii*.[21]

In this theory of vision through the impact of the efflux (*eidolon*) from objects, the particles or films convey shape and color.[22] In Aristotelian perception, light never occurs without color, which overlies the transparent and is visible only as a particular color is visible.[23] The matter of color indicates the aesthetic, not religious, context of Petrarch's poem. Its coloristic adjectives "gold" and "topaz" have been criticized as ironic inversions of scriptural and contemplative symbolism. Petrarch allegedly adores his idol in violation of the psalmist's avowal to love the commandments more than gold and topaz.[24] This reference is arbitrary. There were in the late medieval arts various competing systems of color symbolism, so that they effectively cancel each other out. The humanist Lorenzo Valla would frankly mock the enterprise. Unless there is a contextual cue, such as a heraldic device or a liturgical vestment, for deciding the meaning of a color, the detection of a secret code is futile.[25]

The issue of color was not historically one of "meaning" but of the tension and transition between material and skill. Petrarch was a participant in this important artistic debate. Color meant the application of pigment, but especially the application of colors manifested in objects as illumination altered lights and darks. Color coincided with the reception of light, and it involved the art of manipulating tones and hues, so overlapping with relief. Petrarch's poetic twining of gold and topaz is in reference to an artistic sensitivity to the relative splendor of hues as a medium of emphasis. Importance was designated in medieval art by accenting with a valuable pigment, especially gold, the quality of which was stipulated in contracts. The eye was attracted by expensive colors ground from precious metals and stones before the cheap colors of plain earth. Yet by the fifteenth century there was a general shift from medieval gilt splendor. The conspicuous display of gold was replaced by artistic skill as the natural alternative to precious pigment. The most consistent and prominent motif in the discussion of the arts in the early Renaissance, whether aesthetic or ascetical, was the dichotomy between the quality of material and the quality of skill. A proponent of skill was Leon B. Alberti, who argued that artists should represent golden objects not with real gold but by an application of yellow and white pigments mixed.[26]

Yet the principle had already been famously chiseled in stone by Abbot Suger over the central portal of the Abbey Church of St-Denis:

> Whoever thou art, if thou seekest
> to extol the glory of these doors;
> Marvel not at the gold and the expense
> but at the craftsmanship of the work.

His poetic admonition argued the aesthetic that the architectural carvings should enlighten the mind, not merely dazzle the eye. Those who entered through its golden door should arrive at the true door, or Christ. The dull mind rises to truth through what is material; in seeing its light it is resurrected from submersion in matter.[27] This was an ideal to which Petrarch aspired, although he hardly found its execution easy. He introduced the argument in a dialogue in which Reason rebuked Delight for reveling in the costly expense of vain colors like real gold.

It is this text, *De remediis utriusque fortunae,* and not *De secreto conflictu mearum curarum,* that provides the hermeneutics for Petrarch's *idolo.* In this dialogue Reason criticizes Delight for gawking at paintings in ignorance of the self, which surpasses all art and nature. Art should prudently direct the gaze of the mind to the archetype and to its Creator. As to sculpture, it is closer to Nature and to virtue than is painting. Yet an image of gold should not be esteemed for its cost more than one of clay, but evaluated for the quality of the workmanship. What is noble may be made of vile matter, while what is of pure gold may be rude. Reason argues the examples of a massive "gold" image of the kings of Assyria and a great "topaz" image of the queen of Egypt as promoting wonder more at the material than at the skill. It is this argument in Petrarch's own literature that provides the context of the "gold and topaz" in the poem: the fundamental artistic debate concerning material and skill. What is the correct coloring of images? How to represent the aesthetic light? Reason argues that images should not be enticements to the eyes but monuments to virtue, such as the statues erected in honor of Scipio Africanus, the liberator of Italy. They should honor wise and learned men—the humanist ideal—not merely pander to the vanity of rich merchants. Art must serve virtue. In that service Petrarch exalted skill over material.[28] He aspired to color his poetry not with the crass gilt of rhetorical ornament but with a skillful mixture of pigments, as in the more sophisticated understanding of invention and imitation.

Petrarch's *idolo* is not an idolatrous parody of religion but a humanist *paragone* of art. The comparison of literature with painting and sculpture was a topic of classical rhetoric. In Petrarch's imitation it was axiomatic and prescriptive, a prototype of the humanist habit.[29] His *idolo* is a sculpture: "my image carved in living laurel."[30] The visual image of his poetics is a wood carving; perhaps, as was the fashion, painted polychromatically and set with jewels. But it was not an idol.

An idol was in medieval thought derived from "fraud" (*dolus*), because the devil conveyed to a created object worship appropriate to the divine being. Idolatry was the vice of the alien heathen. Idolators were the ancient pagans whose culture endured in texts and art, the Moslems against whom Christians warred to regain the Holy Land, and the Jews who rejected the gospel. The conventional artistic forms were the figure on a column and the statue within a shuttered niche. Idols could be fat little creatures, elegant nudes with shields, amorphous gobs of gold, or, most radically, blanks on the page. The most common idols were depicted as devils, naked and black, and the most ubiquitous of these had the attributes of Mars. In the fourteenth century idols were extended from these types to include objects of daily symbolic value like money, so that the common usurer could be an idolator before the god Money. Templars and homosexuals were also accused of idolatry.[31]

There is in modern criticism an erroneous concept of medieval idolatry that is essential to a certain reading of "courtly" literature as sacral in significance. Woman is construed as an image on a pedestal to be adored by the lover or demolished by the iconoclast.[32] The interpretation of Petrarch's poetic image as an idol belongs to this sectarian school by parallelism, if not by derivation, of argument. Its premise of a monolithic ecclesiastical culture is gratuitous. To borrow the felicitous metaphor of one of its legion of critics: it assumes that medieval society was a gigantic monastery presided over by the spectre of Augustine.[33] All authors were ruled by his doctrine of charity, so that if one should seem to write a secular poem, he must be understood as writing a religious one, by allegory or irony. The real irony is the survival in Italian criticism of this moralism, which has been rejected by most medievalists for the other vernacular literatures.

The quality of Petrarch's poetic image is aesthetic vividness not religious perversion: "my image carved in *living* laurel." In writing on the visual arts, "lifelike" was a commonplace, as in Ovid's waxen image of a husband away at war that evokes embraces from the wife,[34] or in Dante's angel so gracefully carved that it seems poised to move and speak.[35] With the medieval revival of sculpture, the sculptor was called "master of living stone" to acknowledge the power of the three-dimensional medium for resemblance. Sculpture was considered superior to painting because of its tactile presence, not as a picture reflecting but as an object confronting.[36] Petrarch conventionally praises as almost breathing the bronze horses of San Marco in Venice and a polychrome stucco relief at Sant'Ambrogio in Milan.[37] His poetic image as "carved in living laurel" is a humanist comparison of the arts emphasizing this virtue of realism: vividness.

A clarity so vivid as to render the absent present was *enargeia*. This was the classical term for the representation of reality that evoked a physical, primarily visual, scene in all its line, texture, and color. It was a stylistic effect that appealed to the senses and so described the object that the listener became a spectator. With emphasis on the sense of sight, it thrust itself upon his notice by displaying facts in living truth to the eye of the mind. This vivid pictorial description penetrated to the very emotions. It was the essential painterly skill in literature. As an ornament its achievement was the greatest of all rhetorical gifts.[38] As *en-argeia* means a "bringing into light," and to bring things into the light is to bring them into a field of visual perception,[39] Petrarch's use of the optical term *idolo* is appropriate to the rhetorical ideal. His poetry aspires to be as vivid as sculpture in the representation of reality. The issue of Petrarch's *idolo* is not religious but aesthetic: not whether to adore it but how to adorn it.

Although the interpretation of an idolatrous poetics has discerned religious import where there is none, the more common interpretation of Petrarch has failed to discern it where it is. Humanists like Petrarch developed a rhetorical theology that deserves understanding and appreciation. It should not be dismissed as false and meaningless because its expression is neither scholastic nor monastic. The important and incontrovertible fact is that Petrarch did not capitulate to asceticism: he did not quit writing poetry. This was not, as Augustinus and his sympathizers would allege, because he was a slackard and a sinner. It was because he was able to summon from the scriptural norm, traditional resources, and personal conscience a theological alternative. This book examines how he justified his decision, how he developed his vocation.

What, then, is to be understood by Petrarch's assertion that he practiced an art that was sacred by a genius divinely endowed? Irony? idolatry? ambivalence and ambiguity? The moralizing in literary criticism has been based on judgments that are not literary but religious. Yet although historians have addressed Petrarch the poet as theologian,[40] no theologian yet has. The responsibility for misinterpretation thus reverts not to scholars of Petrarch but to those who are not scholars of Petrarch: the theologians who have ignored this and other major authors in the Christian tradition. Although the reasons for this neglect vary within the Catholic and Protestant traditions, they share a common denominator in intellectualism, whether the intellectualism of reason or of faith. It is because rhetoric historically was orientated affectively toward the persuasion of the will that it has been professionally disdained. It was composed religiously on Augustine's model of condescension to a human frailty that needs to be stimulated and entertained toward morality.[41] Rhetoric was especially a sop to the laity. In the medieval tradition into which Petrarch was born, it was the academic business of theology to translate scripture as divine baby talk (the nursing mother was a favorite metaphor for the text) into human adult language by dialectically elevating its images to ideas.

A hermeneutical and exegetical revolution since the late nineteenth century has through historical and literary criticism restored scripture as rhetoric to its legitimate religious status. This validation of scripture as rhetoric is filtering through the history of theology to an evaluation of the tradition as rhetoric. The research may prove as revisionist as in scriptural studies. This orientation on Petrarch the poet as theologian is by a theologian who is a specialist in the history of method, particularly the rhetorical tradition. It is derived from a reading of his complete literature,[42] to integrate the standard division of labor by which critics read the poetry and historians the prose, so as to promote better collaboration between the disciplines. Although the emergent portrait may vary from that of the collective imagination, it seems cogent to relinquish moralizing about Petrarch the sinner and resume research on Petrarch the humanist.

I

Hail, True Apollo!

The ancient march commenced in the Campus Martius, processed through circuses and theaters, circled the Palatine, and then by the Via Sacra traversed the Roman Forum to ascend the Capitoline to Jupiter's temple.[1] Yet Petrarch braved the ideal route of Scipio Africanus, for it was his poetic celebration of that hero that merited him the laurel wreath on 8 April 1341:

> I too, when fifteen centuries had passed
> through their appointed cycles, greatly strove
> with all the means my meager strength allowed
> to follow o'er the rough and thorny path
> those precious traces and to imitate
> with similar crown, like site, and glorious name,
> the ancient heroes and their dignities
> sublime, lest what the Greek bard had foretold
> of me might prove a faulty prophecy.[2]

At his departure from Avignon for this momentous journey, he had anticipated the envy his triumph might provoke. Despite his insistence that his art was considerable,[3] his epic *Africa,* although conceived three years prior, was still in progress.[4] Two decades later friends continued to importune its publication. Petrarch died, however, refusing to release the manuscript, which was only rescued by intrigue from the flames, if not from the revisionists. Only with the turn of the century was the heralded epic published.[5]

Before the laurel had wilted on his brow, however, Petrarch, inflated by the praise, was inspired to revive the desultory project.[6] The most ambitious epic since antiquity, *Africa* was to honor in nine books the military exploits of Scipio Africanus the Elder during the Second Punic War to defeat Hannibal's encroachment on the Roman empire. Already Petrarch had shown—probably recited—a partial manuscript to King Robert of Naples, whose patronage of the Roman coronation he had solicited. Impressed with the endeavor, the monarch had asked for its dedication to himself,[7] which request the poet obliged, while promising a worthier sequel to praise the valor of that modern hero.[8] This royal approval of *Africa* issued in a document that conferred on Petrarch not only the coveted insignia of the laurel wreath but also the privilege of crowning other poets; the faculty of reading, debating, and interpreting ancient and modern literature, and the rights of the professors of the liberal arts; the titles of honorific "great poet and historian" and of academic "master"; and Roman citizenship.[9] Although the epic would fail to equal the formal excellence of classical verse, its enterprise was historic. Petrarch's celebration of Scipio's brave deeds in noble words was designed to elicit patriotic spirit by a new humanist reconciliation of history, poetry, and philosophy.[10] Its program absorbed the poet and the monarch in conversation and in contest just prior to Petrarch's coronation. In these private and public examinations, Petrarch excelled in the defense of poetry.[11]

Petrarch's presentation at court rehearsed the oration he would deliver on the Capitoline. In that brief collation on a Vergilian verse, he declaimed the mutual difficulty and desire of poetry, its allegorical truth, and its reward of glory, immortality, and the laurel.[12] In that oration a motif emerged that distinguished Petrarch's poetics: the *sacred* art. A Christian tradition had countenanced poetry as a figurative imitation of the truth, and thus a reflection of divine verity. As Petrarch acknowledged this theory anagogically, poetry beheld the same light as did philosophy or history, but by oblique illumination. He argued that although poetry clouded this truth in fiction, its perception might prove the sweeter for its arduous discovery.[13] This native difficulty of the art, and its delight, Petrarch related to the necessity of divine inspiration. By reviving a classical equation of poetry with theology, he exceeded and challenged Christian poetics, which had tolerated the art as a mere propadeutic to theology. "The inherent difficulty of the poet's task lies in this," he proposed, contemplating his own ascent of Parnassus, "that whereas in the other arts one may attain his goal through sheer toil and study, it is far otherwise with the art of poetry, in which nothing can be accomplished unless a certain inner and divinely given energy is infused in the poet's spirit." He cited Cicero's testimony in *Pro Archia,* a manuscript of which he had enthusiastically discovered, that "'whereas attainment in other activities depends upon talent, learning, and skill, the poet attains through his very nature, is moved by the energy that is within his mind, and is as it were inspired by a divine inbreathing—so that Ennius fairly calls poets sacred in their own right, since they appear to be commended to us by the possession of a divine gift.'" He also recalled the nobility of mind and the indomitable spirit that Juvenal ascribed to poets as beholding the faces of the gods. And he exclaimed with Lucan: "Sacred and great is the task of the poets."[14]

This sacred status Petrarch notably expounded in an apologetical epistle for his first eclogue. The pastoral genre of the *Bucolicum carmen*, he explained, suited his intention of commenting safely on controversial matters through a veil of ambiguity that few readers would penetrate, although many would enjoy it.[15] Such poetic artifice would not, he feared, charm his brother Gherardo, who was contracted as a Carthusian cleric to asceticism. Petrarch argued with him, therefore, that his poetic eclogue was not the antithesis of religious fervor. "In truth," he wrote, "poetry is not in the least contrary to theology. Does this astonish you? I might almost say that theology is the poetry of God." This definition of theology as rhetorical rather than dialectical, in humanist confrontation with scholastic method, Petrarch reinforced with examples of scriptural figures rather than syllogistic conclusions. "What else is it if not poetry," he asked, "when Christ is called a lion or a lamb or a worm? In Sacred Scripture you will find thousands of such examples too numerous to pursue here." Indeed, he continued, the Savior himself invented parables or allegories, the very texture of poetry, which weaves together the subjects of God and man. Petrarch traced the pedigree of the poet as theologian to the authority of Aristotle. He offered the etymology of *poet* as further proof of this identity, for the word originated in the effort of primitive man to create a religious homage not in common speech but in uncommon language, one that was artful, exquisite, and novel, in Greek called *poetices*. To the anticipated rejoinder of his brother that poetic sweetness contradicted religious severity, Petrarch adduced the precedent of the Hebrew prophetic and sapiential literature, especially the psalms, whose author deserved the title "the poet of the Christians," since he sang metrically of Christ. In patristic literature, moreover, Ambrose, Augustine, and Jerome employed poetical forms and rhythms, as did those devout Christian poets Prudentius, Prosper, and Sedulius. A practice so approved by the saints should not be spurned, Petrarch proposed. As a principle one should rather embrace the intended meaning of a text, if it is true and salutary, regardless of its style. "To praise food served in an earthen vessel while feeling disgust at the same meal served on a golden platter is either a sign of madness or hypocrisy," he concluded.[16]

It was fitting, therefore, that in the exordium of his coronation speech Petrarch termed his oration "theological," although he declared that he would refrain from elaborating the distinctions that were usual in such declamations. It was theological precisely because it lauded poetry defined as an allegory of the truth.[17] Before him Albertino Mussato, who had been awarded the laurel in 1315 at Padua,[18] had proclaimed poetry a heaven-sent knowledge, a science by divine right. Poetry was a philosophy to rival Aristotle's. It was "a second theology." This poetics had provoked an altercation between Mussato and the friar Giovannino of Mantua concerning the divine versus human origin and nature of poetry.[19] In the reverberating debate Petrarch championed poetry as divine in origin, holy in purpose. As he had concurred with the ancient author, "Sacred and great is the task of the poets."[20] These exalted sentiments countered the modest role that poetry had been assigned in Christian apologetics. As rhetor and doctor of grace, Augustine defined its status for centuries of Latin authors by cleaving Horace's designation of poetry as a unity of profit and pleasure: poetry as "useful and enjoyable."[21] In Augustine's distinction the enjoyable rendered men blessed, while the useful merely aided and sustained their movement toward blessedness. A confusion of the useful with the enjoyable impeded and deflected men from their true course, restraining or even preventing by the shackles of an inferior devotion their attainment of sanctity. Although he acknowledged that truth, wherever discovered, was universally the Lord's, Augustine advised that the arts and sciences were not to be embraced, but rather to be assessed soberly for their utility, and then applied moderately to the quest for beatitude. He appropriated the Mosaic principle of despoiling the Egyptians (Ex. 3:22, 11:2, 12:35–36), by which the Christian might plunder the treasuries of antiquity while eschewing their idols. The Christian was to be ever mindful in this practice, however, that in comparison with biblical wisdom, pagan knowledge was slight and neither promoted nor ensured salvation.[22] This theology was the fruit of Augustine's tortuous conversion from the ardor and ambition of a secular profession to that of a sacral vocation. His own experience of subordinating, then sublimating, aesthetics to rapture recapitulated a patristic tradition that had asserted the unique claims of the gospel by reducing, if not denying, those of the arts. Guilt dogged Christians who favored the Muses. Reflecting in senescence on his literature, Augustine regretted that he had attributed so much to the liberal arts, when many saints were ignorant of them and many learned in them were not saints.[23]

From the perspective of his own old age, Petrarch defended poetry by indicating that the Fathers had established doctrine on a foundation of the classics, as fortifying and consoling human experience. While he thus exploited the Christian appreciation of secular study, he subverted and exceeded it by rebuking the remorse of the elder Augustine. If learning was unnecessary to piety, Petrarch ventured, neither was it an impediment. "I know of many who have attained to extraordinary sanctity without literature," he acknowledged, "but none do I know who has been hindered from it by literature." In considering the diverse paths to salvation, he stated that, although every such pilgrimage was blessed, "the more enlightened and sublime the route is, surely, the more glorious, whence the devotions of the cultured and the rustic are incomparable." Propose any saint from the illiterate herd, he challenged, and he would counter with a holier one from the learned class.[24] The ray, however oblique, that had symbolized poetry in his coronation speech, Petrarch still affirmed as more gracious than the pall of ignorance and more pious than blind faith.

This reversal of values was famously argued in *De secreto conflictu mearum curarum*,[25] Petrarch's fictional dialogue with a mock Augustine cast in the role of philosopher-physician. Assiduously the saint plied the poet with the ascetical commonplaces. A vivid and profound reflection on death and misery, he advised, together with a passionate desire and drive for ascent, would repel all worldly seductions. By subjecting the carnal to the spiritual in accordance with the golden mean, virtue would yield Franciscus true happiness in triumph over poetic melancholy. Yet this voluntarist theodicy, in which perfect knowledge of one's evil condition assured perfect will to supersede it, faltered on Franciscus's own experience. The poet summoned Truth itself as a witness to the futility of such a cure. To Augustinus's rejoinder that his will for health was merely self-deception, Franciscus initially agreed. "From my youth upwards I have had the increasing conviction," he said, "that if in any matter I was inclined to think differently from yourself I was certain to be wrong." Observing that Franciscus was agreeing with his argument "more out of deference than conviction," Augustinus invited him, "Pray feel at liberty to say whatever your real judgment suggests."[26]

As the dialogue progressed, the abrasion of Augustinus's asceticism on Franciscus's passion goaded him to the formation of conscience: a mature conscience as established in his experience rather than one merely derived from authority. He dared to state that the honored maxims Augustinus adduced were to him but "paltry pleas." He boldly asked: "But I beg you will produce some more solid arguments than these, if you know any, for experience has taught me that all this is more specious than convincing." Augustinus's appeal to Franciscus's conscience as an incitement to shame for his base affections testified contradictorily to the poet's ardent love for things eternal. Poetry, he eloquently parried, has a mind disdainful of earth, zealous of heaven; a visage radiant with divine beauty; a character of perfect honor; a voice and vision of immortality; a form and rhythm unique. This affirmation Augustinus angrily denounced as falsehood. The charm of poetry, he charged, had only allured Franciscus to a ruinous neglect of virtue. "She has detached your mind from the love of heavenly things and has inclined your heart to love the creature more than the Creator." To Franciscus's protest that "the love which I feel for her has most certainly led me to God," Augustinus retorted that it had rather "inverted the true order." Creatures were to be cherished for their Creator, not the Artificer for the art. Yet Petrarch refused to concede, and avowed that he would remain steadfast even under torture against such allegations of depravity. He had loved the soul more than the form of his mistress, he declared. He thus rejected as impossible Augustinus's moral of a flight to freedom, or at least to imprisonment by a milder discipline. There was no substitute for poetry, which he continued to compose.[27]

The conversation was classically therapeutic.[28] It healed Franciscus's wounds, not by application of the patent medicine Augustinus prescribed, but by perception of the truth, which the dialogical process itself manifested. Augustinus was ultimately not the magistrate, however well he may have served as the master. Both interlocutors were subject to Truth, the silent judge of their colloquy. Franciscus expressed his gratitude for its patient witnessing of their discourse. He then concurred with Augustinus's parting admonition to be true to himself—for he could not be faithful to God if he betrayed himself—and turned to his daily occupations. These, especially poetry, were so much of himself that to renounce them ascetically would transgress the principle of truth.

"To her," he explained in personifying his poetic art, "to her I owe whatever I am, and I should never have attained such little renown and glory as I have unless she by the power of this love had quickened into life the feeble germ of virtue that Nature has sown in my heart. It was she who turned my youthful soul away from all that was base, who drew me as it were by a grappling chain and forced me to look upwards."[29] In celebrating his art in the vernacular verse of his *Rime sparse,* Petrarch lauded poetry as a heavenly Idea born in paradise, who is divinely revealed yet clothed in humanity. She is an illumination that manifests heaven on earth, a testimony to its beatitude. Her eyes, he affirmed, beam "a sweet light that shows me the way that leads to Heaven." By her glance she turns his thoughts toward salvation. "She is indeed blessed," he exclaimed, "who can make others blessed with her sight."[30] Franciscus thus concluded his deliberations with Augustinus: "I am not ignorant that, as you said a few minutes before, it would be much safer for me to attend only to the care of my soul, to relinquish altogether every bypath and follow the straight path of the way to salvation. But I have not the strength to resist that old bent for study altogether." To Augustinus's reluctant blessing on his choice Franciscus added: "May God lead me safe and whole out of so many crooked ways; that I may follow the Voice that calls me."[31]

That "heavenly siren" who lured him was the "invisible form" of truth, as liberated in paradise from the poetic veil; or the "naked" truth that language cloaks on earth. That "voice, pleasing even in Heaven" called Petrarch from beyond, admonishing him to spurn the attractions of the world, begging him not to delay in elevating his soul. "From there she rules me, from there she forces me," he stated. "Nor do I beg her to set me free, for all other paths to Heaven are less straight."[32] Petrarch thus rejected the ascetical commonplace expressed by Augustinus that poetry, like all secular science, is a deviant occupation that deflects men from beatitude. Considering the path to salvation, he asserted that "no one who participates in honorable activity may be excluded" from it.[33] His declaration that poetry is the most direct path inferred that it is also the most honorable. Petrarch defended poetry vigorously against the dialectical argument that since it was by the Horatian canon for pleasure and for ornament, it was therefore less noble in proportion as it was less necessary. Madness! cried Petrarch. "If necessity enobles the arts, the most noble of all would therefore be the shoemaker's, the baker's and the other lowest of mechanical trades." But as Aristotle himself affirmed, he reminded the critics, while these trades were more necessary than philosophy and all the arts that render life blessed, cultivated, and adorned, they were not more worthy.[34] Petrarch insisted that it is the poetic laurel that indicates "the straight way to Heaven"; indeed, all other paths are less direct.[35]

Thus it was that Petrarch honored poetry:

> "From her comes the amorous thought that, while you follow it, sends you toward the highest good, little valuing what other men desire;
>
> "from her comes the courageous joy that leads you to Heaven along a straight path, so that already I go high with hope."[36]

And, he prayed: "Let her meet me, and let her draw and call me to herself, to be what she is in Heaven," for as he averred, "my highest desire is to be permitted to follow her . . . by a straight and unimpeded road." Praising his heavenly guide, he wrote:

> She teaches me to go straight up, and I, who understand her chaste allurements and her just prayers with their sweet, low, pitying murmur,
>
> I must rule and bend myself according to her because of the sweetness I take from her words, which would have the power to make a stone weep.[37]

Ignorance—"the level road of the lazy"[38]—Petrarch thus rejected for the heady ascent of Parnassus, at whose cloud-capped summit he gazed from the Capitoline on that triumphal Easter of 1341. Had not Augustinus unwittingly urged him there? "You would indeed be of all men the most miserable were you to try to arrive at the truth through the absurdities of the crowd, or to suppose that under the leadership of blind guides you would reach the light," the saint had advised. "You must avoid the common beaten track and set your aspirations higher; take the way marked by the steps of very few who have gone before, if you would be counted worthy to hear the Poet's word—

> On, brave lad, on! your courage leading you,
> So only Heaven is scaled."[39]

His mentor hardly imagined the ironic subversion of this advice, by which Petrarch would abandon *him* as purblind. Nor did Augustinus perceive the ambiguity in his own liberal citation of classical poets to illustrate his refutation of their art. From the tedious compendium of ascetical rules the "saint" proffered, Petrarch selected this essential principle: "Listen only to that Holy Spirit who is ever calling, and in urgent words saying, 'Here is the way to your native country, your true home.' You know what He would bring to mind; what paths for your feet, what dangers to avoid. If you would be safe and free obey His voice. . . . Follow the lead which the inspirations of your own soul give you."[40] Franciscus prayed in response: "May God lead me safe and whole out of so many crooked ways; that I may follow the Voice that calls me."[41]

In a celebrated letter narrating an allegorical ascent of Mont Ventoux,[42] Petrarch illustrated the divergent paths to blessedness: the shortcut, direct but steep, of religious profession and the highway, smooth but meandering, of secular occupation. At its unclouded summit, a visionary Petrarch imitated the conversionary experiences of Augustine and Anthony, but as prompted by reading a different sort of text. The conversions of the bishop and anchorite, as symbolizing the active and the contemplative offices in the Church, had been through ascetical precepts: "Not in revelling and drunkenness, not in debauchery and licentiousness, not in quarrelling and jealousy. But put on the Lord Jesus Christ, and make no provision for the flesh, to gratify its desires" (Rom. 13: 13–14); and, "If you would be perfect, go, sell what you possess and give to the poor, and you will have treasure in heaven; and come, follow me" (Matt. 19:21). The text of Petrarch's admoniton was illuminative rather than purgative: "And they go to admire the summits of mountains and the vast billows of the sea and the broadest rivers and the expanses of the oceans and the revolutions of the stars and they overlook themselves." This injunction of Augustine's provoked Petrarch to rage because of his admiration from Ventoux of the natural scenery rather than of the human mind. From the exterior vista he thus turned his eyes to interior reflection.[43] The dictum "What could be found within they go seeking without" became monitory for Petrarch's own poetic quest for the truth.[44] It guided him "from thought to thought, from mountain to mountain," as he ascended and descended poëtizing, ever elevating his mind by the contemplation of the beautiful idea.[45] In retrospect from that insight, the physical altitude of Ventoux seemed to him squat in comparison with the spiritual loftiness of man, once unstuck from the mud in which he had wallowed since the Fall, and uplifted to the dignity of his standing in Christ.[46] "Tear off the veil; disperse the shadows," Augustinus had urged.[47] On Ventoux, Petrarch stood entranced. There above the clouds in the sacred ether common to Athos and Olympus, he perceived the translucent truth to which his allegorical path had led him.[48] The veil was rent, the shadows were banished. The summit of sanctity was revealed through interior vision. And in such introspection, in obedience to the interior vision rather than the exterior spectacle, Petrarch was to encounter his genius.

Classically, genius was innate talent, particularly as associated with invention. It was opposed to art as the skill learned by rule and imitation. The phrase "art and genius" (*ars et ingenium*) became a critical and polemical concept in the medieval defense of poetry.[49] In medieval authors the term *genius* acquired associations that created a dimension of meaning, on a scale from cleverness to prophecy, that had not been inherent in the classical texts from which they derived the antithesis.[50] In psychology and poetry it became a mental faculty that comprised noble and base impulses: the capacity of the will toward comprehension of the arts and its curiosity toward transitory images.[51] In the usage of Dante, the constituents of genius were natural instinct, intuition for the investigation of reality, perception of sensory impressions, and transmission to memory. Genius encompassed the ability to discern the particular purposes and ends of life and the poetical source and origin of the imaginative and aesthetic world. It was an instinct to be controlled by reason, as in rhetorical invention, lest the mind be determined toward a distorted object.[52] Yet from the classical poetics derived from Platonism and recorded by Cicero, Horace, and Seneca there endured a concept of genius as involving inspiration and insight that are divine. The poetic theory of the Renaissance was profoundly influenced by this, and it was in this tradition that Petrarch wrote.[53]

A genius was originally the tutelary spirit that so animated nature as to reside in every plow, every plot, for the peasants who cultivated the Italian soil in antiquity. This animism was particularly embodied in the genius of the family, whose generative power spiritually symbolized physical semen. The Latin word *genius* was derived from *gignere*, "to engender," a fitting description for the spirit who ensured the propagation of the crops and the clan. In the earliest literary allusions to it, in the comedy of Plautus, the concept was extended beyond the paterfamilias to represent the vital fluid of every male, his virility, his energy. With the introduction of Greek polytheism and philosophy to Italian culture, this generative spirit was transferred to other paternal figures—the founders of cities and of institutions, then the gods, the senate and the plebs, the emperor, and finally the Roman state. As deified, the genius was the personal double of every man, guiding him from womb to tomb, regulating his fortune for good or evil, and demanding honor and propitiation. In Horace's important verse, the genius was "the companion which controls the natal star; the god of human nature, in that he is mortal for each person, with a changing expression, white or black." These popular beliefs were elaborated philosophically by the ascription of a genius, functioning as an agent of generation or of fate, to the universe. Astrologically, the genius as natal god determined the constellation or horoscope of an individual, and hence his temperament or destiny. Cosmologically, the procreative power of the genius was identified Stoically with the immanent reason of paternal Jupiter as world-soul.[54]

Although the Theodosian edict (A.D. 392) finally imposed capital punishment for sacrifice to the genius on one's birthday, the deity survived. The genius proved an impregnating spirit indeed in the fertile imaginations of medieval poets. The Roman piety of indulging the genius with sensual pleasures, especially food, so as to be "genial," promoted a medieval equation of genius with appetite, or concupiscence. The pagan genius, conforming to its phallic origin, was thus adapted for Christian moralizing. By appropriation from the Horatian definition of the genius as "the god of human nature," he was personified in Bernardus Silvestris's *Cosmographia* as the agent of natural descent, the concupiscent soul of microcosmic man. In Alain de Lille's *De planctu Naturae* this generative role was translated into a moralistic censure of homosexuality. The sacerdotal role by which, as priest of Nature, the genius also wed form and matter and excommunicated perverse sinners was appropriated and complicated in Jean de Meun's *Roman de la Rose*. There the genius as instinct, or cosmic priest of Nature, condemned chastity, while as reason, or earthly bishop of God, he exhorted virtue. A dualistic identity was maintained in John Gower's *Confessio Amantis,* in which the genius, as priest of Venus, shrove a lover and instructed him in the seven deadly sins by relating classical tales of distraught paramours.[55]

Not only did medieval allegorists exploit the procreative power of the genius for moralizing about lust and chastity. They also explored its creative power for developing a poetic theory, thus elevating natural genius to artistic invention. The Greek analogue of the Roman genius had been the daemon, or divine messenger. Traditionally he consorted with men through dreams and visions, whose phantoms became associated with the figures of poetic artifice. The dream-vision, which disguised the truth by integument, became incorporated into a literature of descent to the underworld. *De planctu Naturae, Roman de la Rose,* and *Confessio Amantis,* in which the genius figured allegorically, were all compositions of this genre. In that of Alain de Lille, Genius represented the archetypal poet Orpheus as the source of the artificial creation that secreted truths in a figurative envelope. In the vision of Jean de Meun, however, Orpheus was condemned as a poet and a pederast, and the falsity of his images was imputed to demonic provocation or human illusion. Gower concurred that fantasies disrupted psychosomatic harmony, and thus alienated man from Nature, but he argued that poetry, by concealing truth in fiction, soothed the soul, reconciled it to the body, and thereby regenerated man.[56] As metamorphosed in each author's vision, the internalized genius of the poet could thus serve a beneficent or a maleficent purpose. That fickle spirit, white or black, had so varied human fortune ever since antiquity.

When, in pondering his epic *Africa,* Petrarch expressed great confidence in his genius, he therefore acknowledged a complex convention sprung from the very soil on which he reclined in that secluded Tuscan valley of his own invention. As in the medieval allegories, the figure of his genius emerged in a dream-vision; moreover, one that adumbrated his poetics. At the climax of *Africa,* the bard Ennius theorized about poetry as an integument of truth, as had Petrarch in his coronation speech. Whoever would essay a poem, he said, must first establish

> "a firm foundation of the truth whereon
> he then may build a cloud-like structure, sweet
> and varied, veiling the foundation."

The labor of divining the truth would then be the sweeter for the exertion, he instructed. Poetic license extended to the subjects of history, natural science, and moral philosophy, yet not as those disciplines exposed the truth:

> "but to be disguised beneath
> a covering cloak, or better, a light veil
> which tricks the watcher's eye and now conceals
> and now discloses underlying truth."

A fabricator, one who did not compose from the truth, was neither a poet nor a seer, but a liar. This theory Ennius ascribed to Homer, of whose specter he had just dreamed during the Carthaginian contest. In his imaginary company, Ennius spied a youth plaiting a laurel wreath in contemplation of some noble task. Homer divulged his identity as one Franciscus, a Florentine who would in the future lure the exiled Muses back to Helicon with his song. Peerless for ten full centuries, he would worthily assemble the exploits of Scipio into a volume called *Africa*.

> "How great will be his faith in his own gifts [*ingenium*]!
> How strong the love of fame that leads him on!"

Finally, Homer prophesied, Franciscus would ascend the Capitoline in triumph to be crowned with the laurel whose fashioning he now rehearsed.[57]

Such confidence in the poetic genius as to attract the notice of those ancient bards exceeded the norm of Christian apologetics, however conventional Petrarch's explanation of the art as truth veiled in fiction was. His defense against the asceticism exemplified by Augustinus and Gherardo was to attribute to his poetic nature a divine origin: a genius, a lofty genius given him by heaven.[58] Its bestower he named as the god Apollo. This was no reversion to pagan religion, however, as Petrarch subscribed to anthropomorphism. The inventors of the arts, he thought, had been deified by the ill-advised gratitude of mortals, who were in fact committing sacrilege. "The harp," he stated, "has made a god of Apollo."[59] In adopting Apollo as his benefactor, Petrarch nevertheless departed from the tradition that had associated the genius, a paternal spirit, firmly with Jupiter.[60] The classical provinces of Apollo were prophecy, music, and medicine. Yet Petrarch in his coronation speech affirmed him as the source of his courage for the aspiration to Parnassus by ascent of the Capitoline. The triple impediments of poetry, he said—failed inspiration, bitter fortune, and public disdain—were surpassed by its triple allurements—the honor of the republic, the charm of personal glory, and the stimulation of one's confreres. "And I do not deny," he continued, "that in the struggle I have had the advantage of a certain genius given to me from on high by the giver of all good things, by God himself—that God who may rightly be called, in the words of Persius, 'Magister artis ingenique largitor' [Master of the arts and bestower of genius]." In lauding the laurel as a fitting reward, Petrarch specified his divine benefactor. A touch to the head with its foliage was believed to make dreams come true, and poets were said to sleep on Parnassus, he explained. Since the laurel moreover foretold the future, it was singularly the emblem of Apollo, the god of prophecy. "Accordingly," he concluded, "since Apollo was held to be the god of poets, it is no wonder that deserving poets were crowned with the very leafage of their own god, whom they regarded as their sustaining helper, whom they called the god of genius."[61]

As a precedent for this attribution, Petrarch described in *Africa* the genius of Ennius as Apolline:

> "since great Apollo gave you at your birth
> the heavenly talent [*ingenium*] which has won you fame,
> and goddesses, while you were still a child,
> immersed you in the sweet Castalian spring of sacred
> Helicon and led you forth
> to the high hills, bestowing on you there
> the pen and voice and spirit of a bard."

So the ancient poet praised "kind Apollo / the god of genius."[62] Although there was no historical evidence for the attribution of the natal genius to Apollo, Petrarch may have been inspired to it by a fragment of Ennius preserved in Cicero's *De divinatione*. That treatise defined the human soul as endowed with "an inherent power of presaging or of foreknowing infused into it from without, and made a part of it by the will of God." The abnormal development of that power was termed *furor*, a state in which the soul withdrew from the body and was vehemently excited by a divine impulse. Cicero illustrated the theory with a citation from Ennius's tragic *Alexander*, which thus explained the sudden rage and burning eyes of the prophetess Cassandra:

> "I have been sent to utter prophecies:
> Against my will Apollo drives me mad
> To revelation make of future ills."[63]

By identifying his natal genius with Apollo, Petrarch expressed the divine endowment of his poetic nature. It was one excited by a desire he was unable to curb, as Franciscus stated, despite the admonitions of Augustinus.[64] His would be a different devotion. Even the "saint" had recognized that in his zeal for poetic excellence Franciscus was "borne up on the wings of genius," although he had decried poetic genius as touched with madness.[65] It was not Augustinus, however, but King

Robert whom the aspirant Petrarch considered among all men "the judge of [my] genius."[66] Indeed, Petrarch compared him as the singular judge of the poetic gift with Augustus, the patron of Vergil.[67] In addressing Augustinus, whose advice he declined, Franciscus explained how the exigency of the human condition deflected him from the pursuit of higher values. With the ancients he attributed this psychic duality to a divine source. "It is not without reason, I imagine," he said, "that the poets of antiquity dedicated the double peaks of Parnassus to two different divinities. They desired to beg from Apollo, whom they called the god of Genius, the interior resources of the mind, and from Bacchus a plentiful supply of external goods." This perspective was recommended to him by the testimony of the wise and corroborated by his own experience. "Moreover," he continued, "although the plurality of deities may be ridiculous, this opinion of the poets is not devoid of common sense. And in referring a like twofold supplication to the one God from whom all good comes down, I do not think I can be called unreasonable, unless indeed you hold otherwise."[68]

Augustinus did hold otherwise. He wished Franciscus to descend not only from the base peak of Bacchus but also from the illusory peak of Apollo. Who was Apollo, his eponym had once asked, but a seer and physician identified with the sun by deluded pagans? In the very book that is Petrarch's first recorded purchase of a text, *De civitate Dei*, Augustine had scoffed at "poetical theology" and had refuted the very concept of the genius. "And what is Genius?" Augustine had inquired. Consulting Varro, he observed its worship as the potentate of everything born, or Jupiter, and again as the rational soul of every man. This contradiction, he argued, permitted the absurd conclusion that every man's soul was a god.[69] Petrarch, however, was not embroiled in polemics against paganism. From the secure perspective of a Christian culture he could envision a continuity of art and religion. Pagan symbols could be appropriated poetically, as in the stunning conceit of *Africa* in which Jupiter prophesied his incarnation:

> "Now hearken well. It is my fixed intent,
> since now the splendor of the earth is dimmed,
> once more among you to descend, assuming
> the shape and flesh and bondage which are man's;
> aye, and for love to suffer shameful death.
> . . . .
>   Already I
> am captive to a Maid, whose tender breasts
> seem now to soothe me with their flowing milk."[70]

When Petrarch identified the god of his genius as Apollo, he transgressed classical piety, which associated genius and Jupiter. When he further identified this genial Apollo with Christ, he affronted Christian piety. In the apology for poetical theology addressed to his brother Gherardo, Petrarch offered a key to the interpretation of his first eclogue. The shepherds Silvius and Monicus who conversed about their distinct vocations to the active and contemplative life were Petrarch and Gherardo themselves. In their rivalry over the superiority of classical or biblical verse, the figure of John the Baptist at the Jordan was recalled:

> "This I have heard: it is said that once on the shores of that sparkling
> River a hirsute youth laved the golden limbs of Apollo.
> Blest were the wavelets that were, if the tale I heard is a true one,
> Privileged to touch that immortal body."

"Apollo," Petrarch explained, "the son of Jupiter, is called the god of genius. For him I interpret Jesus Christ, true God and true son of God, the God, I emphasize, of genius and wisdom."[71]

With this allegory Petrarch upset the tradition of Christian apologetics that had refuted pagan religion by unmasking Apollo as a demon and discrediting his oracles as frenzied hallucinations. It was an argument that Petrarch certainly knew.[72] Origen had elaborated on it by ridiculing the method by which the Pythia at Delphi received Apollo's sacred utterance through a spiritual penetration of her womb. "Consider then," he proposed, "whether this does not indicate the impure and foul nature of that spirit in that it enters the soul of the prophetess, not by open and invisible pores which are far purer than the womb, but through the latter part which it would be wrong for a self-controlled and sensible man to look upon or, I might add, even to touch." The Pythia's frenzy and fainting in the oracular experience also evidenced to him a demonic origin, since true communion with a deity ensured clarity of vision. Origen further marveled that Apollo should have preferred to prophesy through a vulgar woman—and a married woman rather than a virgin at that—instead of through a wise man. Reflecting on the claim that the disembodied Apollo passed into the Pythia through her genitals, he preached: "But we hold no such opinion about Jesus and his power; the body born of a virgin consisted of human substance, capable of suffering wounds and death like other men." Christians, he summarized, "will not tolerate it if you compare Jesus with Apollo."[73]

As Lactantius (whom Petrarch cited) argued, the sign of the cross terrorized such demons. A pagan priest had no power to cure a demoniac by invoking the name of Apollo, whereas the same demons would flee in fear at the name of Christ. Indeed, at the name of the true God, the seer of Apollo would himself shudder, and Apollo would depart from him as quickly as a demon from a demoniac, since the pagan gods were merely impersonations of demons.[74] Gregory the Great verified this notion with the legend of the founding of the Benedictine oratory on Monte Cassino. The site was an ancient shrine of Apollo, in which groves the local peasants even in the Christian era still worshipped him with sacrifices. Saint Benedict destroyed the idol, overturned the altar, and cut down the groves. In the temple of Apollo he constructed a chapel in honor of St. Martin, and on the location of the pagan altar, a chapel in honor of St. John. He also converted many in the region by his preaching. The devil whom he had expelled from the site appeared to him in an open vision as a most foul and fiery creature who raged against him with flaming mouth and eyes.[75]

While most Christians might be assured by Saint Benedict's example that the Apolline demon could be abjured simply by prayer,[76] it was also observed that among the pagans Daphne alone had escaped the corruption of that prophet.[77] Tatian exulted: "You now I laud, O Daphne!—by conquering the incontinence of Apollo, you disproved his power of vaticination; for, not foreseeing what would occur to you, he derived no advantage from his art."[78] Like that chaste maiden who foiled Apollo's grasp, Christian poets obedient to such apologetics also spurned his art, or so they feigned. The exemplar of this rejection of the classical convention of poetry was the tenth poem of Paulinus of Nola. This verse was composed in the fourth century during its author's ascetical transit from a literary education and consular career, both as a pagan, to the office of a Christian bishop. Responding to the inquiry of his friend and mentor Ausonius, it delineated lucidly a conflict between classical and Christian modes of being a poet.[79]

> Why, father, do you bid the deposed Muses to return to my charge? Hearts dedicated to Christ reject the Latin Muses and exclude Apollo. Of old you and I shared common cause (our zeal was equal if our poetic resources were not) in summoning deaf Apollo from his cave at Delphi, invoking the Muses as deities, seeking from groves, or mountain ridges that gift of utterance bestowed by divine gift. But now another power, a greater God, inspires my mind and demands another way of life.[80]

That vocation demanded of Paulinus, as he testified, the surrender of his life to its divine source. It required the renunciation of the leisure that had traditionally fostered poetry. It bid him spurn the fictions of literature, which clouded the divine light with poetic invention. Of poets he wrote:

> These men steep our hearts in what is false and empty. They form only men's tongues, and bring nothing to bestow salvation or to clothe us in the truth. What good, what truth can they possess who do not have the Head of all, God who is the Kindling and the Source of truth and goodness, whom no man sees except in Christ?

As he evoked this new inspiration: "He is the light of truth. . . . He is the Sun of justice [righteousness]. . . . He has flashed his rays over our hearts."[81] With this resolute displacement of Apollo by Christ, refulgent in the solar imagery of the deity deposed, Paulinus affirmed his conversion. Like Augustine disciplining his concupiscence by Truth, he exposed his poetic fiction to the Light. "I was wayward," he confessed of his secular career in poetry, "my eyes enveloped in falsehood's darkness, wise in what God brands as foolishness, living on death's sustenance."[82]

Not all Christians who composed poetry shared his stern conviction of the incompatibility of artistic and religious commitments. Paulinus himself had attempted a reconciliation of classical and Christian pieties with a metaphor of Christ as repairing in his body the broken cithara of humanity, by plucking its strings while he hung crucified like a lyre.[83] Prudentius integrated the fractured commitments by giving a religious perspective to literary culture in a manner deserving of the title of Christian poet. Without artificial compromise he liberated pagan convention for new purpose, as inspired by an intellectual engagement with his faith.[84] Yet the search for an accommodation of the secular impulse toward poetry and the sacred injunction toward piety was fraught with tension. Could the Christian poet dismiss Paulinus's cry that the Muses were only "deaf nobodies," invocations to whom dissipated in the wind?[85] Was it not more certainly salvific to imitate his example and supplant the classical invocation to Apollo and the Muses with a prayer to Father, Son, or Spirit?[86] As Prudentius declared:

> I shall not summon Castalian Muses, the ghosts of poets, nor rouse deaf Phoebus from the Aonian rock. Christ will inspire my song, for it is

through Christ's gift that I, a sinner dare to tell of His saint and of heavenly things.[87]

Resounding with the new song of Christ, even Prudentius polemicized: "Apollo writhes when the name of Christ smites him, he cannot bear the lightnings of the Word, the lashing tongue torments him sorely whenever the praises of the God Christ's wonderful works are sounded."[88] And thus he spurned the classical emblem of coronation that Petrarch would covet:

> Put away, my Muse, the paltry ivy-leaves wherewith thou hast been wont to encircle thy brows; learn to weave mystic garlands and tie them with a band of dactyls, and wear thy hair wreathed with the praise of God.[89]

This was a decision Petrarch rued. In his visionary catalogue of poets, "Laurea occidens," the tenth eclogue of *Bucolicum carmen*, Petrarch surveyed the consequences of Christian poets spurning the laurel and the Muses:

> I saw a tawny-haired tiller [Arator], with clumsily fashioned plowshare
> Furrowing a sacred meadow, turning a soil rich and fertile;
> And as he labored, two workmen, one prudent [Prudentius], one
>   sedulous [Sedulius], followed,
> Striving with rigid harrows to break up the stubborn earth clods.
> Fecund the soil but the oxen were weary and there was no laurel
> Nor ivy nor myrtle nor any green for a garland, nor zealous
> Cult of the Muses, and voices were weak.[90]

As the cultural confrontation waned with the evangelization of Europe, however, poets ventured to revive the classical invocation, even in manifestly Christian verse. Dante apostrophized Apollo in undertaking *Paradiso:*

> O good Apollo, for this last labor make me
> such a vessel of your worth
> as you require for granting your beloved laurel.
>
> Thus far one peak of Parnassus has sufficed me,
> but now I have need of both, as I enter
> the arena that remains.
>
> Enter into my breast and breathe there
> as when you drew Marsyas from the sheath
> of his limbs.

> O divine Power, if you do so lend yourself
> to me that I may show forth the image
> of the blessed realm which is imprinted in my mind,
>
> you shall see me come to your beloved tree
> and crown me with those leaves of which the
> matter and you shall make me worthy.
>
> So rarely, father, are they gathered,
> for triumph of caesar or of poet—
> fault and shame of human wills—
>
> that the Peneian frond ought to beget
> gladness in the glad Delphid deity
> whenever it causes anyone to long for it.
>
> A great flame follows a little spark:
> perhaps, after me, prayer
> shall be offered with better voices that Cyrrha may respond.[91]

Yet this address was no more serious than similar invocations by classical poets when the religion that had inspired such entreaty dwindled to convention. Apollo would indeed find "a better voice" in Petrarch. He would be echoed by such a humanist as Giovanni Pico della Mirandola, who in his *Oratio de hominis dignitate* lauded "the true Apollo—not the fictive one—the one who enlightens every soul coming into this world, Christ himself."[92] Well after Petrarch composed his bold invocation to that deity, however, John Milton was still repeating the traditional Christian rejection of Apollo in his poem "On the Morning of Christ's Nativity":

> The Oracles are dum,
> No voice or hideous humm
>   Runs through the arched roof in words deceiving,
> *Apollo* from his shrine
> Can no more divine,
>   With hollow shriek the steep of *Delphos* leaving.
> No nightly trance, or breathed spell,
> Inspires the pale-ey'd Priest from the prophetic cell.[93]

Petrarch was inclined rather to the judgment of Lucan: "But the Delphian oracle became dumb, when kings feared the future and stopped the mouth of the gods; and no divine gift is more sorely missed by our age."[94]

While the ancient Christian poets replaced Apollo resolutely with Christ, and their medieval posterity revived him experimentally, Petrarch symbolically synthesized the god and God. He introduced *Africa* with a double invocation to pagan and Christian spirits:

> Muse, you will tell me of the man renowned
> for his great deeds, redoubtable in war,
> on whom first noble Africa, subdued
> by Roman arms, bestowed a lasting name.
> Fair sisters, ye who are my dearest care,
> if I propose to sing of wondrous things,
> may it be given me to quaff full deep
> of the sweet sacred spring of Helicon.
> Now that a favoring Fortune has once more
> restored me to clear springs and pleasant meads,
> the welcome shelter of the sun-bathed hills,
> and the soft stillness of the lonely fields,
> inspire, I pray, within your bard the song
> and give him heart.
>   Thou too, Who art the world's
> securest hope and glory of the heavens,
> Whom our age hails above all gods supreme
> and victor over Hell; Whose guiltless flesh
> we see scarred by five gaping wounds, O come,
> all-highest Father, bear me succor here.
> Full many a reverent verse shall I bring back
> to Thee—if verses please Thee—from the crest
> of high Parnassus. If they please Thee not,
> then Thine shall be the guerdon of those tears,
> which long since I might fittingly have shed
> save that my wretched blindness checked their flow.[95]

The initial invocation was addressed to the muse of heroic poetry, Calliope, its succeeding verse to an Apolline Christ. The conflation of the "all-highest Father" with the crucified Christ was no expression of patripassianism, but a classical attribution in imitation of Vergil. At the original shrine of Apollo in Delos the altar was erected to him as "the Father." It was at this site that Aeneas had worshipped, with Vergil observing the proper style by addressing Apollo as "Father."[96] This appellation Petrarch also knew from the *Saturnalia* of Macrobius, which synthesized the diverse cults of Greek and Roman cultures into the honor of one god: the sun personified as Apollo.[97] In essaying his epic *Africa,* Petrarch thus revived the classical invocation to the Muses and Apollo, but Apollo in a new manifestation as Christ. The equation was justified by the medieval adaptation of the myth of Python to the drama of salvation. As Christian allegorists compared these gods, just as at Delos Apollo had slain the monster Python, so at Calvary did Christ slay Satan.[98] Nor did Petrarch scruple to introduce his vernacular lyrics, *Rime sparse,* with the invocation, "Apollo, if the sweet desire," while concluding with a Christian counterpart, "Beautiful

Virgin."⁹⁹ It was a matter of knowing, he explained, what is due to Apollo the cither-player and what is owed to Mary the Virgin Mother, and to her Son, the redeemer, true God and true man.¹⁰⁰

Petrarch did not merely juxtapose these classical and Christian fonts of inspiration. He conflated them, equating Apollo and Christ¹⁰¹ in the first eclogue and in the prologue of *Africa*. A single verse, once attributed to Paulinus but of uncertain provenance, appears to be the ancient precedent. In apostrophe to Christ, slayer of Satan as Apollo was of Python, a poet wrote: "Hail, O true Apollo, Paean renowned!"¹⁰² Other legendary attributes of the deity also suggested parallels. Like Christ, Apollo was a human god; indeed, as the son of Zeus and the titaness Leto he was firstborn of the god-men. As early as the Homeric Hymn he was celebrated as a revealer, the herald of Zeus's paternal secrets. An expiator and sufferer, exiled on earth for slaying Python, he also anticipated Christ's role as the Savior.¹⁰³ The medieval vogue for reading pagan mythology as an allegory of Christian doctrine exploited these parallels. Scholia and glosses recreated an Ovid so edifying that even nuns could peruse his amorous tales.¹⁰⁴ The twelfth-century commentary by Arnulf of Orleans allegorized a solar Apollo who dessicated the noxious humors of earth, Python. As wise reason Apollo exterminated Python as false credulity. His futile pursuit of the chaste nymph Daphne became a moral on virginity preserved.¹⁰⁵ John of Garland moralized poetically on the virtuous victory over evil:

> Phoebus subdues Python,
>   and wisdom, wickedness,
> And he tramples human error beneath reason.

In the human mind the tree of wisdom he so ardently pursued would shoot forth a victorious and verdant rod:

> It is the rod of Phoebus,
>   wisdom made a crown,
> The laurel wreath which man
>   seeks with desirous mind.¹⁰⁶

In an *Ovide moralisé*, composed during Petrarch's formative years, an anonymous Franciscan friar baptized the Apolline fables by immersion. The malevolent serpent Python that terrorized and devoured men was the devil. "But Phoebus, also named Apollo, god of wisdom, namely Jesus Christ, the true sun and light of the world, so fights on behalf of man that he vanquishes and overcomes the devil and delivers man from imprisonment in limbo." Apollo, the god of wisdom who indoctrinated everything, was proposed to be Jesus: the light of the world who illumined everyone, was master of every discipline, art, and science, and who for love of humanity joined himself to Mary, as Apollo desired to unite with Daphne.[107] This identification of solar Apollo with Christ as "the true sun and light of the world" was the immediate inspiration for Petrarch's poetics, as for allegories by his artistic intimates Pierre Bersuire and Giovanni Boccaccio and even by his spiritual advisor, Dionigi da Borgo San Sepolcro.[108] The most elaborate of these contemporaneous expressions was in Bersuire's *Reductiorum morale,* a moralizing compilation that proposed to harmonize pagan thought with Christian dogma by purifying the mythology. Apollo represented the glorious victors of virtue over vice, especially as the god of wisdom, that is, Christ, the wisdom of God the Father. He was inflamed with undying love for Daphne as the human soul with whom he sought perfect union. For its refusal the soul was transformed into a laurel, the cross Phoebus, or Christ, the sun of righteousness, bodily embraced.[109]

Petrarch justified his own portrayal of Christ in Apolline figure "because he is the god of genius and wisdom."[110] This dual attribution reflected the Pauline appellation of Christ as "the power of God and the wisdom of God" (1 Cor. 1:24). The identification of Christ as the personified Wisdom of the Hebrew scriptures was consistent in patristic literature, although medieval piety often transferred the attribution to Mary. As Petrarch explained his Apolline metaphor for Christ, "As is well known among theologians, among the attributes of the persons of the supreme and undivided Trinity, wisdom is attributed to the Son and he is the very wisdom of the Father."[111] He cited copiously from Augustine's theology of the Son as wisdom, and therefore the true end of the philosopher as a lover of wisdom.[112] "The true wisdom of God is Christ," he declared, "so that in order to philosophize rightly we must first love and cherish Him."[113] Petrarch did not explain, however, why he presumed to call Christ "the god of genius" as well, although he did repeat of him the phrase "master of arts and bestower of genius," which he had originally ascribed to Apollo in his coronation speech.[114] The Greek noun *dunamis* of the

Pauline verse (1 Cor. 1:24) probably suggested the idea, however. The noun means not merely "power," but specifically any natural capacity or faculty that may be applied for good or evil. This definition coincides with the common understanding in antiquity of the genius, once the Italian natal god fell under the spell of the Greek daemon.[115] The probable source of Petrarch's attribution was Horace's definition of the genius as "the god of human nature,"[116] the classical meaning that governed the medieval allegories of that figure.[117] In the Christian creed the ascription of human nature could only be to the Son, and so it was plausible for Petrarch to term Christ as the god of human nature the god of genius.

This adoption of Christ in Apolline figure as the genius of his poetic vocation was a moral justification of art against asceticism. The classical definition of the genius as a personal double who regulated fortune was perpetuated in Petrarch's belief in a guardian angel who had been assigned him as a companion to ensure virtue by his monitory presence. More profoundly, the concept of the genius related to his "even more impressive and awe-inspiring belief" in the omnipresence of Christ to him as a witness of his thoughts and actions. "There is absolutely no Christian who doubts," he wrote, "that Christ himself is always present in the most secret recesses of the soul, examines what goes on there and sees everything as though it were openly exposed."[118] For himself Petrarch did not need to resort to the ascetical device of an imaginary witness to incite shame for base deeds and desires. He believed rather in this presence of Christ, "Christ alive and real and always present to us." Thus he invoked as a testimony to his rectitude: "I call to witness our Apollo, the only son of the heavenly Jove and true God of wisdom, Christ."[119] It was this interior presence that singularly associated Christ with Apollo in Petrarch's theology, in advance over the medieval allegorizations. As Franciscus stated to Augustinus in defense of poetry, Apollo as the god of genius represented "the interior resources of the mind."[120]

Christians had not been as reticent in the plastic arts, as they had been in literature, to synthesize their faith and pagan culture as did Petrarch the humanist. At the beginning of the fourth century, during which the Christian rejection of Apollo dominated poetry, an ageless Christ modeled on manly heroes began to appear on sarcophagi. Just after the Edict of Toleration (A.D. 311), his prototype became the geniuses in the seasonal depictions on triumphal arches, the geniuses who as sons of the gods promised the empire constant good fortune. The beautiful style of the midcentury created from these pagan examples a youthfully innocent Son of God, who adorned sarcophagi and ivory carvings and was depicted by a famous statuette.[121] The impressive portrayal of Christ as Apollo, however, was the mosaic forming the vault of a small burial chamber in the cemetery beside the Via Cornelia in Rome, now beneath the Vatican. At its splendid golden apex of intertwining vines is the figure of Christ with the Apolline attributes of a quadriga and horses. Seven rays emanate from his nimbused head in evangelical allusion to the light of the world (John 8:12, 9:5, etc.). This solar personification, which reappeared in a fifth-century mosaic in Sant'Aquilino, Milan, was characteristic of Christian iconography in the era preceding and contemporaneous with Constantine.[122] The nimbus with seven equidistant rays, similar to the radiated crowns on Greek and Roman coins, especially symbolized Apollo as the sun, beaming to each planet a ray.[123]

Although Apollo was not a solar deity in Greek religion, his Roman domestication converted him into one. His prophetic role as the exclusive interpreter of Zeus favored him during the monotheistic critique of divination. Apollo became associated with the power and virtue of the sun as a beneficent cosmic force. Through a convergence of political fortune with religious currents as diverse as the Pythagorean, Mazdean, and Mithraic, the attribution expanded into cult. The decisive impetus for this piety was Apollo's reputed epiphany in the miracle of Actium (31 B.C.), in which battle Octavian defeated Antony in the civil war. As the first Roman emperor, Caesar Augustus appropriated Apollo as his personal god, constructing in his honor a temple on the Palatine adorned with a solar quadriga. As Horace memorialized it:

> O quickening Sun, that in thy shining car usherest in the day and hidest it, and art reborn another and yet the same, ne'er mayest thou be able to view aught greater than the city of Rome!

The heroization of the Roman emperor was thus symbolized and sanctioned by a cult of the invincible sun, personified as Apollo.[124]

The identification of Christ with this triumphal, solar deity, as in the notable mosaic, developed from the evangelical metaphor of light. The nocturnal course of the sun from west to east suggested to theologians the gospel of Christ's burial and descent to hell and his ascent and resurrection to heaven.[125] Especially significant was the ascription to him of the prophesied title "the sun of righteousness": "But for you who fear my name the sun of righteousness shall rise, with healing in its wings" (Mal. 4:2a). This scriptural symbolism was prominent in the Easter liturgy and in the baptismal rite, as Jerome testified: "In the mysteries first of all we renounce him who is in the west [Satan], and we die to ourselves with our sins, and thus turned toward the east, we enter a covenant with the sun of righteousness [Christ], and we promise that we will serve him."[126] The imagery was transmitted to Christian poetry particularly through the Ambrosian hymns that hailed Christ as the "true sun" who dispelled the darkness of sin.[127] In medieval piety Francis of Assisi composed his canticle to brother sun in specific memory and honor of Christ's title as "the sun of righteousness." As a memoir recorded, "And because he deemed and said that the sun is fairer than other created things, and is more often likened to our Lord, and that in Scripture the Lord Himself is called 'the Sun of Righteousness,' therefore giving that name to those Praises which he had made of the creatures of the Lord, what time the Lord did certify him of His kingdom, he called them 'The Song of Brother Sun.'"[128]

> Praised be You, my Lord, with all your creatures,
> especially Sir Brother Sun,
> Who is the day and through whom You give us light.
> And he is beautiful and radiant with great splendor;
> and bears a likeness of You, Most High One.[129]

It was not fortuitous that this same prophetic phrase, "sun of righteousness," illumined the conclusion of Petrarch's own *Rime sparse*. Shot through with Apolline-Christian light, the entire *canzoniere* lauded and lamented a sun that allured and eluded Petrarch with its rays of inspiration. The personification of his poetics was a lady who was among ladies a "sun," a "living, sweet sun." The day of her birth was the most beautiful the sun ever opened. She descended like the dawn. Her growth was like the diurnal course of the sun, whose rising and setting alternately enlightened and darkened, gladdened and saddened the poet. Her countenance was so radiant as to equal, to rival, even to surpass in beauty and antiquity the splendor of that celestial body at high noon in summer. Her burnished golden hair made the sun envious; so did her eyes, for they were brighter than the sun. Their opening was like the Orient. The lady's glance was sunlight itself; her gaze, sunbeams. Their light shone in him "as a sunbeam penetrates glass." This sun dazzled him. Gazing into her clear lovely eyes, as "holy lights," enraptured him to heaven. He melted like a snowman in their incandescent rays. He sought the sun as the sole object and hope of his vision.[130] It was this illumination that inspired Petrarch to compose.

> She who among ladies is a sun, moving the rays of her lovely eyes in me, creates thoughts, acts, and words of love.[131]

This solar Apolline imagery was explicitly Christian. It was Christ himself who once in his humble incarnation "coming to earth to illuminate the pages that for many years had hidden the truth," now in his risen glory granted another "sun" in this lady. Her gentle eyes vivified the poet with their "high divine beauty"; their solar rays warmed, ignited, and kindled his inspiration to compose.[132]

The epic *Africa* reflected this Apolline light: the sun's course through the heavens charted the heroic contest of Scipio, from the failure of the god to shine upon Italy to the restoration of his smile. No aloof divinity, Phoebus Apollo was especially active in the lovers' tale, although dimmed by Sophonisba's dazzling beauty. In pity for her lover Massinissa, Apollo dipped his fiery chariot into the sea in mournful memory of his own thwarted passion for Daphne. He concluded their sad affair by appearing radiant at dawn, until Sophonisba saluted him with a suicidal toast. Yet it was Scipio Africanus whom Apollo bathed in such excellent radiance that the sun itself marveled at his human rival.[133] Scipio's course of life was indeed solar in its energy, ending in an apotheosis reserved for the divine.

> He, moving as it were from setting sun
> in headlong brilliance to the break of dawn—
> for so his conquering course may be described—
> will raise the name of Italy aloft
> up to the stars. Before him all will bow,
> and Fortune, generous in triumphs, will
> reward the victor.[134]

In considering the course of the epic itself, Petrarch would entreat the preservation of its exploits in defiance of "the circling sun that burns away the centuries."[135]

Yet it was not the sheer aesthetic light that attracted Petrarch to poetry, but its prophetic virtue. Prophecy captivated him and allied him with Apollo. Had not his own advent and triumph as a poet itself been prophesied, and by the eminent seer Homer?[136] In the epics of that bard, as in other classical poets, such forecasts had issued most often from omens, either chance sightings, especially avian flight and behavior or chance sounds, especially thunder. Dreamed phantoms in the shape of friend or kinsman, mantic pronouncements of seers, and even epiphanies, were also means of divine revelation.[137] Among the gods it was supremely Apollo who, as the elected voice of Zeus, prophesied through oracles. The oracles of Apollo were singular in Hellas for their reliance on a single person in a permanent office at a fixed site, rather than on the usual divinatory devices. Indeed, they were singular in the ancient world and since.[138] From the sixth century B.C. on, the most frequented of these oracles was at Delphi, which site attracted powerful and wealthy clients, cities as well as individuals from Hellas and beyond. Although its prestige popularly orientated it with the foundation of the world, its historical origins are uncertain.[139] From its zenith between 580 and 320 B.C., the Delphic oracle declined after the age of Alexander through the Hellenistic and Roman eras, but still proffered responses at least until the third quarter of the fourth century A.D. when the Theodosian edict silenced it.[140] Its propagandists were priests, poets, and aristocrats who composed an intellectual and social elite. Creating an efficacious imperialist myth during Greece's era of colonization, they assimilated the ancient regional gods who presided over certain local rites to Apollo, and then subordinated the various versions of Apollo to the glorious Pythian god of the Delphic cult. Almost all colonial cities attributed their foundation to a consultation with the consent of that god through a Delphic oracle. Under the patronage of Apollo a moral empire developed in which the authority of that oracle governed common ideas and laws, much as Christianity imposed a certain unified perspective on medieval Europe. The intervention of the Delphic oracle in the evolution of Greek cities was well attested, since tradition attributed an oracular source to the most venerable and important institutions of government, law, and religion.[141] It was this identity of the civic with the prophetic through Apollo that Petrarch would appropriate for the restoration of the empire and the papacy to Rome.

In the mantic session at Delphi, the Pythia, attended by priests and officials, mounted a tripod, from which seat she pronounced Apollo's response in direct conversation with the inquirer. Although enthusiastic in her inspiration, the Pythia was not hysterical. Whether in verse or in prose, she prophesied articulate, if sometimes ambiguous, oracles in her own voice. The frenzy reported to be characteristic of her behavior by Christian polemics was an allegation derived from a single passage in Lucan that lacks credibility. The Platonic term *mania*, designating telestic, poetic, and amorous rapture or ecstasy, was commonly mistranslated into Latin as *insania*, which connotes psychotic behavior.[142] It was thus that Augustinus had warned Franciscus of perilous poetic "madness."[143] Yet it was knowledge that Petrarch sought as the fruition of his Apolline genius, a knowledge that coincided with the end of the Christian illuminative way.[144] "There is no doubt," he affirmed, "that the only true knowledge is to know and to honor God, whence it is written: 'Piety is wisdom.'" The most noble and sacred study of all, theology, had been conferred on man for the achievement of this wisdom. Corrupt human vanity, Petrarch complained, had debased theology into dialectic.[145] Criticizing those who usurped the title of "theologian" and professed a knowledge of divine affairs, he stated: "Instead of theologians, they are dialecticians, sophists at that; instead of lovers of God, they are knowers of God, nor do they wish to be that, but only to seem to be so; thus although they could follow Him in silence, they pursue Him with raucous voices. Behold the level to which the studies of mortals [have] descended! Oh, if you only knew the drive I feel and the passion that inflames me to speak at length on these matters!"[146] Petrarch would champion a poetical theology as oracular of divine truth, as in Apollo's utterances at Delphi.

While legendary occasions for consultation of that oracle ranged from plague to pregnancy, in the extant responses from contemporaneous records the pronouncements generally concerned sanctions of religious laws and proposals and prescriptions of cultic acts. Whether direct or indirect, complete or incomplete, quotations of Delphic oracles and allusions to them were preserved in a variety of historical, literary, and philosophical texts, as well as in public and private inscriptions.[147] Petrarch culled from these classical testimonials a dozen examples of such consultations with Apollo, which he recorded with commentary in his *Rerum memorandarum liber*. As derived from the conclusion of Cicero's *De divinatione*, the manuscript was an exposition of the virtue of prudence in the service of rhetoric. Its books examined the parts of that virtue as memory, understanding, and

"providence through which a certain future event is seen before the fact." In reflecting on providence and divination, Petrarch admonished the reader to rejoice and give thanks that as a Christian he had been led forth from the ambiguities of shadowy oracles into the serene light of true revelation. Yet the Apolline utterances testified, Petrarch thought, to the custom of mortals possessed by divine spirits to predict the future. Of the Delphic pronouncements, one that was surely stated without mask or lie he considered to be this: "Socrates is the wisest man of all who have lived."[148]

Apollo might have designated other philosophers as exemplars of Delphic wisdom. Pythagoras by some accounts received his doctrine directly from the Pythia. Plato founded his ideal republic on the sanctuary of Delphi, as not only the center of religious life and the origin of moral and political laws, but as the supreme authority dominating that city. As priest of that shrine, Plutarch personally united the Greek philosophical tradition with the Delphic religion, exalting Apollo as the master of morality.[149] Yet the oracle that so esteemed Socrates above all was, as Petrarch suggested, "not falsely stated," at least in Apolline judgment. Socrates regarded himself as "the consecrated servant" of Apollo, from whom he had received his own prophetic gifts. He counseled his friends to consult the oracle of Apollo through the Pythia.[150] Saliently he established his philosophy on the most famous, although inauthentic, of the Delphic oracles, the gnomic "Know thyself."[151] This utterance advised a knowledge of the distinction between man and the gods, and thus a prudence in not exceeding one's proper nature. "Know thyself" was related to the other famous Delphic maxim, the cautionary "Nothing in excess." The essence of Delphic doctrine was a religious spirit that expressed itself in a central moral rule of discretion, or *sōphrosunē*. In recommending that man take stock of his nature as distinct from the divine, it established him as the center of moral life and invested him with new value. "Know thyself" was inserted into the mouth of Apollo as not only the master of oracular science but also the master of wisdom and piety who located the good in moderation and reverence.[152] The oracle served ironically as a pretext for the accusation of atheism that occasioned Socrates' death.[153] So would the anthropocentric revival of Petrarch and other humanists be misjudged as irreverent, even irreligious.

Although the maxim "Know thyself" was also attributed to the seven sages, Petrarch identified it as Apolline.[154] The command was decisive in his life and for his literature. Its citation as the only Delphic oracle in Macrobius's commentary on the *Somnium Scipionis*,[155] a principal source for Petrarch's *Africa*,[156] is particularly suggestive of its influence. There the Apolline oracle occurred during a philosophical consensus that souls originated in the sky and that perfect wisdom acknowledged that the soul, although inhabiting a body, recognized this source. "A man has but one way of knowing himself... if he will look back to his first beginning and origin and 'not search for himself elsewhere.'" Recognizing its dignity, the soul would thus assume the virtues that would elevate it to that sky.[157] The citation of Persius's counsel to search for oneself not corporeally but spiritually, not externally but internally, recalled the text of Augustine that enlightened Petrarch: "And they go to admire the summits of mountains and the vast billows of the sea and the broadest rivers and the expanses of the oceans and the revolutions of the stars and they overlook themselves."[158] As assimilated from the classical into the Christian tradition,[159] the oracle "Know thyself" coincided with the mandate of self-examination in Petrarch's *Secretum* and with the revelation of self-importance in his epistolary ascent of Mont Ventoux. Petrarch espoused this Delphic wisdom in deliberating with another poet, Tommaso da Messina, concerning the rough and uncertain path to the borders of antique learning. The subject of their mutual investigation was the location of the island of Thule. Surveying the conflicting testimonies and conjectures of geographers and travelers concerning this remotest western land, Petrarch exclaimed: "Alas, how much disagreement! Indeed to me the island seems no less hidden than truth itself." Its location hardly mattered, he decided, "provided that virtue, which is centrally placed, does not lie hidden, and likewise the path of this short life over which a great portion of men proceeds trembling and staggering, hurrying to an uncertain end over an obscure trail." Petrarch advised his perplexed friend to seek information about the obscure problem of Thule from a more learned scholar. As for himself, he averred like Socrates: "If it is denied to me to search out these hiding places of nature and to know their secrets, I shall be satisfied with knowing myself. It is here that I shall be open-eyed and fix my gaze."[160]

What Petrarch essayed to discover interiorly was not ego but Christ. By this knowledge he hoped to attain to the role of the true theologian. As he counseled concerning the one good: "If you desire it fully and sacredly and reasonably (otherwise such a great thing cannot be desired), you will find that what you seek is already with you. Seek and you will find Him whom you desire deep in your soul. You need not wander outside of yourself in order to enjoy him."[161] It was this interior presence of Christ as the author of his genius that established Petrarch's poetic vocation. In Petrarch's experience the emergence of self from tradition, especially from the asceticism that constrained his art, was founded in such consciousness as fostering the formation of conscience. Justifying his decision to continue as a poet, despite the cry against it, he ironically inverted Augustinus's sermon in *Secretum* on the vanity of eloquence: "What boots it that others shall approve of what you have said," argued the saint, "if in the court of your own conscience it stands condemned? For though the applause of those who hear you may seem to yield a certain fruit which is not to be despised, yet of what worth is it after all if in his heart the speaker is not able to applaud?"[162] He reversed Augustinus's deprecation of the Capitoline crowd that had honored him with the laurel by applying the norm of conscience to the saint's own words. He thus relativized his authority. Was Augustinus's disapproval to outweigh Robert's approval? or either external judgment to overbalance that of his own conscience? In Petrarch's struggle for spiritual integrity he confuted authority with authority, arguing Augustinus against Augustinus to exploit on behalf of self the ambiguity and contradiction of tradition. Sometimes he regressed to melancholic doubt; sometimes, however, he advanced to inspiring probity.

The "very insistent and uncertain battle for the control of my two selves," as he termed his difficulty from the peak of Ventoux,[163] was for the integration of carnal and spiritual man, as symbolized in the poetic synthesis of Apollo and Christ. Petrarch experienced the grief and frustration of the purgative way, which demanded the subordination of the one self to the other, until in the presence of Truth he rejected asceticism for being discipline but not wisdom. On the illuminative way of poetry—more enlightened, more sublime, more glorious, as he claimed[164]—he sought to create a spirituality of the secular that would allow, transfigure, and honor his poetic genius. Petrarch's conjunctive method was through a mediation of culture and experience in which he examined and judged the Christian apologetics against poetry by a hard stare in the mirror of his own conscience. His volumes thus comprised a journal of self-encounter and self-expression. The ascents of Ventoux, of the Capitoline, and of Parnassus itself were simultaneously a descent into himself: the external climb of poetry, the internal tunnel of psychology. Or, rather, this exploration was theology, for Petrarch discovered his genius as the divine presence of an Apolline Christ. The psychological search for a personal identity was paralleled by historical research for the public identity, as exemplified in his epic *Africa*. Petrarch's artistic vocation was one of creation through restoration, of stripping the veneer that had accrued during "the dark ages"[165] on the pristine truth of ancient revelations, classical and Christian. In this art of pentimento Petrarch discovered prophecy.[166]

2

The Sylvan Citizen

A poet, Petrarch declaimed from the Capitoline, is a prophet. As divinely inspired, he exercises an Apolline genius in the sacred task of articulating the civil destiny, and so of fostering patriotic zeal. Petrarch declared himself impelled to his arduous ascent by love. The same love of the fatherland that had animated Scipio now prevailed upon him to seek Roman citizenship and the laurel wreath. In praise of that bough he related that its touch to the head of a poet would realize dreams and foretell the future.[1] This equation of the poet and the prophet was as ancient as the Roman ruins he surveyed from that vantage, for it was in the Augustan age that Petrarch's customary term *vates* had been extended from its denotation of "priest, soothsayer" to include "poet." The neologist was Vergil, and he introduced this usage to convey a solemn religious significance to the art.

Occurring first in the sense of "poet" in the *Eclogues,* the term recurred four times as "seer" in the *Georgics,* a verse of which Petrarch selected as the text for his coronation speech: "But a sweet longing urges me upward over the lonely slopes of Parnassus." After this Vergil consistently preferred *vates,* and the term *poeta* appears only once in his entire literature, and then only to refer to Greek practice. In his famous profession, moreover, he affirmed: "But as for me—first above all, may the sweet Muses whose holy emblems, under the spell of a mighty love, I bear, take me to themselves, and show me heaven's pathways."

Vergil's definition of the poet's role thus coincided with that of Posidonius concerning the Gaulish *ouateis*. Emphasizing the hieratic function of the poet, metaphors in the exordium of the third book of the *Georgics* derived from the temple and its sacrifice. The foundation of the Palatine temple of Apollo, the library and votive offering, was especially important for Augustan poets, as in Horace's celebration of the solar quadriga as an imperial emblem. Vergil appropriated its foundation and cult as a principle of his epic *Aeneid.* In its first five books the term *vates* was a leitmotif especially associated with Apollo, while in the sixth book, as Aeneas prayed at the Delian altar, the term was applied to the god himself. The hero's prayer promised precisely the foundation of the Palatine temple to Apollo by the emperor Augustus. It was under the protection of that god that the *vates* Museus thus guided Aeneas to his father, and the *vates* Sibyl enlightened his conversionary descent to the underworld. It was, therefore, in a context of Apolline service that Vergil restored the term *vates* to honor, both in its old sense as "priest" and in its new as "poet" by combining religion and art. The *vates* as poetic spokesman was inseparable from the god Apollo.[2]

Although in Vergil's verse, as in Roman cult, Apollo retained his Greek character (indeed, as the most important of the Hellenic deities), the poet emphasized his association with Rome through the Sibylline oracles and the patronage of the Augustan poets, as well as of Augustus himself. Apollo was originally imported to Italy early in the fifth century B.C. as a god of medicinal healing, but his prophetic gift soon emerged. From the colony of Cumae he transmitted the Sibylline oracles that were destined to inspire Roman religion. With the possible exception of Jupiter, Apollo or Phoebus was mentioned more frequently by Vergil than any other deity. The poet acknowledged Apollo's manifold nature as medicinal, poetic, musical, and solar, but he especially emphasized the prophetic. Elevated from his popular pose in the *Eclogues* as solver of riddles, Apollo assumed in the *Aeneid* the more dignified role of inspirer of oracles. Apolline oracles were integral to the numinous structure of that epic, for they revealed the divine will. The hero Aeneas consulted Apollo at Delos and at Cumae, where the frenzied Sibyl so famously dramatized her possession by that god.[3]

By associating the poetic *vates* with Apollo, Vergil elevated the status of poet to an extraordinary prophetic ideal. As *vates* the poet was entitled to propose morals and manners to the citizenry and to control the national myth, if not the national destiny. Vergil referred to himself as *vates* in the explicit context of Aeneas's promise of the foundation of the Palatine temple to Apollo and of the revelation of Rome's future glory. This exaltation of the art in early Augustan poetry declined, however. Although Horace initially employed the word *vates* in a solemn sense, he later reduced it to the mere equivalent of *poeta*. In Augustan verse the *vates* acted as a leader and educator of the populace; the *poeta* played a neutral, lesser, or pejorative role. Tibullus dallied with the term *vates;* Propertius used it to acknowledge his position. Professing to be a *vates* who was forced by Cupid into the service of love, Ovid further depreciated its meaning by extending the title to all poets. With this disintegration of the Vergilian ideal, the concept failed, and Hellenistic ideas again triumphed.[4] Petrarch's ambition was a revival of this Vergilian ideal by which poets as spokesmen of the gods established public morality and religion. The poet was again to be a man of vocation, set apart by his *vis mentis,* to recall Varro's etymology of *vates,* his inspiration or genius.

Vergil was himself endowed with the Apolline grace, poetic and prophetic, that Petrarch would claim. With an intimate knowledge of magical practice and belief, Vergil described the charms and spells of Italian folklore: the evil eye, the witch's potion, the amorous incantation. As dramatic devices he also employed omens. Such natural events, especially the meteorological and the avian, were piously regarded as indicating the divine will: the oak struck by lightning, a croaking crow, bloody wine. The traces in his literature of these omens as influencing fate or foretelling the future reflected primitive superstition. More sophisticated was the appeal by his characters to a deity for confirmation of such omens. More religious still was their belief in omens as deliberately willed and conferred by the gods. As incorporated into an elaborate Roman system of augury, formal divination involved either a sign voluntarily sent by a god and requiring interpretation, or a sign petitioned for by man and granted by a god in response. Auspices were specifically the omens undertaken to determine whether or not the gods approved of an endeavor, especially the assumption of office or engagement in battle. Vergil recorded the traditional vocabulary and observance of omen and augury with precision. Rivaling in his verse these more primitive notions were prophecy and oracle. To the Italian notion of a gifted human or an animistic spirit as uttering a divine word he added the Greek influence of the dream-vision. More important, he employed the anthropomorphic concept of divine revelation through the instrumental oracle of a human priest or priestess at a sacred site. Apollo was the exemplar of this method, and his oracular seats such as Delos and Cumae, where Aeneas consulted the god, were renowned in the Augustan age. For Vergil, Apollo was supreme in prophecy.[5]

Yet it was not Vergil's Apolline service as seer that prevailed after the Augustan age. The assiduous medieval study of his texts perpetuated rather the ideal of linguistic perfection that had also elevated him to fame in classical antiquity. Vergil and grammar became synonymous. His verses were mined for the practical instruction in Latin that was the aim of their exposition in the medieval schools. While grammar dominated the study of Vergil, there was, nevertheless, a philosophical sympathy for him as a pure and noble soul, a Christian before Christ. The *Aeneid* was explored as an allegory of the vicissitudes of human life in its aspiration toward a perfection that was not only linguistic but moral. The golden bough that admitted its hero Aeneas to the underworld symbolized Vergil's own wisdom as the entry to secret truths. The medieval commentaries that both examined and invented this profundity were synthesized and surpassed in the *Commedia* of Dante, who elected Vergil as his guide through the hazards of hell.[6] It was perhaps such adulation of his extraordinary knowledge of natural secrets that fostered Vergil's reputation for magic. John of Salisbury initially reported in his *Policraticus* that Vergil had provided Naples with a talismanic fly to rid the city of that pest. Such necromantic legends, emerging in the twelfth century, were multiplied by the tongues and pens of chroniclers, encyclopedists, and troubadours. Vergil, who had lived in Naples, was particularly portrayed as expressing his affectionate concern for the welfare of that city by granting such talismans as a miniature model of the city in a bottle as a palladium against attack, a bronze horse that healed infirm ones, a butcher-block that preserved meat from decay, and a bronze statue of an archer with drawn bow and ready arrow aimed at Vesuvius to prevent its eruption. Vergil also reputedly banished all serpents in the city to beneath one gate and provided the populace with therapeutic baths. Whenever his bones were exhumed and exposed, the atmosphere would darken and the wind would rise so that the sea swelled and raged about the Neapolitan castle in which they had been interred. Imitative Roman legends were invented that identified the poet with various monuments of the city he had once called golden. Most ancient and most popular was the tale of a marvelous palace Vergil had constructed, whose statues rang bells of alarm whenever the provinces meditated revolt.[7]

Vergil's role as a civic benefactor paled, however, when Christian moralists interpreted these innocent marvels as diabolical sorceries. For his own enthusiastic embrace of the ancient poet, Petrarch was himself accused of magic by the plenary papal court of Avignon. "See what I have received when I ought to have won a reputation for integrity," he exclaimed of the slanderous whispers in advance of the trial:

> the suspicion of exercising new machinations and malicious cunning against the very finest men. Perhaps—as has often reached my ears by chance when I was in the company of great men, great by fortune but not by talent—perhaps, I say, by this time I appear to many as a necromancer and magician. I no doubt appear so because I am frequently alone and because, as those experts say and I do not deny, I read the works of Virgil, an opinion which elicits in me bile mixed with laughter. I have indeed read them. There is the reason for mistrust; there is the reason for the bad reputation of studies![8]

As he also related of the incident, "I shall say something that will make you laugh even more. I myself, the greatest enemy of divination and magic, am oftentimes called necromancer by these excellent judges because of my admiration for Virgil. How low our studies have sunk! O hateful and laughable nonsense!"[9] In his formal examination for the poetic coronation, Petrarch had been questioned by King Robert, about whose capital of Naples the necromantic legends concerning Vergil had just been published.[10] Of the popular tale that Vergil had by incantation bored a tunnel through Mount Posilippo near his tomb at Pozzuoli overnight, Petrarch jokingly replied that he had never read that Vergil was a stonemason. The king nodded a severe assent to his judgment that the tunnel had been created not by magic but by tools. In a later description of that landscape Petrarch ventured as his own explanation of the legend the presence of Vergil's bust at the site.[11] He also knew of the talisman of the enchanted egg that Vergil had reputedly fashioned to protect the fortress on which he founded Naples.[12]

Petrarch's revelation of the Vergilian secrets that so astonished his royal patron exceeded such Neapolitan lore, however. It was precisely his knowledge of the sublime meaning veiled in Vergil's poetic fiction, as Petrarch attested to Boccaccio, that had secured him the laurel wreath with honorific titles and Roman citizenship.[13] Petrarch did record on the flyleaf of his manuscript of Vergil the pious legend of St. Paul's visit to the tomb of Vergil, as expressed in a sequence chanted on the feast of the apostle's conversion. Reverently shedding a tear at the site, St. Paul exclaimed: "What would I have not rendered thee if

I had found thee still living, O greatest of poets!"[14] The singular Vergilian mystery that captivated the imagination of Christians, however, was the song of the Cumaean Sibyl in the fourth eclogue:

> Now the Virgin returns, the reign of Saturn returns; now a new generation descends from heaven on high. Only do thou, pure Lucina, smile on the birth of the child, under whom the iron brood shall first cease, and a golden race spring up throughout the world! Thine own Apollo now is king![15]

These verses, celebrating a universal regeneration through the birth of a child, were acknowledged by theologians no less severe toward pagan poetry than Augustine as an inspired prophecy of Christ's nativity.[16] Petrarch was inclined to suspect in the Sibylline oracles, as in the Apolline ones, "the fallacy of extremely inimical spirits." Except he did allow that Christian doctors gave credence to them as predictions of Christ, especially the oracles of the Erythraean Sibyl, an apocryphal manuscript of which he possessed.[17] Petrarch thus wrote of "the Sibyls, those divine women with a single name, who were prophetic and cognizant of the divine plan." Indeed, he continued, "they had made so many predictions about the end of the world and especially about the coming of Christ that, when the latter was fulfilled, this name common to all the Sibyls was included by our learned men among the names of the holy prophets."[18] Concerning the celebrated song of the Cumaean Sibyl, he thought that Vergil's literal reference was to the birth of Caesar Augustus, and that pious readers had subsequently interpreted it to be that of the celestial emperor, Christ. Yet he believed that faith legitimated the interpretation of the Christ Child. To those whom God has graced with Christian faith, he explained, "all these events are clear without any external witnesses, and thus rays of divine light flood the eyes of the faithful so that there is no blind man who does not perceive with his mind Christ, 'the sun of righteousness.'" He was convinced that, if this true light had shone into Vergil's eyes, "undoubtedly" he would have referred the prophecy of the golden age literally and not figuratively to Christ rather than to Caesar.[19]

Whether this Sibylline oracle was interpreted as intentionally or inadvertently pronounced of Christ, it was revered by Christians as a testimony among and to the nations of divine providence. The popularity of the text, promoted in homily and drama, coincided with the medieval adulation of Vergil, so that he was often depicted in literature and in art as the companion of the Sibyl. And, just as in the solemn funereal sequence "Dies irae" the advent of Christ was "testified by David and the Sibyl" so Vergil himself was elevated to the status of the canonical prophets of scripture.[20]

A significant display of this honor was the inclusion of Vergil in the medieval design of the tree of Jesse. This iconography depicted Isaiah's prophecy of a Messianic rule of idyllic peace, justice, and piety:

> There shall come forth a shoot from the stump of Jesse,
> and a branch shall grow out of his roots.
> And the Spirit of the Lord shall rest upon him,
>   the spirit of wisdom and understanding,
>   the spirit of counsel and might,
>   the spirit of knowledge and fear of the Lord.
> And his delight shall be in the fear of the Lord.
>
> (Is. 11:1–3)

By vocalic exchange the shoot, *virga* (Vg), was as early as the third century interpreted as a prefiguration of the Virgin Mary, *virgo,* while the rod signified Christ. The artistic type, which emerged at the end of the eleventh century and developed by the fourteenth into complex forms, was a recumbent figure of Jesse, from whose body grew a tree on which appeared the ancestors of Christ and at its top Christ himself.[21] Petrarch constructed an epistolary exhortation to humility on this popular theme. Indicating that Christ despised the fame of birth from noble lineage and chose rather the obscure family of Jesse, the poet lauded his ancestors as exemplars of that virtue: the impoverished widow Ruth amid an alien people, Jesse himself, David the callow shepherd, a humble ancestry regressing to the patriarchs Abraham, Isaac, and Jacob, who were not splendid regents but lowly herdsmen.[22] The figure of Vergil was introduced into this biblical genealogy in the thirteenth century. The impetus for the association was his renowned citation of the prophecy of the Cumaean Sibyl, who herself became included in the tree of Jesse. Since her oracle of the virgin was traditionally interpreted as being of the Virgin, portrayal of the Sibyl and of her spokesman Vergil was deemed an appropriate addition to this Marian and messianic iconography.[23] It was this concept of a prophetic Vergil, who could be grafted, although pagan, onto the very tree of Jesse as an ancestor of Christ, that informed the frontispiece of Petrarch's famous manuscript of the Mantuan seer.

That cherished codex featured the major poetry of Vergil—
Eclogues, Georgics, and *Aeneid*—framed by the paragon of medieval
commentaries, that of Servius. Petrarch himself annotated these texts
and also recorded on the flyleaf of the volume important personal
notices.[24] The literary value of the manuscript was enhanced artistically by a unique painting, executed on the verso of the first folio by
the Sienese master Simone Martini (1283–1344). The scene allegorically illustrates Vergil's mastery of the classical rhetorical styles—the
lowly, the average, and the lofty—as symbolized by a shepherd, a
farmer, and a general, corresponding to the *Eclogues, Georgics,* and
Aeneid. Each of these figures is portrayed with an appropriate instrument from the medieval scheme of "Vergil's wheel": the shepherd
with a crook, the farmer with a pruning hook, and the soldier with a
lance. As they pause in their occupations, the commentator Servius
indicates to them, with an emphatically extended arm, an open book
on the lap of their author, the poet Vergil. Two winged inscriptions
by Petrarch, who apparently commissioned the painting, announce:

> Bountiful Italian earth, you nourish distinguished poets,
> but this one enabled you to attain the goals of the Greeks.
>
> Servius disclosing the secrets of Vergil to speak aloud
> so that they might be manifest to knights, shepherds, and farmers.

A third couplet below, also by Petrarch, praises the illustrator:

> Mantua bore Vergil, who composed such songs,
> Siena, Simon, who with a finger painted them.

If the arm of Servius, which creates the dynamism of the composition,
is continued imaginatively, it aligns with his text on the complementary folio, which describes the three rhetorical styles. The illustration
thus exemplifies the Vergilian ideal of eloquence.[25]

Although Petrarch declared his own genius to be one of agility,[26] his
poetics comprised more than such rhetorical versatility. Above all Latin
geniuses he revered Vergil as excelling by the divine artifice of his style
in the elegance and enlightenment of doctrine beneath the poetic veil.[27]
Petrarch had declared in his coronation speech that poetry was allegory,
the veiling of truth in fiction, and the background of Martini's illustration includes such a veil, suspended before three trees in a bucolic
setting. Although the action of the scene has been described as Servius

pulling the veil away from Vergil,[28] Vergil is already disclosed. He reposes visible in full figure, with pen in hand and book in lap, in a state of contemplation. Servius is not drawing the veil from Vergil but rather from the central image of the illustration, a laurel tree. His hand is superimposed on its trunk, which coincides with the vertical axis of the composition. If, moreover, the illustration is subjected to a geometrical analysis according to the root-two construction that Martini often employed, the arc passes through Vergil's eyes.[29] Although this aspect of the design may only suggest the poet's inspiration, there is a plainer visual correlation. The arc passes through Vergil's eyes directly to the lofty foliage of the central tree. Vergil is not musing vacantly into some space beyond the page but regarding the laurel. If again an arc is extended from the curvature of the pen poised in his hand, it too coincides with the laurel, at the branching of its trunk. This is iconographically appropriate, as according to legend Vergil's mother dreamed in pregnancy that she bore a laurel bough, which when it touched the earth immediately grew into a mighty tree laden with blossoms and fruit.[30] This structural focus on the laurel emphasizes his eloquent style, for which that tree served as a symbol in the medieval "wheel." Servius's direct gaze at the general, the type of the *Aeneid* in that "wheel," reinforces the excellence of the eloquent style.

Yet the allegory is profounder still than this allusion to the poetic laurel that wreathes Vergil's head in the illustration. The posture of the poet is reminiscent of the figure of Jesse in the medieval depictions of Isaiah's prophecy (Is. 11:1–3). Just as in that iconography the tree of Christ grew from the body of Jesse, so in this example the laurel rises from Vergil's. Its roots are secured near his feet. In the exemplar, especially in French art, Jesse was not necessarily recumbent but was often seated, as is Vergil here. Nor did the Jesse tree necessarily portray an explicit genealogical motif or represent Christ or the Virgin in human form.[31] Simone Martini's illustration derives from the artistic and literary tradition that included Vergil among the Hebrew prophets who foretold the advent of Christ. The vertical axis passes directly through the middle of the laurel to the middle of the shepherd, who symbolizes Vergil's *Eclogues*. It was in that very work that the poet had uttered the "messianic" oracle of the Cumaean Sibyl that elevated him among Christians to the status of a prophet. The laurel at which Vergil gazes and to which his pen points is, then, a symbol of Christ. It is his cross in bloom. Although its verdant foliage is revealed, as is the base of its trunk, which disappears into Vergil's body, its middle is veiled. This veiled section of the tree corresponds to the area of the cross on which the body of Christ hung with outstretched arms. Flanking this tree in exact alignment, while inclining toward it in pathetic fallacy, are two other trees. These are of a species different from laurel; perhaps myrtle, as suggested by their silver-blue color in distinction to the yellow-green pigment of the central tree. These represent the crosses on which the two thieves executed with Christ hung to death. The laurel that wreathes Vergil's head is a significant prophecy of the crown of thorns to circle that of the crucified Christ. This will prove to be an emblem of Petrarch's poetics.

The other figures in the illustration deviate from the medieval iconography of Vergil's "wheel." The general holds a lance rather than the sword, the usual symbol of the *Aeneid*, perhaps in reminiscence of Martini's crucifixion scenes, in which lances are prominent. The shepherd is milking goats rather than sheep; the farmer is pruning a barren thornbush rather than a luscious fruit tree. These deviations from, even reversals of, the medieval scheme may allude to the evangelical parables of judgment in which the antitheses of the sheep and the goats (Matt. 25:32) and of the fruit tree and the barren tree (Matt. 7:16–20, 21:18–19) figure. Judgment will prove to be the act of Petrarch's prophesying. As his couplet interpreted this pictorial allegory, Servius was not revealing Vergil but "the secrets of Vergil." The Latin noun *arcana* was specifically religious, denoting sacred secrets or holy mysteries. It was the same disclosure of the secrets of Vergil that had engaged Petrarch in formal examination by Robert of Naples and secured for him the poetic laureate.[32] His own wreath, unlike that of Vergil, which is depicted as laurel intertwined with myrtle, was of laurel alone. That bough symbolized for him the crown of Latin poetry, the eloquence of the *Aeneid*, which he essayed to imitate in his *Africa*.[33] And although the laurel may also have symbolized a Laura, a noble lady upon whom Petrarch lavished in exquisite lyric his ardent yet plaintive love,[34] that interpretation seems, like his very definition of poetry, a fiction of the truth. As the sacred branch of Apollo, the laurel symbolized his own prophetic vocation and the personal and patriotic glory that genius would merit. Ultimately it signified the arboreal mystery on which all true oracles converged for that Christian poet, the cross of Christ.

On the flyleaf of the manuscript, in the position corresponding exactly to the laurel of Martini's illustration, Petrarch recorded this famous remembrance: "The laurel, illustrious through its own virtues, and long famed through my verses, first appeared to my eyes in my youth, in the year of our Lord 1327, on the sixth day of April, in the church of St. Clare in Avignon, at matins . . ." Although this reputedly relates an encounter with a Laura, Petrarch wrote "laurea," not "Laura." It was coincidentally, as he continued his memorial, "and in the same city, also on the sixth of April, at the same first hour, but in the year 1348, that light was withdrawn from the light of day."[35] These initial and final dates were confirmed by the recurrence of the phrase "the sixth of April" and "at the first hour" in two of the commemorative poems of *Rime sparse* and again in *Triumphus mortis*.[36] It was also coincidentally on the sixth of April, in 1338, that Petrarch conceived of his epic *Africa*.[37] The third poem of *Rime sparse* convinced commentators as early as the quattrocento that the sixth of April indicated Good Friday. As Petrarch wrote of his enamorment:

> It was the day when the sun's rays turned pale with grief for his Maker when I was taken, and I did not defend myself against it, for your lovely eyes, Lady, bound me.
>
> It did not seem to me a time for being on guard against Love's blows; therefore I went confident and without fear, and so my misfortunes began in the midst of the universal woe.[38]

Did this not recall the miraculous eclipse of the sun during the crucifixion of Christ, as creation hid its beauty in mournful shame at the death of its Creator (Luke 23:44–45)?[39] Did the poet's onset of misfortune not match the lugubrious solemnity of the liturgy? Although the feast of Good Friday did not coincide with the sixth of April in any of the years Petrarch cited—in 1327 and 1338 that date was Easter Monday, and in 1348, two Sundays before Easter—the association has persisted since the Renaissance. Although historically inaccurate, the date has been considered ideal. It has been supposed a synthesis of an imagination sacred and profane in which these highlights of the poet's career were incorporated into the universal history in which man was created on the sixth day and redeemed on the sixth day.[40]

The date was apposite for enamorment. April, as Petrarch knew, was the month of Venus, from *aphros* for the foam from which she sprang, or better, as Macrobius thought, from *aperilus*, because in the spring Nature opens (*aperio*) in leaf and blossom.[41] The sixth day of any week was also consecrated to this goddess of love, according to the custom universal since the first Christian century of naming the seven days after the seven planets.[42] Yet although the crucifixion of Christ would prove in Petrarch's poetical theology to be the perfect expression of passionate love, his reference to the sixth of April may have been not fundamentally sacred but secular, not Christian but classical. The phrase "the sixth of April" may indicate the rhetorical figure of adynaton, the hyperbolic impossibility. Adynaton initially appeared in a poetic fragment of Archilochus that complained of the reversal of the world during a total eclipse of the sun at Thasos on 6 April 648 B.C.[43]

> Nothing will surprise me anymore, nor be too wonderful
> for belief, now that the lord upon Olympus, father Zeus,
> dimmed the daylight and made darkness come upon us in the noon
> and the sunshine. So limp terror has descended on mankind.
> After this, men can believe in anything. They can expect
> anything. Be not astonished any more, although you see
> beasts of dry land exchange with dolphins, and assume their place
> in the watery pastures of the sea, and beasts who loved the hills
> find the ocean's crashing waters sweeter than the bulk of land.[44]

In explaining its device of making another speak censure in one's place, Aristotle cited a verse of this influentially in his *Rhetorica:* "There is nothing beyond expectation, nothing that can be sworn impossible."[45] The entire poem was also preserved in the *Florilegium* of Stobaeus, a collection of Greek poetical and ethical texts dating to the late fifth century A.D.[46] Petrarch included Archilochus in his own visionary catalogue of inspirational poets thus:

> Next I saw one who, destroying the firmest of hopes, could stir anger.
> And with his blazing iambics bring about death and destruction.[47]

The coincidence of two eclipses on the sixth of April, in the poetry of Archilochus and in the poetry of Petrarch, suggests imitation, although a precise Latin intermediary for that date remains elusive. The fragment of Archilochus marveling at the total upheaval of the laws of Nature during the eclipse of the sixth of April did inspire rhetorical imitation. While the figure of adynaton as the reversal of the natural order was employed with restraint in Greek drama and poetry, its form was varied. The figure encompassed as its types such proverbs as counting hairs or grains of sand; such fables as the hare and the tortoise or the wolf allied with sheep; and such folkloric and poetic impossibilities as the sceptre that blooms or the pine tree that bears pears. Other motifs were derived from the observation of Nature: cosmic and astronomical impossibilities, such as the sun changing its course, the stars fading, and the sky plunging into the sea. There were also paradoxical unions, such as heaven joining hell, or day, night: human reversals, such as a man without reason; and historical examples, such as Achaeus aiding Troy. The Greek origin of the figure in popular speech was perpetuated in the vivid Latin expressions for "Impossible! never!" that punctuated the comedies of Plautus. In the classical period, however, adynaton acquired a different aspect. Elaborated even to five hexameters, it achieved tone and rhythm and certain literary figures and motifs. With the decisive examples of Vergil, such as the "messianic" prophecy of the fourth eclogue in which the lion and the lamb coexisted in peace, adynaton attained a remarkable status in Latin poetry. The verse of Ovid especially aggrandized this imperious and ingenious hyperbole. The figure, whether apt or abused, was most frequent in bucolic and elegiac poetry, especially in the expression of personal sentiment, whether that of the author or of his characters. Since its theme often accompanied a promise of fidelity, of attachment, or of recognition, it flourished principally in the elegy. Adynaton was nationalized in the Augustan age, which envisioned an eternal Rome as so conforming to natural law that its fall was patriotically imagined as the emphatic impossibility, the supreme adynaton.[48] Persisting in the Latin poetry of the postclassical and Carolingian periods, the figure also survived in Old French and Provençal poetry.[49]

Petrarch typically employed adynaton to express the impossibility of embracing his elusive beloved, as figured in Daphne's thwarting of Apollo's embrace:

> May I be with her from when the sun departs
> and no other see us but the stars,
> just one night, and let the dawn never come!
> and let her not be transformed into a green wood
> to escape from my arms, as the day
> when Apollo pursued her down here on earth!
>
> But I will be under the earth in dried wood,
> and the day will be lit by the tiny stars,
> before the sun arrives at so sweet a dawn![50]

His wish to possess her ever before his eyes was foiled:

> Then my thoughts will have come to shore
> when green leaves are not to be found on a laurel;
> when I have a quiet heart and dry eyes
> we shall see the fire freeze, and burning snow.[51]

Again, echoing the adynaton of Archilochus (cf. Wis. 19:19) in which the solar eclipse beached dolphins, he lamented:

> Alas! snow will be warm and black, the sea without waves, and all the fish in the mountains, and the sun will lie down beyond where Euphrates and Tigris have their one source,
>
> before I find in this either peace or truce, or Love or my lady learn another fashion, who have plotted wrongfully against me.[52]

His enamorment was impossible of fulfillment:

> I have never had a tranquil night,
> but have gone sighing morning and evening
> since Love made me a citizen of the woods.
> Before I rest, the sea will be without waves,
> and the sun will receive his light from the moon,
> and the flowers of April will die in every meadow.[53]

Again he asserted:

> The sea will be without water and the sky without stars when I no longer fear and desire her lovely shadow and no longer hate and love the deep wound of love that I hide so ill.
>
> I do not hope ever to have rest from my labors, until I am disboned and dismuscled and disfleshed or my enemy feels pity for me.
>
> Every impossible thing will happen before another than she or Death heals the wound that Love made in my heart with her lovely eyes.[54]

The prominence of the figure of adynaton as presaging "every impossible thing" argues that Petrarch's citation of "the sixth of April" for the decisive events of his poetic vocation indicated not a calendrical date but a rhetorical figure. By identifying the visionary appearance and disappearance of the laurel wreath and also the conception of *Africa* with this commonplace of the world upside down, he declared their astounding, their prodigious, their impossible defiance of the laws of Nature. The description in the sonnet of enamorment would thus refer not to the eclipse of Good Friday but to the classical invention of adynaton. The failing light in Petrarch's memorial of the death and burial of the laurel wreath was similar imagery. As he recorded, he first spied the laurel at the hour of matins, at dawn, and again on the sixth of April "that light was withdrawn from the light of day."[55] If Petrarch referred by that date of eclipse to adynaton, he announced the stupendous import of the vision and withdrawal of the laurel wreath and of the conception of *Africa*. He was certainly confronted with the supreme adynaton of Vergil: the eclipse of eternal Rome in the absence of empire and papacy.

The event of envisioning the laurel wreath and of being stricken with desire for it was related to the Apolline tradition of the prophetic quality of that bough. In composing poetry Petrarch allied himself, as had Vergil, with Apollo. The initial version of his *Rime sparse,* begun in the year following his coronation, was introduced by a salutation to that diety:

> Apollo, if the sweet desire is still alive that inflamed you beside the Thessalian waves, and if you have not forgotten, with the turning of the years those beloved blond locks;
>
> against the slow frost and the harsh and cruel time that lasts as long as your face is hidden, now defend the honored and holy leaves where you first and then I were limed;
>
> and by the power of the amorous hope that sustained you in your bitter life, disencumber the air of these impressions.
>
> Thus we shall then together see a marvel—our lady sitting on the grass and with her arms making a shade for herself.[56]

This inaugural poem commemorated the myth of Apollo's pursuit of the nymph Daphne. According to the Thessalian version Ovid adopted, Apollo defied Love, who in revenge wounded him at the sight of Daphne's seductive beauty. The nymph resisted the wooing of his amorous discourse, then fled at his bolder attempt to subdue her by force. Invoking her father, the river god Peneus, she was metamorphosed into a laurel on his nurturing banks. Apollo embraced the tree, consecrated it to his divine person, and bestowed upon it immortality. Daphne the laurel became the perfect symbol of the desire for the unattainable so celebrated in the medieval poetry of troubadour and "courtly" love: a perpetual insatisfaction in an amorous quest that frustrates desire but provokes admiring praise.[57] This pursuit of the unattainable beloved as poetic truth motivated Petrarch's lyrics.[58] In the inaugural apostrophe to Apollo, the poet allied himself with that god by whose inspiration "we shall then see together a marvel." He identified the object of his pursuit as the same as Apollo's desire, "our lady." Petrarch named her "Lauretta" or "Laura," the French and Latin versions of Daphne. As his confidant the poet Boccaccio stated: "That illustrious Lauretta should be taken allegorically for the laurel wreath."[59]

Petrarch located his laurel conventionally in a pleasance, the beautiful, shaded natural site that had been the principal motif of descriptions of Nature since the Roman empire. Its typical features were one or several trees, a meadow, a spring or brook and variously, flowers, bird song, and a breeze. The classical source was the Vale of Tempe, the cool, wooded valley between the steep slopes of Ossa and Olympus through which the river Peneus coursed. Such a landscape afforded to poetic invention the charm of a river valley and the grandeur of a rocky gorge.[60] The site was Apolline, for it was at Tempe that the god had pursued Daphne until she was transformed on the bank of the Peneus. It was to such a pleasance that Petrarch recommended the recourse of the poet "to sow the seeds of new projects in the field of his genius," so that upon returning to his chamber the germinating thoughts might achieve perfect expression. The recollection of literature and the mental composition through which the poet aspired were most effectively achieved, he was persuaded, in such locales. As Petrarch advised in *De vita solitaria,* the princes of eloquence, Vergil and Cicero, adhered to this practice of solitary refuge amid oaks, beeches, and poplars, accompanied only by the sounds of breezes, birds, and rippling waters. In such retreat they imitated Plato, who conceived his republic and its laws in such a site.[61]

Petrarch described the laurel by the properties he had praised in his coronation speech: its fragrance, shade, incorruptibility, verdure, and immunity to lightning. The laurel was lofty, noble, even regal. It was redolent with a fragrance that surpassed the rarest perfumes of Orient and Occident, wafting its incense even to heaven. Eternally green, preserving its leaf through the change of seasons, it flourished to propagate an entire wood from a single tree. Its sweet shade, exceeding less beautiful pleasures, was marvelously formed by the arms of his lady seated on the grass. Petrarch envisioned her there under this canopy of virtue, chastely seated with his lord. It was in the laurel's shade that he also spied the symbolic white doe. Adopting the classical motif of composing poetry on the grass beneath trees and near a spring, Petrarch interjected himself into the landscape. He wrote both light and lofty thoughts in the shade of the laurel to the sound of waters. The shade gave repose to the cares of his weary life, and it made his feeble genius flourish. To it he escaped, "fleeing the pitiless light that was burning down upon me from the third heaven." Fearful of being seared by the celestial bolt of judgment, he sought refuge beneath the graceful branches of "the tree most favored in heaven." In its shade he was sheltered from harm. Its honored status rendered it and him immune from lightning, Jove's bolt. As a symbol of immortality, it was thus a fitting crown to honor famous brows, the sole ensign of the twin valors of the emperor and the poet.[62]

The laurel was most nobly, however, what Petrarch termed it in the inaugural apostrophe to Apollo, a "holy" tree.[63] This religious denotation repeated from the coronation speech his praise of it as "a sacred tree, to be held in awe, and to be reverenced." He had cited Vergil's testimony of the erection of altars in its groves and of the garlands of laurel the priests of Apollo wore at sacrifices. The bough was indeed worthy to adorn temples and the very Capitol from whose site he declaimed it.[64] The very word *laura*, as Petrarch ingeniously demonstrated, teaches "LAU-d and RE-verence."[65] In yet another conceit, in which love planted within the poet's heart a laurel rooted in virtue, he even worshiped the tree:

> With his right hand Love opened my left side and planted there in the midst of my heart a laurel so green that it would surpass and weary any emerald.
>
> My pen, a plow, with my laboring sighs, and the raining down from my eyes of a sweet liquid have so beautified it, that its fragrance has reached Heaven, so that I do not know if any leaves have ever equaled it.
>
> Fame, honor, and virtue and charm, chaste beauty in celestial habit, are the roots of the noble plant.
>
> Such do I find it in my breast, wherever I may be, a happy burden, and with chaste prayers I adore it and bow to it as to a holy thing.[66]

This sentiment reflected the primaeval belief that forests were pervaded with mystery. They evoked awe as a numinous environment in which spirits were thought to dwell in the branches of trees and to whisper revelations in the rustling of their leaves. Sanctity was attributed to trees because of their organic life as displayed in growth. They manifested the divine vitality inherent in all living things. Their vegetative cycle of birth and renewal, creation and rejuvenation, also engendered the concept of the "tree of life." In ancient civilizations it was an enduring symbol of the values of life and creativity.[67] This symbolism of vegetative regrowth was also an important type of the self-awareness of the Renaissance artist.[68] It was from this tree of life that Petrarch's laurel was sown as a symbol of the waxing and waning and waxing again of his poetic invention. Although the laurel represented the chastity of Laura, the ideal form of truth that eluded him, just as Daphne had foiled Apollo's embrace, it was as a tree of life also an emblem of the fertility of his invention.

There was allusion in Petrarch's laurel to an archetypal fertile woman of antiquity, the Magna Mater, or Phrygian goddess Cybele, who was mistress of trees. Her iconography as seated beneath her ensign, the evergreen pine, receiving the offering of the first fruits of her bounty,[69] suggests Petrarch's portrait of Laura seated beneath the evergreen laurel receiving the homage of his verse.[70] The laurel was a feature of the ideal landscape in epic poetry[71] and a particular symbol of Vergil's *Aeneid*.[72] So, too, in Petrarch's *Rime sparse* did it particularly represent his own epic *Africa*, which he conceived in imitation. And in *Africa*, at the climax of his famous description of the gods whose portraits adorned the palace of Syphax, he honored Cybele:

> Last comes the great mother Cybele, to whom
> no land is fairer than Mount Ida's slope.
> In ease disposing her vast body's bulk,
> in garb of many hues the ancient dame,
> revered for her great sceptre and the key
> she holds, is seated. Rich in progeny,
> she wears upon her head a lofty crown
> of Phrygian towers. The old legend tells
> that she brought forth the family of the gods,
> aye, and the Thunderer himself. 'Tis true
> her fickle womb likewise the Giants bore,
> a scourge to all the world in ages past.
> Yokèd lions draw her chariot.[73]

Although this supreme honoring of a Phrygian goddess in an Ethiopian palace is anachronistic, Petrarch's poetic reverence and emphasis was apt, even prophetic. It was the transference to Rome at the dictates of the Sibylline books of the black stone in which Cybele was incarnate that stemmed the tide of Hannibal's army at the end of the Punic wars in 204 B.C. Cybele drove the enemy from Italy. In jubilee her stone, a meteorite, was installed on the Palatine in the Temple of Victory, and a festival in her honor, the Megalesia on 10 April, was proclaimed.[74] Thus the evergreen laurel was for Petrarch a symbol of fecundity, in allusion to maternal Cybele, whom he hoped would once again ensure a Roman victory through the inspiration of his epic *Africa*.

It was the fertility of Laura, as expressing her carnal nature, that Augustinus despised. In lecturing Franciscus he scorned her as worn out with excessive childbearing.[75] This was probably an allusion not to a matron of Avignon but to the source of all poetic invention, Mother Rhetoric herself. Petrarch especially esteemed Carmenta. In mythology Carmenta was a prophetess. It was she who taught the Aborigines to write. Like Daphne, she was a woodland nymph. She was also the goddess of childbirth, revered by matrons. Carmenta herself was a mother, the mother of Evander, the original settler of Rome. Prophecy, literacy, rusticity, fertility, and the settlement of Rome were all united in her cult. In his peripatetic epistle on the arts and ruins of Rome, it was the palace of Evander and the shrine of Carmenta that Petrarch first visited.[76] In *Africa* he described it thus:

> Here dwelt the mild Arcadian spirit, here
> took place the greatest wonders of all time:
> the finding of the books, the works of love
> wrought by Carmenta, prophetess benign
> to be revered through all the years to come
> for her endowment of the Latin arts.[77]

The verse expressed Petrarch's belief that Latin secular literature was born from Carmenta the inventress.[78] The concept of the book as a child was a popular personal metaphor, diffuse in medieval literature and a favorite of Renaissance authors. It originated in Plato's doctrine of Eros, in which certain men by converse with a noble soul in a beautiful body spiritually engender poetry. Their verses, as if children, ensure an eternal fame, which endures beyond the monuments of physically begotten progeny.[79] As Plato wrote:

> Those who are pregnant in the body only, betake themselves to women and beget children—this is the character of their love; their offspring, as

they hope, will preserve their memory and give them the blessedness and immortality which they desire for all future time. But souls who are pregnant—for there certainly are men who are more creative in their souls than in their bodies, creative of that which is proper for the soul to conceive and bring forth: and if you ask me what are these conceptions, I answer, wisdom, and virtue in general—among such souls are all creative poets and all artists who are deserving of the name inventor.[80]

It was the fecundity of poetic verse that Petrarch sought in the shade of Laura. She was a symbolic tree of life that engrafted to it the fertile Carmenta, who had engendered the first settler of Rome, and the fertile Cybele, who had saved the city from foreign conquest. By their inspiration Petrarch hoped to populate and protect Rome once again.

The laurel was a "holy tree,"[81] the object of his cult. He was its prophet, priest, and poet. His vocation demanded of him the sublime experience of rapture, for, as he wrote of poets, they "raise themselves aloft on the wings of their genius, for they must needs be carried away by more than human rapture if they would speak with more than human powers."[82] Aesthetically, he was an ecstatic, "rapt by Love's hand I know not where."[83] He confessed that at the sight of his beloved, "my soul trembles to rise in flight."[84] At the prompting of Love, who "gathers her wandering breath into a sigh and then looses it in a clear, soft, angelic, divine voice":

> I feel my heart sweetly stolen away and my thoughts and desires do change within me that I say: "Now comes the final plundering of me, if Heaven reserves me for so virtuous a death."
>
> But the sound that binds my senses with its sweetness, reins in my soul, though ready to depart, with the great desire for the blessedness of listening;
>
> so I live on, and thus she both threads and unwinds the spool of my appointed life, this only heavenly siren among us.[85]

Yet he could not check the impulse of his soul decisively, for it was seized by a mad, uncontrollable desire:

> So far astray is my mad desire, in pursuing her who has turned in flight and, light and free of the snares of Love, flies ahead of my slow running,
>
> that when, calling him back, I most send him by the safe path, then he least obeys me, nor does it help to spur him or turn him, for Love makes him restive by nature;

and when he takes the bit forcefully to himself, I remain in his power, as against my will he carries me off to death.[86]

Petrarch depicted his soul as driven, mastered by a "humble wild creature" that visited him "in human appearance and in the shape of an angel," so whirling him about "in laughter and tears between fear and hope, that she makes uncertain my very state." If this instability was not soon resolved, the poet predicted his demise, for "my fragile and weary strength cannot any longer bear so many changes; for in the same moment it burns, freezes, blushes, and turns pale."

> If she does not soon either accept me or else free me from the bit and bridle, but still, as she is wont, keeps me between the two, by that sweet poison I feel going from my heart through my veins, Love, my life is over.[87]

The poet was, in a cluster of metaphors that pervaded his *Rime sparse*, "yoked," "chained," "snared," and "netted."[88] The bonds were symbolized by Laura's hair, in an extension of the metaphor of the Song of Solomon 5:7, which described the lover as netted in the tresses of the beloved.[89] Since golden tresses often vied with solar rays in the medieval poetry derived from an aesthetic of light,[90] her golden locks were also an Apolline symbol of inspiration. When they were loosened on the breeze they signified Petrarch's ecstatic seizure. A consistent classical description of ecstasy, especially of Maenadism, was the tossing back of long hair in the wind, as when the possessed Cassandra "flings her golden locks when there blows from God the compelling wind of second sight."[91] It was precisely when Laura's "golden hair was loosed to the breeze, which turned it in a thousand sweet knots" that from her eyes burned the light from which the poet caught fire. She seemed to him then "an angelic form, . . . a celestial spirit, a living sun."[92] As he again acknowledged the agent of his captivity:

> nor can I shake loose that lovely knot by which the sun is surpassed, not to say amber or gold: I mean the blond locks and the curling snare that so softly bind tight my soul, which I arm with humility and nothing else.[93]

When Laura's locks were spread to the wind, he was bound: "No one shall ever set me free from that golden snare, artfully neglected and thick with ringlets."[94]

At this moment of entanglement in her hair, the inspirational breeze assumed over the poet the power of Medusa, the monstrous Gorgon of Greek mythology whose eyes could turn men into stones. The rays of celestial light that beamed from Laura's eyes and shone from her locks petrified him. Since Gorgo had snakes for hair, an evil allure might be attributed to Laura's locks, as if to ensnare him in sin. The Gorgon's head was an apoptropaic symbol, however, one that warded off evil, not that enticed it.[95] A religious rather than moralistic reading is appropriate to this image of poetic inspiration. The snake was the common Roman totem for the natal genius.[96] When Petrarch confessed himself captured by Laura's golden locks, those solar rays of illumination that exercised a serpentine power over him, he referred to his epic *Africa,* since the snake was the legendary symbol of the genius of Scipio Africanus. As Petrarch repeated from Aulus Gellius the lore of his hero's celestial issue:

> 'Tis said a glittering serpent oft was seen upon his mother's bed, that terrified all who beheld it. Hence came the belief, now held in many corners of the land, in origin celestial. And for sure the child thereafter born, as he grew up, in semblance seemed no mortal man.[97]

The poet's entanglement in Laura's curling, snaky locks, which she loosened ecstatically in the heavenly breeze, thus symbolized the conception of the epic that would express Petrarch's natal genius and win him the laurel. This inspiration, he confessed, "has the power over me that Medusa had over the old Moorish giant, when she turned him to flint."[98] The beams of inspiration that enlightened him could be withdrawn at divine will, so that the poet froze in the shade and trembled with fear. Or they could assume a different aspect, as judgmental lightning-bolts that struck at his audacity and with a superior glance turned him "to marble," to "an almost living and terrified stone." Embedded in this rock, Petrarch trembled when his lady angrily rebuked him: "I am not perhaps who you think I am!" He speculated that Apollo might be incensed that a mortal tongue should presume to speak of his eternally green bough.[99] The rock into which the poet was metamorphosed in such ecstatic moments asserted the transcendence of his vision and signified his religious fear of the numinous: literally he was "petrified."

The knots that fastened him, the snaring, serpentine locks of Laura that symbolized his Apolline genius, were "the bonds of Venus."[100] The intimacy of love and prophecy that inspired Petrarch to veil his prophetic ecstasy in lyrics of love derived from the Socratic theory of Eros. The art of divination, according to Plato's *Symposium,* was discovered by Apollo under the guidance of Love, so that the prophet was necessarily a disciple of love. Love was the intermediary spirit between the divine and the human. "Through him the arts of the prophet and the priest, their sacrifices and mysteries and charms, and all prophecy and incantation, find their way."[101] As a prophet Petrarch was thus captive to Love. "I am not deceived, but beset by forces much greater than magic arts," he responded to the doleful lecture of Augustinus on self-deception. "I see what I am doing, and I am not deceived by an imperfect knowledge of the truth; rather Love forces me." As any saint should know, "No human defense avails against Heaven." Although Petrarch acknowledged that his aspiration to express truth in verse surpassed the history of rhetoric in prose and poetry, Latin and Greek, he was compelled to the task: "Mortal tongue cannot reach her divine state; Love drives and draws his tongue, not by choice but by destiny." Again he declared: "Alas, Love carries me off where I do not wish to go, and I see well that we are crossing beyond what is permitted."[102]

Petrarch was thus enraptured to the ecstatic state, divinely induced in the poet. In this rapture he typically described himself as captive to extremes of sense and sensibility:

> Peace I do not find, and I have no wish to make war; and I fear and hope, and burn and am of ice; and I fly above the heavens and lie on the ground; and I grasp nothing and embrace all the world.
>
> One has me in prison who neither opens nor locks, neither keeps me for his own nor unties the bonds; and Love does not kill and does not unchain me, he neither wishes me alive nor frees me from the tangle.
>
> I see without eyes, and I have no tongue and yet cry out; and I wish to perish and I ask for help; and I hate myself and love another.
>
> I feed on pain, weeping I laugh; equally displeasing to me are death and life. In this state am I, Lady, on account of you.[103]

As he described his poetic transport "from thought to thought, from mountain to mountain":

> as Love leads it on, now it laughs, now weeps, now fears, now is confident: and my face, which follows wherever my soul leads, is clouded and made clear again, and remains but a short time in any one state; and at the sight anyone who had experienced such a life would say: "This man is burning with love and his state is uncertain."[104]

It was to the shade of the laurel tree that Petrarch had initially fled for refuge from divine judgment:

> To the sweet shade of those beautiful leaves
> I ran, fleeing a pitiless light
> that was burning down upon me from the third heaven;
> . . . .
> so that, fearing the burning light,
> I chose for my refuge no shade of hills
> but that of the tree most favored in Heaven.[105]

And he acknowledged that "a laurel defended me then from the heavens."[106] In its shade he discovered a divine delight:

> In a young grove were flowering the holy boughs of a laurel, youthful and straight, that seemed one of the trees of Eden,
>   and from its shade came forth such sweet songs of diverse birds and so much other delight that it had me rapt from the world.[107]

There he succumbed to Love, who transported him ecstatically "for he gives wings to the feet and hearts of his followers, to make them fly up to the third heaven." That sphere Petrarch declared the celestial site of those love poets Guittone d'Arezzo, Cino da Pistoia, Dante Alighieri, and Franceschino degli Ablizi, whose souls had preceded him in death.[108] It was more famously to the third heaven that St. Paul had been rapt in the ecstasy that became a paradigm of Christian mystical experience: "I know a man in Christ who fourteen years ago was caught up to the third heaven—whether in the body or out of the body I do not know, God knows. And I know that this man was caught up into Paradise—whether in the body or out of the body I do not know, God knows—and he heard things that cannot be told, which man may not utter" (2 Cor. 12:2–4). Petrarch wrote of his own poetic ecstasy that he was "rapt by Love's hand I know not where." Echoing St. Paul's assertion that the pleasures of paradise are inconceivable (1 Cor. 2:9), he continued by saying of his revelatory voice, "he could not conceive it who has not heard it."[109]

Unlike St. Paul, who dared not reveal these mysteries, Petrarch divulged the speech of his lady during his poetic rapture to the third heaven:

> My thought lifted me up to where she was whom I seek and do not find on earth; there, among those whom the third circle encloses, I saw here more beautiful and less proud.

> She took me by the hand and said: "In this sphere you will be with me, if my desire is not deceived; I am she who gave you so much war and completed my day before evening.
>
> "My blessedness no human intellect can comprehend: I only wait for you and for that which you loved so much and which remained down there, my lovely veil."

In remembrance the poet sighed: "Ah, why did she then become still and open her hand? for at the sound of words so kind and chaste, I almost remained in heaven."[110] He thus saluted the heavenly state of poetry "who made so bright and famous in the world her virtue and my madness."[111]

He was reduced to "raving" at sheer contemplation of the unattainable truth.[112] As the madness of prophecy was presided over by Apollo, Petrarch appropriately invoked him as his native deity. In the inaugural verse of the *Rime sparse* in its original form, Petrarch invoked Apollo: "Thus we shall then together see a marvel—our lady sitting on the grass and with her arms making a shade for herself."[113] A gaze "as full of wonder as anyone who ever saw some incredible thing" reinforced this marvelous nature of his poetic vision. And he exclaimed, "What a miracle it is, when on the grass she sits like a flower!" He praised this manifestation as "the high new miracle that in our days appeared in the world." Again, its image was a "miracle," "a noble miracle."[114] Its depiction became his poetic task:

> The high new miracle that in our days appeared in the world and did not wish to stay in it, that Heaven merely showed to us and then took back to adorn its starry cloisters,
>
> Love, who first set free my tongue, wishes me to depict and show her to whoever did not see her, and therefore a thousand times he has vainly put to work wit [genius], time, pens, papers, inks.
>
> Poetry has not yet reached the summit, I know it in myself and anyone knows it who up to now has spoken or written of Love;
>
> he who knows how to think, let him esteem the silent truth which surpasses every style, and then let him sigh: "Therefore blessed the eyes that saw her alive."[115]

Again: "I bless the place and the time and the hour that my eyes looked so high, and I say: 'Soul, you must give great thanks that you were found worthy of such honor then.'"[116] And, heeding this inspiration he blessed his inaugural prophetic vision, and all its consequences, bitter and sweet:

> Blessed be the day and the month and the year and the season and the time and the hour and the instant and the beautiful countryside and the place where I was struck by the two lovely eyes that have bound me;
>
> and blessed be the first sweet trouble I felt on being made one with Love, and the bow and the arrows that pierced me, and the wounds that reach my heart!
>
> Blessed be the many words I have scattered calling the name of my lady, and the sighs and the tears and the desire;
>
> and blessed be all the pages where I gain fame for her, and my thoughts, which are only of her, so that no other has part in them![117]

His soul, unable to endure the radiant presence of beloved poetry at the gate Love has barred shut, sighed: "Oh, blessed the hours of the day when you opened this path with your eyes!"[118]

It was for the perpetuation of this vision that Petrarch invoked Apollo:

> Life-giving sun, you first loved that branch which is all I love; now, unique in her sweet dwelling, she flourishes, without an equal since Adam first saw his and our lovely bane.
>
> Let us stay to gaze at her, I beg and call on you, O sun.

Yet he lamented the daily solar course that refused his prayer: "and you still run away and shadow the hillsides all around and carry off the day, and fleeing you take from me what I most desire."[119] He prayed that his beloved image might not elude him as it did Apollo: "and let her not be transformed into a green wood to escape from my arms, as the day when Apollo pursued her down here on earth!"[120] Nevertheless, when he achieved the inaugural vision of the laurel that eluded even the god, he discovered that it was he who was captive, not she:

> I saw that I had come to the piercing, burning, shining arms, to the green ensign of victory, against which in battle Jove and Apollo and Polyphemus and Mars lose, where weeping is forever fresh and green again; and, unable to escape, I let myself be captured, and I know neither the way to escape nor the art.[121]

Petrarch was more than captive to love, however. Love transformed him with the patronage of his lady "into what I am, making me of a livng man a green laurel that loses no leaf for all the cold season."[122] He became a denizen of the sacred grove: "Love made me a citizen of the woods."[123]

It was the sacred, especially the prophetic, character of the laurel tree that symbolized Petrarch's poetic vocation. Even more unusual than the presence of the tripod in the Apolline temple at Delphi had been that of the laurel. Like the olive of the Acropolis or the oak of Dodona, this sacred tree may have derived its status from the Cretan-Mycenaean period when Gaea, or mother earth, was mistress of oracles. The Delphic temple consecrated to Apollo was initially constructed of laurel branches from the valley of Tempe and its site was guarded by a serpent entwined with that foliage. The primitive Delphic oracles were supposed to have issued from the laurel itself. Although classical Greek religion preserved other vestiges of an ancient cult of trees, the Delphic laurel was the singular such presence in the interior of an enclosed temple. Painted vases depicted the laurel rooted next to the festooned tripod as a characteristic element of the decor of the adytum, or inner shrine. Its garlands adorned the temple walls, and in the vicinity laurel groves graced the Muses' fountain and the Sibyl's rock, remnants of which trees still grow in this century. The Delphic plantation and usage of the laurel was attested by many literary sources known to Petrarch. The arrival of Apollo at Delphi was saluted by a Greek chorus chanting of the "fine shady foliage of the laurel." And in a poetic debate between a laurel and an olive concerning their nobility and utility, the former argued from its importance in the Delphic ritual. The laurel was indeed, with the tripod and the fountain, a traditional Apolline source of inspiration. The Pythia pronounced her oracles "by the grace of the laurel," just as Apollo himself had prophesied in the original Homeric Hymn "under the inspiration of the laurel." Prior to the oracular consultation she burnt an incense of laurel leaves and barley. She also slept on a bed of laurel branches. During the ritual session she chewed on laurel leaves, which were sacred to Apollo whose oracle she was about to utter. Crowned with laurel, she held in her hand a branch freshly cut from the same tree, which she shook at the moment of revelation. The role of the laurel in that Apolline cult was indeed so salient that it became symbolic of the Delphic oracle itself.[124]

The practice of chewing laurel leaves was established in ancient folklore as a means by which seers and poets invoked divine inspiration.¹²⁵ Juvenal satirically equated the phrase "to bite the laurel" with the poetic gift.¹²⁶ Although Petrarch evidently did not resort to this method, the laurel was emphatically the symbol of his inspiration. Ruffling through its verdant leaves was a "calm breeze," he wrote as he punned on the tree, *laura,* as the very breath, *l'aura,*¹²⁷ of poetic inspiration. This air struck the poet's brow, stirring in his memory a recollection of his enamorment and revealing in his sight the face of the beloved. It was a "heavenly breeze," "like a spirit of Paradise," even a "sacred breeze." This breeze originated in clearer and happier skies beyond the Alps, where the archetypal laurel was rooted by a running stream. He thus lauded "the breeze that softly sighing moves the green laurel and her golden hair, with sights new and charming makes souls wander from their bodies."¹²⁸ It was this prophetic virtue of poetry to reveal and enrapture that captivated Petrarch and allied him with Apollo and his bough. Had not his own advent and triumph as a poet been prophesied by the bards of Greece and Rome, Homer and Ennius? Had they not spied Franciscus under the laurel, plaiting its leaves into a crown?

> Already in his heart the green frond stirs
> so great a love, a reverence so deep
> that in the Delphic grove alone he finds
> his true content. See how he practices
> to fashion garlands of the tender leaves,
> already comforted by prophecies
> of things to come.¹²⁹

Had not St. Paul compared the imperishable wreath with which the triumphant Christian is crowned to the laurel won by the victor in the athletic contests (1 Cor. 9:24–25)? Had not St. Ambrose sung of the Holy Spirit crowning the evangelist John with the laurel whose leaves were his verses?¹³⁰

The metaphor of the tree had for centuries rooted Christian theology. The tree of the knowledge of good and evil from which Adam and Eve ate occasioned the fall of man. The tree of the cross on which Jesus hung redeemed him.¹³¹ As Petrarch stated, "in theology wood was the first cause of human misery and later of human redemption."¹³² Symbolic trees also served moralists who discoursed on human lives as bearing the fruits of good and evil, virtue and vice. In this fashion Petrarch invented an allegory of a rare tree growing in difficult and solitary locations. Despite this obstacle, it waxed tall, upright, and evergreen, with healthful shade and sweet, abundant fruit. The tree, he explained, was virtue; its branches, the cardinal and theological virtues. It was tended by the husbandman Christ, who vivified it with his blood and with his word. Refreshed by the breezes of pious inspiration, it flourished in the soil of a tranquil mind and clear conscience, and so bore the fruit of its virtue. The other features of the pleasance were also symbolic: the plants signified virtuous actions; the flowers, the beauties of morality and the fragrance of good repute; the bright color, the shining quality of virtue; the fountain and stream, good deeds.[133] Petrarch's laurel was a symbol of virtue, the virtue he was convinced poetry would inspire.

It was profoundly a symbol of the virtue of prophecy, like the laurel that graced the Delphic shrine and the frontispiece of his manuscript of Vergil. Of all the trees that flourished metaphorically in medieval culture, none loomed so important as the visions of the exegete Joachim of Fiore, which incited a powerful prophetic movement. Joachim's trees were organic figures of universal history as germinating, growing, and fructifying. In his *Liber figurarum* he employed the tree to symbolize the continuity of history, with branches sprouting and spreading throughout the centuries. The two eras of the Old Testament and the New culminated in the first and second advents of Christ, in incarnation and in judgment. History was, moreover, divided into a triune pattern of states, governed by Father, Son, and Spirit. Joachim envisioned these states as the trunks of three massive trees. The first, rooted in Adam, sprouted twelve branches in Jacob, signifying the Israelite tribes, and then stretched bare from Oziah to Christ. The second, rooted in Christ, sprouted twelve branches, signifying the apostolic churches, and then rose bare to St. Benedict. The third tree, not only mysterious but even mystical, defied precise delineation, for its limbs aspired to the celestial consummation of time.[134]

Petrarch's vatic symbol of the laurel did not involve such genealogical import, except for the inclusion of Vergil among the prophets of Christ in the Martini frontispiece. It did share with Joachim's arboreal figure a significant allusion to his prophetic identity, however. Joachim had described those triune trees, which he viewed from the summit of the mountain of contemplation, as the cedars of Lebanon of which the prophet Ezekiel had discoursed (Ez. 27:22). The genealogy from Adam to the consummation of the ages that he fashioned into tree trunks replicated those of that messianic oracle. As Ezekiel had envisioned, Yahweh would pluck a tender twig from the cedar of Lebanon and replant it on the mount of Jerusalem, where it would bear boughs and fruit.[135] Ezekiel was the prophet of the Babylonian Captivity of Israel, perhaps himself a hostage. In imitation a Babylonian theme informed the prophecy of Joachim. He schematized history on the Apocalyptic pattern of the seven seals or ages of the old covenant and seven openings or ages of the new; each age had corresponding persecutions, and each covenant culminated in the sabbath. The sixth seal of the old dispensation coincided with the era from Daniel to Ezekiel; its conflict was the Babylonian Captivity. The corresponding sixth opening of the new dispensation predicted the immanent fall of the new Babylonian kingdom and the rebuilding of the holy city. The age was associated with the great crisis of the Antichrist preceding the seventh opening, the sabbath in which the new Jerusalem would ultimately triumph over the new Babylon. Joachim equated this new Babylon with the German imperium since Henry I, who had involved the Church in the investiture controversy. For this schism and this tribulation, for transgressing the divine command to keep the peace and defend the faith, Joachim prophesied that the empire would be punished by the sixth angel, who would pour a phial of wrath on the Euphrates to dessicate it; for Rome had indeed become Babylon. Joachim considered its fall with lamentation, already sensing its onset in the defeat of the army of the emperor Frederick.[136]

Joachim paralleled his own generation with that of Jeremiah and prophesied the imminence of a new Babylonian captivity.[137] Already captive in Babylon, Petrarch imagined himself to be Ezekiel revived. Like that prophet who had remonstrated with the evil shepherds of Israel, he prayed: "I rely on Him who rules the world and shelters His followers even in the wood to lead me now with merciful staff among His flocks."[138]

3

The Babylonian Captive

The coronation pageant descended the Capitoline and traveled the Via Sacra to the palazzo by the Castel Sant'Angelo,[1] where the Ponte women, the scribe, the barber's widow, the saddler, pruner, and goldsmith perhaps all paused to stare, and then it bridged the Tiber. The street lined with ancient tombs focused on the basilica of St. Peter, whose entrance faced east to greet the rising sun, designed so during the reign of Constantine to eclipse the Roman cult of solar Apollo with homage to the light of Christ.[2] The processional approach to the basilica was itself a triumphal route, as delineated architecturally by its monumental triple gateway and spacious atrium. Petrarch crossed the courtyard, passed the ablutionary font, and entered the royal door leading to the symbolic throne of God. He strode the long nave between twenty-two massive columns, all spoils of war, and beneath a double tier of frescoes depicting Old Testament episodes. Once in the transept, flooded with sun through huge windows and oculi, he approached the altar and hung his laurel there. The gesture repeated the traditional vernal offering of the first fruits, as he said.[3] In pentimento it recalled the fate of the wasted instrument of the desolate psalmist who refused to sing hymns in an unclean land:

> By the waters of Babylon,
> there we sat down and wept,
> when we remembered Zion.
> On the willows there
> we hung up our lyres.
>
> (Ps. 137:1–2)

Petrarch hung his laurel on an abandoned altar. The See of Peter was vacant, its pope exiled in a parallel "Babylonian captivity" of the Church.

In a city teeming with processions, the most triumphal had been those marking papal coronations. The inaugurated pope, flanked by a subdeacon with a ceremonial cloth and a servant with an umbrella, and preceded by sixteen waves of celebrants, from a caparisoned horse to the cardinals, marched from the Vatican to the Lateran, symbolically uniting the See of the Church with the See of the world. Along the route he was cheered by the faithful, who were incensed profusely and showered with coins in remembrance of Peter's reply to the paralytic beggar, "I have no silver and gold, but I give you what I have" (Acts 3:6a).[4] Whether the procession of the poet rivaled that of the pope is unknown, but Petrarch's march to the Vatican had a definite papal context and significance. His vatic vocation was the restoration of the papacy to Rome for the pacification of Italy.

The term of the papacy in exile at Avignon (1305–78) virtually coincided with the span of Petrarch's life (1304–74). He witnessed its entrenchment from the age of eight when in 1312 his father, an exiled Florentine notary, settled his family with other Italian expatriates in Carpentras, a town about fifteen miles distant. In Petrarch's infancy, Clement V (1305–14), pressured by demands of the French crown for resumption of the lawsuit against his predecessor and for suppression of the Templars, and further debilitated by illness, had failed to achieve his professed intentions of returning to Rome. Late in the summer of 1308 he established court provisionally at Avignon. As the first of the exiled popes, he initiated a centralization of the Church through the selection of bishops and the granting of benefices, and he indulged the abuses of nepotism, bribery, and taxation. At his death violence erupted in Carpentras, where the Curia was quartered. As an inhabitant of the town, Petrarch must have known the brawls between the Italian nationals employed at the papal court and those of the Gascon faction, whose deaths resulted in retaliation. The French murdered Italians, burned and looted in the town, and in a mass rally in the square threatened death to the Italian cardinals then in conclave. Just after the election of John XXII (1316–34), Petrarch departed for legal studies in Montpellier, and later in Bologna. He quit the scene of a court disrupted by vacancy, a treasury depleted by extravagance, and an office compromised by the political intrigues of the French and threatened by the wars of the Italians and the Turks. On his return in 1326 at the death of his father, he encountered a papal power consolidated through the astute administration of finances and government and through the brutal intimidation of a revived Inquisition. Prompted by a diminished inheritance, Petrarch himself soon accepted the tonsure and perhaps even minor orders. He entered the service of Giovanni Cardinal Colonna in 1330, then traveled to Paris, the Lowlands, the Rhine valley, and to Rome. In 1337 Petrarch returned to the vicinity of Avignon. The modest residence he purchased at Vaucluse contrasted with the palatial fortress the successor to the papacy, Benedict XII (1334–42), was constructing. Despite necessary and laudable reforms of the court and clergy, and decent personal conduct, this inquisitor and polemicist of a pope was determined, or resigned, to stay. Petrarch's own literary leisure there was interrupted in 1341 by the honor of the laurel, after which ceremony he lingered in Italy until political fortunes impelled his return to Provence in the spring of 1342. Those fortunes may be recorded by the letter maligning the reputation of a dying pope that is the first entry in Petrarch's *Liber sine nomine,* an epistolary execration of the Avignon papacy.

Benedict's successor, Clement VI (1342–52), restored papal benefices and extravagant expenditures, although he evidenced a fine diplomacy and a genuine charity, especially during the great pestilence of 1348. Although Petrarch twice pleaded with him to return to Italy, Clement built a sizeable addition to the palace. The poet protested that "the pope has deserted his proper See (against nature I do believe), and strives to act the head of the world forgetful of the Lateran and Sylvester." When missions to Italy resulted in the lucrative offer of a bishopric and secretariat, Petrarch declined these rewards for his service. It was during this period that he composed his Babylonian sonnets. At the opportunity in 1347 of being installed in a canonry in Parma, however, he departed again for Italy, where after an unsatisfactory appointment he traveled extensively. In the summer of 1351, having lived intermittently in the shadow of the Avignon papacy for about fifteen years, Petrarch returned there decisively. He had been summoned by two cardinals, he said, to a papal audience on an undisclosed topic. The enticement was likely a cardinalate. When Petrarch was again only offered a papal secretariate at an episcopal rank, he refused it. Two years later he left Avignon, this time forever.[5]

Petrarch crossed the Alps to settle in northern Italy; the papacy remained. Innocent VI (1352–62), a zealous reformer but inept diplomat, contended with rebellious friars, depleted coffers, mercenaries and marauders, and yet another plague. Urban V (1362–70) was a monk on the throne, observing the Benedictine rule strictly but liberally patronizing scholarship and art. Petrarch died halfway through the pontificate of his successor Gregory XI (1370–78), aware of the reforming impulse that had revived the Inquisition but not of that which restored the papacy to Rome.[6]

It was an act Petrarch had persistently implored. As early as the pontificate of Benedict XII he composed a metric epistle in which Rome, personified as a distraught matron weeping amid the ruins of her honor, begged for the return of her negligent spouse, the pope. As a widow Rome also importuned his successor, Clement VI.[7] Both poems imitated the first of the biblical Lamentations, a national dirge composed just after the fall of Jerusalem into Babylonian Captivity.[8] The device had been introduced into Italian poetry by Jacopone da Todi, who moralistically portrayed the Church as an abandoned, widowed matron, lamenting her bereavement of her true sons and bewailing her bastards, who earned her the epithet of "whore."[9] Dante politicized the figure as Rome the weeping widow who begged Caesar to return.[10] By the pontificate of Urban VI, an elderly Petrarch abandoned the personification for a bold plea in the name of Christ himself. Prophetically he assailed the pope as the very vicar on earth of "the sun of righteousness" and demanded justice. By this title Petrarch appealed to the ancient belief in the sun as the god of law and justice who observes everything.[11] The poetic inspiration the solar rays symbolized in his verse secured its end in justice, and the justice Petrarch required of the Apolline Christ and his vicar was a Roman papacy. "I believe that Christ Jesus our Lord is beginning to have mercy on his faithful, and I think he wills to impose an end to the evil which we have seen for these many years," he wrote the pope concerning the Avignon exile. "He wills, on behalf of the inauguration of the golden age, to recall his Church, which he has long allowed to wander on account of the sins of men, to its ancient and proper seats and to the state of its pristine faith."[12] Thus, like the oracles of old, spoke Petrarch the divine will.

His concentration on Rome was fostered by a patriotism that most famously allied him with the ill-starred revolution of Cola di Rienzo, but that was also expressed constantly in fervent literature and diplomatic mission. This patriotism had as its object the salutation of the triumphal risen Christ, which Petrarch echoed in poetry and in person: "Peace be with you."[13] The laurel was thus his fitting emblem, for symbolically it was a harbinger of peace, and to hold its branch between enemy armies was a token of the cessation of hostilities.[14] Petrarch imagined an Italy purged of strife and of vice and reunited under the Roman aegis. The vessel of this restoration he believed especially to be that son of an innkeeper whose fascination with monumental inscriptions and ancient histories had inspired the revival of an idealized Rome as in the Augustan peace, Cola di Rienzo. His eloquence, which so impressed Petrarch, roused the Roman populace to such enthusiasm that he was on 20 May 1347 proclaimed master of that city. An exultant Petrarch hailed him as a liberator in the very image of Scipio and panegyrically declared that liberty was at hand. He invented a waking dream of Cola surrounded by masses of brave men in the center of the world on a peak that pierced the skies. Illumined by the sun, he was elevated on a shining throne so resplendent that he rivaled Apollo. The meaning of this marvel, Petrarch decided, was that the liberator was awaiting his fortune. As that fortune declined the poet shifted his own attitude toward the revolution from exultation to defense to rebuke to grief.[15] Yet this was only the most egregious episode of his patriotism, and however Petrarch varied that investment of hope, whether in Robert of Naples, Cola di Rienzo, Charles IV, this pope or that, he persisted in his loyalty to Rome. No matter how disheveled, neglected, and unruly it had become, it was still a regal city, "the see of the true faith, the foundation of the church and the empire of the world."[16] No phrase, he stated, struck a more responsive chord in the human heart than "the Roman republic."[17] The glorification of Rome he understood and undertook as his personal duty, an office conferred upon him at his coronation. Acknowledging his debt, he wrote, "She has bestowed on me the remarkable privilege of being called a citizen, perhaps hoping that I would not be the last defendant of her name and of her diminishing fame in these times." In response he continued, "When her welfare is involved, it is not only shameful, but inhuman and ungrateful, for me to remain silent."[18]

Petrarch's praise of Rome was established not only in his citizenship but also in his office as "historian," a title conferred at his coronation. "For what else is all history," he wrote, "other than the praise of Rome?"[19] The rules for the praise of cities formulated in the rhetoric of late antiquity, that is, the description of the site and its excellences, were extended in medieval practice to glorify its martyrs and confessors, prelates and theologians.[20] In an epistolary tour of Rome, Petrarch conventionally catalogued the marvels of the city by succeeding the pagan ruins with Christian sites. The Christian examples did not supplant the pagan ones, however, although the martyrdom of Agnes religiously surpassed that of Virginia. The Roman exploits whose memory their monuments evoked maintained their own integrity. Their function in Petrarch's rhetorical reminiscence was precisely monumental: to be impressive: to evoke, to elevate, to excite the mind and tongue, as he himself stated, so that deeds both base and noble might be considered and then judged. The aim of his peripatetic habit amid the ruins was virtue, and in this cause Roman truths might be exemplary of Christian ones.[21] As he reinforced this belief in another letter, "No eloquence could express how highly I esteem those glorious remnants of the queen city, those magnificent ruins and the many impressive signs of her virtue that afford light and point the way for those who have entered upon either the heavenly or the earthly journey."[22] Petrarch defined his vatic vocation as the service of the public morality, and he believed that this civic virtue was to be achieved through the same Apolline wisdom that inspired his personal conversion: self-knowledge.[23] As he explained his lady laurel: "She alone is a sun, not merely for my eyes, but for the blind world, which does not care for virtue."[24] And so, climaxing his epistolary praise of Rome, he lamented: "Today who are more ignorant about Roman affairs than Roman citizens? Sadly do I say that nowhere is Rome less known than in Rome. I do not deplore only the ignorance involved (although what is worse than ignorance?) but the disappearance and exile of many virtues. For who can doubt that Rome would rise again instantly if she began to know herself?"[25] As Petrarch assayed his poetic mission, it was to enlighten Rome with such self-knowledge as to elevate it from depravity.

> If Love or Death does not cut short the new cloth that now I prepare to weave, and if I loose myself from the tenacious birdlime while I join one truth with the other,
>
> I shall perhaps make a work so double between the style of the moderns and ancient speech that (fearfully I dare to say it) you will hear the noise of it even as far as Rome.[26]

His exaltation of Rome was religious in import. In an eloquent letter to Cola di Rienzo and the Roman populace on the initial victory of the revolution and the promulgation of the constitution, Petrarch praised Rome as not merely a secular capital but a sacred site. It was God, he declared, who willed Rome to be the supreme head of the world. Thanksgiving was to be rendered on that occasion "to God who has not yet forgotten his most Holy City, and could no longer behold enchained in slavery her in whom he placed the empire of the world."[27] The divine ordination of Rome had been declared by many signs, by martial glory and by preeminent virtue.[28] This favor assured its citizens that, however fickle fortune might prove in debasing the city, "what she will certainly never be able to bring about is the establishment of the Roman empire in any other place than Rome, for as soon as it is found elsewhere it will cease to be Roman."[29] Petrarch subscribed to the pagan myth of an eternal and sacred Rome, as baptized by the enrollment of Christ in the census of Augustus and as hallowed by the blood of martyrs, which had been a conventional apology for its providential mission since its foundation.[30] Contemporaries of Petrarch, notably Dante,[31] also revered Rome as the mistress of the church and the world. The divine depository of imperial, papal, and communal ideals, Rome grounded Latin civilization and Christian faith. For Petrarch the city was not vaguely or vastly sacred, however, but endowed with specifically Christian meaning. It was Christ who had selected Rome as the see of his successors, and who had established it as the temporal head of the world and the foundation of religion. It was thus to Christ that Petrarch looked for compassion on the sacred city, a once noble matron now trampled in the dust and stricken down by her own sons even as she attempted to rise.[32] The papal imprisonment of Cola di Rienzo at Avignon in 1352 occasioned this cry to him: "What are you doing, oh Christ, infallible and perfect judge? Where are your eyes with which you usually dispel the shadows of human misery? Why do you turn them away? Why do they not flash out twin balls of fire to destroy this shameful trial?"[33] Yet this appeal to the very "sun of righteousness" availed no more than that to his vicar, and the Apolline light, clouded by the smoke of human vice, sank into an abysmal horizon.

It was as oppressed by evil and terrified by the threats of worse ill, Petrarch stated, "that I have entered this madness and with hard cares rave to you."[34] The gross social disorder that confuted the blessed oracles of peace once uttered by Hebrew and Roman prophets alike now impelled him to compose oracles of malediction. The yokes, chains, and nets of love that bound him to the lady of his vernacular verse were symbols of the captivity of an entire people. His miserable exile from her sweet abodes[35] was a conceit for the exile of the papacy from Rome. "Scattered rhymes" he titled his verse, a fitting summons to dispersed citizens. His vatic vocation was nowhere more stridently evident than in the doom he pronounced against the new Babylon, the Avignon papacy that was obstructing his ideal of a Roman peace.

Petrarch identified the exiled papal court as "the western Babylon (than which the sun shines on nothing more deformed)," exceeding in reputation the eponymous cities of Egypt and Assyria.[36] He referred by "Egypt" to the site between Memphis and On (Heliopolis) at the vertex of the Nile delta on the right bank opposite the pyramids of Gizeh. The strategic fortress of a Roman legion during the early empire, it became the foundation of Cairo following the Muslim invasion. Although classical geography reported its origins as a colony settled by Babylonians in revolt from their conscripted labors,[37] Petrarch identified its founder as Cambyses, the mad son of Cyrus, who murdered his brother, married his sisters, and profaned religion and custom alike.[38] By "Assyria," the latter and more ancient site, Petrarch indicated the celebrated capital of Babylonia, the fertile area of lower Mesopotamia between the Tigris and Euphrates rivers. From the beginning of history through the Greek incursions of the fifth century B.C., the civilizations of western Asia had focused their trade routes on this city, situated on the main highway between the Persian Gulf and the Mediterranean. Flourishing in the eighteenth century B.C. under the law of Hammurabi, it achieved the apex of its power and culture more than a millennium later under the Chaldean king Nebuchadnezzar. It was he who in a second siege devastated Jerusalem and deported most of the noble citizens of Judah into the "Babylonian Captivity" of Israel.[39] This decisive event terminated the culture and conduct of a small center of government, the Davidic dynasty, which had functioned with its officials, priests, and citizens within the political compass of that great oriental power, Babylon. Deprived of the freedom to occupy its promised land and to govern its independent institutions, the Israelite nation lamented with the hostage prophet Jeremiah, "Our inheritance has been turned over to strangers, our homes to aliens" (Jer. 5:2).[40] This exilic age, memorialized in the apocalyptic literature of the priest and prophet Ezekiel and in the oracles of Deutero-Isaiah, became a prototype for Christian political and social bondage. It furnished Petrarch with the poetic and historic symbol for his own prophetic protest.

Medieval knowledge of Babylon was derived from the itinerary of Benjamin ben Jonah, who late in the twelfth century reported that the ruins of Nebuchadnezzar's once splendid palace were now inhabited by snakes and scorpions. Yet the synagogue of Ezekiel with his sepulchre was still a house of prayer for Mohammedans and Jews. A perpetual light burned over the sanctuary, and had reputedly done so since the day the prophet himself had lit it. The traveler also reported sighting the foundation of the tower of Babel.[41] It was thus that the city had first been noted in scripture, as Babel, in the kingdom of the mighty hunter Nimrod, a descendant of Noah (Gen. 10:10).[42] As climaxing the prehistory of mankind, the Yahwist tradition narrated the etiological legend of the tower by relating the Hebrew *bll*, "to confound," with the Akkadian *bâbilu*.[43] The origin of different languages was ascribed to Yahweh's assertion of sovereignty by confounding the construction of a ziggurat (Gen. 11:1–9). With the fall of Jerusalem (2 Kings 24:10–17, 2 Chron. 36:10), Babylon attained notoriety. For its arrogance it was interpreted by the prophets as the instrument of God's vengeance against Israel. Yet for its arrogance it was also interpreted as the victim of his pity for Israel.

The proverbial fertility of Babylon, which had so impressed classical travelers,[44] was debased in prophetic and apocalyptic scripture to the metaphor dominating Petrarch's own depiction, that of harlotry. The rhetorical figure derived from the allegories of Ezekiel on Jerusalem that adopted prostitution as a symbol of its cultic apostasy and of its political alliance with foreign nations. The prophet accused Jerusalem of fornication in the corporate personality of the whore. This symbolized its sin of trusting in its famed beauty, and of thus converting its ornaments into idols, its harvests and even its children into sacrifices. By this device Ezekiel accused Jerusalem of engaging in alien rituals of sacred prostitution and of rendering fees in tribute to foreign powers. For this apostasy, he pronounced, the husband Yahweh, who had once betrothed and cherished Jerusalem, would now allow his imperious whore to be stripped naked before her lovers, tried for adultery and murder, and released to the mob for justice: to be stoned to death and then hacked to pieces (Ezek. 16:15–63). The prophet attributed this wanton apostasy to the alliances of Jerusalem and Judah with the nations, especially with Babylon and Egypt, in breach of Israel's covenant with Yahweh. It was for this infatuation and defilement with aliens that Yahweh delivered Israel over to her lovers, who ravished, mutilated, and murdered her, so that she might never again play the seductress (Ezek. 23:1–49).[45]

In the New Testament, however, the author of Revelation reversed the imputation of this metaphor of harlotry from Jerusalem to Babylon (Rev. 17:1–19:10). As the new Jerusalem the Christian church was being persecuted by the new Babylon, "the great city which has dominion over the kings of the earth" (Rev. 17:18), that is, Rome. Its fornication was its consort with subject nations, as involving suzerainty, idolatry, and vice, all abominations to Christian believers.

> Then one of the seven angels who had the seven bowls came and said to me, "Come, I will show you the judgment of the great harlot who is seated upon many waters, with whom the kings of the earth have committed fornication, and with the wine of whose fornication the dwellers on earth have become drunk." And he carried me away in the Spirit into a wilderness, and I saw a woman sitting on a scarlet beast which was full of blasphemous names, and it had seven heads and seven horns. The woman was arrayed in purple and scarlet, and bedecked with gold and jewels and pearls, holding in her hand a golden cup full of abominations and the impurities of her fornication; and on her forehead was written a name of mystery: "Babylon the great, mother of harlots and of earth's abominations." And I saw the woman, drunk with the blood of the saints and the blood of the martyrs of Jesus.
> (Rev. 17:1–6)[46]

This figure prevailed in Christian poetry, as in the paraphrase of Paulinus of Nola on Ps. 137 (136 Vg.), "By the waters of Babylon." For persecuting the Church in a Babylonian manner, the poet wished the offspring of Rome to be dashed to death on the rock of Christ. He also enjoined the Christian remnant to commit to the same fate its own infantile vices of the flesh.[47] In a commentary on the same psalm, which Petrarch cited as exemplary,[48] Augustine portrayed the Christian as wandering because of sin between two cities, Jerusalem, or the vision of everlasting peace, and Babylon, or the confusion of worldly peace. The waters of Babylon he interpreted as temporal pleasures lapping the roots of barren trees, on which the Christian should mournfully hang up his instruments of salvation, scripture, the divine commandments and promises, and eschatological meditation. Evil desires, the children of Babylon, were again to be dashed against the rock of Christ. He exhorted:

> Brethren, do not cease devoting yourself to the instruments; sing to one another songs of Sion. As you have readily heard, so readily do what you have heard, if you do not wish to be willows of Babylon, fed by its streams and bearing no fruit. But sigh for the heavenly Jerusalem. What your hope precedes, let your life follow: there we will be with Christ. Christ is as a head to us, for he governs us from above. He will embrace us to himself in that city where we will be equal to the angels of God. We should not dare to suppose this concerning ourselves unless Truth

had promised it. Contemplate this, therefore, brethren; think upon it day and night.[49]

Heeding this advice, Petrarch appropriated the antithesis of these heavenly and earthly cities to discourse on spiritual conflict.[50] More notably, he decided that the "prostitution" of the papal court at Avignon, or Jerusalem in exiled consort with a foreign nation, demanded its shocking equation with Babylon. And thus he pronounced:

> Fountain of sorrow, dwelling of wrath, school of errors, and temple of heresy, once Rome, now false wicked Babylon, for whom there is so much weeping and sighing:
>
> O foundry of deceits, cruel prison where good dies and evil is created and nourished, a hell for the living: it will be a great miracle if Christ does not finally show his anger against you.
>
> Founded in chaste and humble poverty, against your founders you lift your horns, you shameless whore! And where have you placed your hopes?
>
> In your adulterers, in your ill-gotten riches that are so great? Constantine will not come back now. But since Hell shelters him, may it carry you off, too![51]

Acerbically Petrarch criticized patristic and medieval equations of Babylon with Rome as "motivated not so much by their desire for truth as by their hatred and envy of the city."[52] He was convinced that Babylon was Avignon, and he excoriated its perversions in *Liber sine nomine* as the infamous whore of Revelation. Like the ancient city of Babylon, webbed by irrigation canals, Avignon too was girded by "many waters," except that the surging of the Rhône, Durance, and Sorge exceeded the swells of the Euphrates or the Nile. Petrarch suggested, following Augustine, that the waters of Avignon could be interpreted as the temporal goods on whose accumulation the papal court firmly sat, mindless of the riches of heaven. While the ancient city was so mammoth in its construction as to merit the title Babylon the Great (Rev. 17:5), the geographical circumference of Avignon only deserved the epithet Babylon the Small. Yet its corruption so surpassed its model as to have made it Babylon the Immense, he judged, for Avignon fornicated with the kings of the earth in meretricious display (cf. Rev. 17:1–2, 4). "Certainly the words that follow apply to you alone and to no other," he wrote, interpreting scripture, "'Babylon, the mother of harlots and abominations of the earth' [Rev. 17:5]. You are the impious mother of the foulest offspring, seeing that every abomination on earth, every harlot, is born of you, and that you continually give birth to them, your womb being always swollen, full and heavy with them." Petrarch alleged that Avignon, like persecutory Rome, was drunk with the blood of saints and martyrs. If the evangelist had marveled at the mere vision of Babylon, how must a Christian react to its plain sight? He must, Petrarch urged in echo of the prophets, flee.[53]

The debasement of a corrupt Church, even the corporate Roman Church, as the whore of Babylon had been a common cry of rigorist sects. The Waldensians, the Cathars, and the Apostolic Brethren all employed the metaphor.[54] Petrarch's identification was influenced by certain Joachimite polemics. Although Joachim of Fiore himself never equated the Church with Babylon, he was criticized by the Commission of Anagni for implying that it was so during the second age.[55] A prophetic brand of Joachimism preached by his disciple Peter John Olivi did condemn the carnal Church as Babylon. Olivi summoned the elect congregation, or Jerusalem, to arise; he repeated the verse of Revelation, "Come out of her, my people, lest you take part in her sins" (Rev. 18:4). Although he did not intend by this to vilify the corporate Roman Church,[56] the Beguins, who regarded his interpretation of Revelation as authoritative, even apostolic, distorted and exaggerated the revelations of their saint to that meaning. Inquisitional depositions taken from Beguins, who flourished in Provence from 1300 to 1325, recorded a consistent identification of the Roman Church with the carnal Church, and therefore as the whore of Babylon.[57] Olivi's even more zealous disciple Ubertino da Casale also regarded the ecclesiastical hierarchy as the whore of Babylon, especially for its persecution of the Spiritual Franciscans, whose emergence was revered by the Joachimites as the confirmation of the sixth age.[58] Although this critique was resolutely condemned by the papacy, it survived and flourished in Petrarch's polemics.

The vice of lust, the drunken fornication of which he accused Babylon, was phrased prophetically.[59] As he cursed the papal court:

> May fire from Heaven rain down on your tresses, wicked one, since doing ill pleases you so, who after eating acorns and drinking from the river have become great and rich by making others poor,
>
> nest of treachery, where is hatched whatever evil is spread through the world today, slave of wine, bed, and food, in whom intemperance shows its utmost power!

Through your chambers young girls and old men go frisking, and Beelzebub in the midst with the bellows and fire and mirrors.

And you were not brought up amid pillows in the shade, but naked to the wind and barefoot among the thorns; now you live in such a way—may the stink of it reach God![60]

The law of the ancient capital of Babylon requiring females to prostitute themselves with strangers in the temple of Aphrodite, and the lewd custom of prostituting wives and daughters with guests, had tainted the reputation of that city among classical authors.[61] Except for the prophetic song in which Babylon was taunted as a virgin only in its sterility (Is. 47:1), it was not indicted for such prostitution in scripture, however. It was rather Jerusalem that was condemned for playing the whore, in betrayal of its troth to the Lord. Petrarch's poetic description of the rise of Avignon from poverty, especially the final stanza of that sonnet, resonated with the oracle of Ezekiel on the origins of Jerusalem as "cast out on the open field," as "naked and bare" in its youth (Ez. 16:5, 8, 22) before Yahweh in his pity clothed it with luxury (vv. 10–13). When the author of Revelation transferred this metaphor of harlotry to Rome, he retained religious idolatry and political suzerainty as the meaning of its fornication. Petrarch's indictment of "debauchery, ravishment, incest, and adultery" at Avignon may have reflected sexual license, as his satire of the lecherous cardinal suggests.[62] Its meaning transcended any carnal fornication, however, to symbolize, as had the image of the whore in the prophetic and apocalyptic literature, consorting with foreign idols and allies. The political import of Petrarch's moralizing about the vices of the papal court was consistently his primary sense. When he cited "a torrent of the most obscene passions, an unbelievable storm of lewdness, and the foulest shipwreck of chastity"[63] he meant that the papacy was fornicating with foreign alliances and alien religion. Only its repentant return to Rome could absolve its sin and restore its integrity.

The avarice for which Petrarch excoriated the papal court[64] was also aptly portrayed by the Babylonian metaphor, for that city had since the Greeks been a proverbial monument of wealth and luxury.[65] "There is only one hope of salvation here, gold," Petrarch wrote of Avignon, and even: "Christ is sold for gold." He equated this covetousness with sheer idolatry.[66] Although the venality of the curia was a staple of medieval satire,[67] the opulence and greed of its establishment at Avignon were corroborated by records of its excessive taxation on ecclesiastical benefices.[68] As Petrarch observed of the cardinals, "Instead of the naked feet of the apostles," there were "the prancing snow-white mounts of thieves, bedecked with gold, covered with gold, champing on gold bits, soon to be shod with gold shoes if the Lord does not curtail this debased excess. What else? You might think that they are the kings of the Persians or the Parthians, to be adored, whom it would be criminal to greet without offering a gift." He dubbed Avignon "the kingdom of Avarice" itself and deplored the arrogance this wealth fostered through the procurement of political and ecclesiastical power.[69] For such pride the Israelite prophets had especially blamed Babylon and predicted its fall (e.g., Jer. 50:29, 30–31). A source of particular grievance to Petrarch was the reason for this extortion of money through physical violence and threatened excommunication. It was not primarily the maintenance of the papal personage and palace that was depleting the coffers, but the Italian wars.[70]

Petrarch also accused the papal court of the vice of drunkenness, perhaps reflecting his personal observation of "rich feasts in place of sober fasts."[71] Traditionally, however, the intoxication of religious leaders was metaphorical, as in the biblical imagery of the priest and the prophet so reeling and staggering with foreign drink as to render fogged and erroneous judgment to the people (Is. 28:7–8). The particular symbol Petrarch appropriated was the drunkenness of fornication, which in scripture dually signified religious apostasy and political alliance.[72] When Petrarch sketched the pope as "soaked in wine,"[73] therefore, he conveyed more than the cameo of a dotty prelate dozing in his cups. Ancient Babylon had been prophetically "the golden cup from which the nations drank to madness" (Jer. 51:7), a sin for which Yahweh would induce an intoxication to perpetual sleep (51:39, 57). This drunken stupor symbolized political destruction. The cup of drink so potent that whoever drained it staggered and fell crazed was a trope for divine judgment on the nations (Jer. 25:15, 17, 27–28).[74] Petrarch repeatedly imputed such drunken stupor, even madness, to Avignon.[75]

Deploring "Oh Avignon, whose vineyard, if we may believe the prophets, will bring forth bitter grapes and bloody vintage,"[76] Petrarch alluded to the parabolic song of Isaiah in which a loving husbandman planted a vineyard on a fertile hill. Despite cultivation, it yielded only wild grapes, symbolizing bloodshed rather than justice

(Is. 51:1–7).[77] Petrarch thus recalled Yahweh's angry curse on Israel's perversions in the Song of Moses:

> For their vine comes from the vine of Sodom,
>   and from the fields of Gomorrah;
> their grapes are grapes of poison,
>   their clusters are bitter;
> their wine is the poison of serpents,
>   and the cruel venom of asps.
>
>   (Deut. 32:32–33)

He also recalled the divine promise that Yahweh "avenges the blood of his servants" (v. 43). Just as ancient Babylon had proffered "the golden cup from which the nations drank to madness" (Jer. 51:7), so had pagan Rome held in her hand the "golden cup full of abominations and the impurities of her fornication" with the nations (Rev. 17:4). Her intoxication was not with wine, however, but with "the blood of the saints and the blood of the martyrs of Jesus" (v. 6). So it was that Petrarch taunted Avignon, "Do you not know yourself, Babylon?"[78] Its intoxication was not merely with the vintages of Provence, but with its politics, its revenues, and even its populace. Imputing to a drunken Avignon "the blood of the saints and the martyrs,"[79] Petrarch indicted the rapacity of the court.

He may have also alluded to the notorious executions of the revived Inquisition, which had in 1319 at Marseilles burned at the stake four Franciscans of the Spiritual observance. Espousing absolute poverty, they had refused to submit to the papal ruling and to the authority of the Order, which maintained the validity of owning communal property. Their execution catalyzed the apocalyptic sect of the Beguins, the band of Provençal laymen who adhered to the Joachimite preaching of Olivi. Relics were salvaged from the charred corpses and venerated. The names of the victims were inscribed in a liturgical calendar and invoked in litanies, as if to saints and martyrs, while the executioner-pope was denounced as Antichrist. For this defiance the Beguins were themselves prosecuted. As the inquisitioner summarized their testimonies during the process of 1321–25, the Beguins accused the Church of "having become drunk with the blood of martyrs, that is of the four friars condemned and burned at Marseilles."[80] It was this indictment of a rapacious papacy that slaughtered those whose evangelical poverty bore witness against its avarice that Petrarch may have echoed in his accusation. Prudently indeed he separated this and other documents on the Avignon rule from his familiar letters and circulated them only privately.

The heinous crime by which the papacy was gorging itself on human blood Petrarch addressed and avenged by an outcry to the blood of Christ. In his plea for the divine justice of "the sun of righteousness" he assumed a prophetic posture. To the Vergilian ideal of the poet as the Apolline oracle who established the national morality, Petrarch assimilated the scriptural role of the prophet who essayed the same vocation as Yahweh's herald. His stance was egregious in his appropriation of biblical verses and images to censure the vices of Avignon. It was also emphatic in his own invention of oracles. Petrarch did cite against the practice of divination the authority of saints, philosophers, and poets. Such illusion and deceit only flourished because of the ignorance of the crowd and its rage to know the unknown, he declared. He exhorted against faith in soothsayers, advising that anxiety concerning the future would only torment the soul. The prognostication of evil events, if false, excited empty fear; if true, wretchedness before the fact. The prediction of good events induced a weariness of anticipation and a preoccupied hope that robbed one of joy. If the prediction proved false, happiness dissipated in the grief and shame of lost hope. Soothsayers should thus be dismissed in favor of Christ, who does speak of the future but from a divine prescience. "He doubtless speaks many things to us constantly through the ears of our heart," Petrarch believed. "If we were willing to listen to Him, we could easily disdain the promises of these mountebanks." This resort he considered necessary, for "until you throw aside the burden of superstition, you can desire but not pursue the blessed life."[81]

Yet Petrarch was fascinated by such superstition. In his *Rerum memorandarum liber* he compiled and commented on examples of providence and divinations, of oracles, of the sibyls, of enraptured prophecies, presages of death, and dreams, of the science of haruspicy and augury, of omens and portents, and of the Chaldean mathematicians and magi.[82] Both interior and exterior signs of the supernatural preoccupied him, especially dreams and portents. Petrarch confessed to being terrified by dream-visions, which wracked his sleep, a "sleep restlessly agitated by threats and ambiguities of dreams." He acknowledged this disturbance as a universal suffering of the human condition, but considered himself especially subject to its passionate stings.[83] He reported dreams as a vast subject considered by the learned and the populace, about which opinions varied. He cited several commentaries, but agreed essentially with the judgment of Cicero's *De divinatione*. To the ancient lore collected in his own *Rerum memorandarum liber* he detailed in a letter two personal reminiscences of predictive dreams. The one was an oracle of the recovery of a dying friend, the other an oracle of a dead patron; in both the personage revealed his future to Petrarch. "I have faith in dreams," Petrarch concluded,

> not because Caesar Augustus, that very great man both as a ruler and as a learned person, may be said to have been of contrary opinion, and there are many today who agree with him; nor because a dream made either my master or my friend appear before me in my anxiety, nor because one died and the other lived, for in both cases I saw either what I wished for or what I feared, and fate happens to coincide with my visions. My faith in dreams is no more than Cicero's who considered that the accidental truth of one of his dreams did not undo the ambiguities of many others.[84]

Like many of his contemporaries,[85] however, Petrarch was willing to exploit this ambiguity for the sake of art. Dream-visions were a common device in his poetry, as in the oracular vision in which Laura stole from heaven into his chamber to console him with a dialogue on the Apolline symbols of the palm and the laurel.[86]

Portents also invaded his poetry, as in *Africa,* where the Roman populace was terrified by:

> the many portents of the gods: the sun
> high in mid-heaven faded and grew dim,
> losing its splendor, while the earth beneath
> shook and yawned wide and swallowed in its cleft
> entire vineyards: then, before men's eyes,
> subsided, leaving a tremendous gulf.
> The Tiber, bearing in its raging flood
> uprooted trees, broke through its barriers
> and with a deluge never known before
> alarmed the city. On the Palatine
> a sudden shower of stones came pelting down.

The ancient Italians sought the meaning of these omens by sacrificing ritually according to the Sibylline prescription.[87] So did their medieval progeny wonder, fear, and pray. Petrarch described his own experience of a Neapolitan storm and earthquake of monstrous violence and destruction that had been predicted by a local bishop-astrologer. Those who had not been terrorized into repentance before the event were soon impelled to it. As Petrarch reported his own response to the prophecy: "I myself was neither hopeful nor fearful, and, though favoring neither side, I inclined somewhat toward fear, for the fact seems to be that things that are hoped for come less readily than those that are feared. I had also heard and seen at that time many threatening signs in the skies which for one accustomed to living in northern climes resembled the supernatural events that occur in the cold of winter, and make one prone to turn to fear and indeed to religion." Troubled by the public alarm, which sent women running through the streets to huddle in the doorways of the churches, Petrarch long observed the aspect of the moon from his window, and then sleepily retired. With the onset of the quake, however, he awoke and hurriedly processed with the religious of the household to the church, where the night was spent "prostrate with much wailing, believing that our end was imminent and that everything around us would shortly lie in ruins."[88] Again he vividly recounted his experience of an earthquake in Rome that he thought portended calamity to the republic, a destruction of peace and liberty to rival the fall of the Roman empire itself. He supposed it the fulfillment of Balaam's last prophecy (Num. 24:24).[89] However Petrarch may have cooly counseled a rational serenity toward the unknown, as fortified with a confident faith in Christ, he could in the grip of catastrophe share the terror of the crowd. Like his contemporaries he too observed and chronicled the apocalyptic signs "of the floods, the storms, and the fires by which entire cities have recently perished, of the wars raging throughout the world that are causing great slaughter of people, or of the plague from heaven that is unequaled through the ages. These are matters known to everyone," he stated, "witnessed by vacant cities and fields without farmers, mourned by an afflicted and nearly deserted world and by the tearful face, so to speak, of nature herself."[90]

Petrarch's own birth had been inauspicious: begotten and born in exile, through such an arduous labor that his mother was long considered dead by both the doctors and the midwives. "Thus," he wrote, "I experienced danger even before being born and I approached the very threshold of life under the auspices of death."[91] He believed himself governed by a cruel natal star, the victim of a cruel cradle and cruel exile, and of the cruel lady who wounded him with her eyes.[92] Petrarch observed his heart of melting snow and judged it "perhaps prophetic of these sorrowful dark days."[93] The failure of his poetical theology to persuade pope or emperor to civic piety seemed yet another apocalyptic sign of the end of civilization. There appeared no favorable omen, no "crow on the right or raven on the left" to sing a happy fate.[94] On the day on which he surrendered his heart to his serious and pensive lady, divested of her usual gay ornaments of rhetoric, he left his life in doubt: "Now sad auguries and dreams and black thoughts assail me, please God may these be false!"[95] In this humor he lamented poetically, "No sparrow was ever so alone on any roof as I am."[96] The metaphor echoed the sigh of the psalmist, who pleaded that the Lord not hide his face on the day of distress, for "I am like a lonely bird on a housetop" (Ps. 102:7; 101:8 Vg.). The affliction of the psalmist was the Babylonian Captivity of Israel. Despite the taunts of the enemy, he confessed himself confident that the Lord would pity the destitute captives and rebuild Jerusalem from the dust, so that all kingdoms might praise his glory in that city (vv. 12–22). Petrarch, who described himself as "an angry exile from Jerusalem, living by the rivers of Babylon,"[97] also composed political verse in hope of a Roman restoration.[98] In his vatic role he especially imitated the prophet of the Babylonian Captivity, Ezekiel, who like the warbling psalmist on the roof had been appointed by the Lord as "a watchman for the house of Israel" (Ez. 3:17a).

In this choice of model Petrarch may have been inspired by Joachim of Fiore's very popular letter to the faithful that prominently cited this verse. Joachim had interpreted the divine injunction as entrusted in the new Babylonian captivity to all those more enlightened than the crowd, and he had justified by it his own office of interpreting scripture and prophesying judgment.[99] Yet Ezekiel was by his historical circumstance the obvious model for Petrarch's imitation. He did indeed affirm that his literature on Avignon as Babylon was from personal experience:

> I speak of things I have seen, not just heard about. As a boy it was my evil fate to be carried off to that country where, despite my revulsion, I was bound until recently by what shackles of Fortune I do not know. There I passed many years in sorrow. I know from experience that there is no piety there, no charity, no faith, no reverence or fear of God, nothing sacred, nothing just, nothing reasonable, nothing serious—in a word, nothing human.[100]

Yet Petrarch believed that genius was exercised in a poetic invention that emulated ancient examples, as bees create wax and honey from the flowers they sample, then abandon. Its aspiration was "to produce in our own words thoughts borrowed from others . . . in a style uniquely ours although gathered from a variety of sources." The more felicitous writers might imitate not bees but silkworms, which produce thought and speech from within themselves. Petrarch considered himself a bee, an emulator.[101] This apiarian metaphor was that of Seneca,[102] one of the classical models whom Petrarch imitated "to assert or discover his own cultural identity through an act of role-playing."[103] He would trace his forebears' path, he said, but not their tracks, in an imitation that is not sameness, "in a resemblance that is not servile, where the imitator's genius shines forth."[104] In an important poem on emulation alluding to the same letter *Ad Lucilium,* Petrarch thus distanced himself from his patron Apollo.

> The son of Latona had already looked down nine times from his high balcony, seeking her who once in vain moved his sighs and now moves those of another;
>
> when, tired with searching, he could not discover where she was dwelling, whether near or far, he showed himself to us like one mad with grief at not finding some much-loved thing.
>
> And thus sadly remaining off by himself, he did not see that face return which shall be praised, if I live, on more than a thousand pages;
>
> and besides, pity [piety] had changed her, so that her beautiful eyes were at that time dropping tears: therefore [but] the air retained its earlier state.[105]

The allusion was to Seneca's theory of imitation, which advised a resemblance to the original without exactness, much as a son might resemble his father. As Petrarch explained it, "While often very different in their individual features, they have a certain something our painters call an 'air,' especially noticeable about the face and eyes, that produces a resemblance."[106] His poetry thus resembled the classical model in that the "air" of Daphne had remained, although piety had changed her into Laura. Reverence of the Christian revelation that superseded pagan mythology required his imitation also of scriptural models, as of the prophets.

Of Petrarch's prophecies, none was more sobering or more dramatic than the series of portents uttered in his renowned visionary poem, "Standomi un giorno solo a la fenestra." It was a pastiche of images presaging the death of his beloved Laura.[107] In its political sense it was also a remarkable imitation of the oracles of Ezekiel on the Babylonian

Captivity. Petrarch constructed the poem according to the Hebrew prophetic convention of an autobiographical announcement and a visionary sequence.[108] In scripture the personal announcement was typically expanded with the circumstance and date of the experience and with the prophet's state or reaction. Petrarch introduced himself as being "one day alone at the window," and as "already almost tired" from the sheer number and novelty of the visions. In biblical imagery the windows of heaven were the celestial counterparts to the fountains of earth through which the cosmic waters issued at divine will (Gen. 7:11; Is. 24:18, Gen. 8:2).[109] The window through which Petrarch saw his portents was similarly not vitreous but symbolic: the luminous eyes of Laura.[110] The eyes of the lady were in medieval poetry not only spiritual windows but even perilous mirrors.[111] Petrarch's solitary witness at the window recalled that of the prophet Daniel in Babylon, who was also exhausted by his private revelations (Dan. 10:8, 16b, 17b). Physical weakness was in Israelite prophecy a commonplace reaction of dismay to the evil content of visions.[112] Although sometimes the canonical prophets merely observed the scene of their visions, usually they participated by expressing an emotion such as grief or fear or by engaging in dialogue, or even by a dramatic action. No mere spectator either, Petrarch displayed his feelings toward the visionary sequence by a sigh, heavy grief, sorrow, then still grieving fear at the memory of the omen, ardent piety and love, persistent weeping, and finally a sweet desire for death. He interposed himself physically only into the fourth vision, in whose scene he seated himself, delighting in its atmosphere. His sole speech was a concluding address to the poem itself in which he anticipated the poem's response to him.

The scriptural types of prophetic vision involved the oracle, the dramatic word, and the revelation of mysteries. The first vision was a brief report dominated by a question-and-answer dialogue in which a simple image provided the occasion for an oracle or divine proclamation through prophetic announcement (e.g., Amos 8:1–2). The second type depicted a celestial scene or action interpreted as a portent presaging an earthly event (e.g., Amos 7:1–6, Ezek. 9:1–10). The third version conveyed in symbolic, sometimes bizarre, imagery secret activities or future events, with a dialogue deciphering the esoteric significance of the report (e.g., Zech. 2:1–2).[113] Petrarch's visionary sequence imitated this last type, but without the dialogical interpretation. When he designated the first portent as "on the right" he signaled an evil omen. In writing of an injury to his left leg, Petrarch stated the custom of referring to what is unfortunate as left-handed or sinister. Yet "I know full well," he continued, "that in prophesying, the left is considered favorable, whence the poet says, 'It thundered on the left,' and thunder on the left is considered favorable because things on our left are on the right of heavenly beings, from whom all good fortune is to be expected."[114] In prophesying, therefore, the right is unfavorable. It was in imitation of that verse of Vergil[115] that Petrarch favored the ancient Italian preference for the right hand as representing an evil portent. What he envisioned on the right were six oracles of doom:

I

Being one day alone at the window, where I saw so many and such strange things that from the mere seeing I was already almost tired,
    a wild creature appeared to me on the right hand, with a human face such as to enamor Jove, pursued by two hounds, one black, one white,
    who at both sides of the noble creature were tearing so fiercely that in a short time they brought it to the pass where, closed in a stone, much beauty was vanquished by untimely death and made me sigh for its harsh fate.

This first portent was inspired by the parable of the lioness in the nineteenth chapter of Ezekiel. In the ancient world the dead were honored by the chanting of laments or dirges that recited their virtues and deeds and bewailed their loss. The Israelite prophets adopted this form (*qinâ*), in which professional mourners narrated the deceased's past, to portray future events that would also evoke bitter lamentation.[116] The wailing of the widow Jerusalem in the lamentations of Jeremiah (1 and 2; cf. Amos 5:1–2), which Petrarch adapted to Rome in his metric epistles on the new Babylonian captivity,[117] was a prime example of this poetry. Ezekiel also raised such a lament under the figure of a lioness who bore and raised many cubs in its lair. As they matured one of these learned to tear its prey, devouring men. For this carnage the nations captured it in a pit and dragged it with hooks to Egypt. Desperate and desolate at this loss, the lioness raised another of its whelps. It too prowled about, tearing its prey, devouring men, and ruining their palaces and cities. Aghast at its roar, again the nations with a hue and cry cast a net over it and caught it in a pit. With hooks they then drew it into a cage and brought it to the king of Babylon, who imprisoned it, silencing its roar forever (Ezek. 19:1–9). As an elaboration of the leonine metaphor of the king of Judah (Gen. 49:9), the lioness represented in Ezekiel's parable the Davidic royal household, especially the influential queen mother Hamutal. It was she who bore the regent Jehoahaz who was deposed and captured by the pharaoh Neco and taken to Egypt, where he died in bondage. His equally awesome successor, Jehoiakin, was similarly deported to Nebuchadnezzar's palace in Babylon, and imprisoned there during the first siege of Jerusalem (597 B.C.). The deportation of the two kings to exile in the west and in the east thus intimated a universal catastrophe for Israel through its captivity by foreign nations.[118]

Petrarch's metaphor *fera* generically signified a wild beast, and particularly designated species as diverse as a boar, horse, stag, wolf, sea-monster, serpent, and ant. The noun also denoted a lion, as in Phaedrus's classical collection of Aesopic fables, which was widely propagated during the Middle Ages in a prose paraphrase attributed to a Romulus. This usage occurred in the tale of an aged, feeble lion who was gored, trampled, and kicked by his foes, the boar, the bull, and the ass. The dying lion complained of such insults as a double death, which moral the fabulist applied to anyone who loses prestige and thus becomes subject in his disaster to abuse by cowards.[119] This tale was appropriate for Petrarch's criticism of the debilitated condition of the Church under the Avignon papacy, its former hegemony now subject to predators. The medieval bestiaries commonly began with a lengthy and complex description of the lion as the king of the beasts. Its royal and sacred nature was underscored in the traditional opening to the first chapter of the early Latin *Physiologus*, from which text the genre of the bestiary evolved. This cited "Jacob's blessing" on the lion of Judah (Gen. 49:9),[120] a text whose imagery Petrarch would repeat in other portents of this visionary poem.

In Petrarch's vision this noble beast was harried by two hunting dogs that flanked it, bit it severely, and herded it into a pass, where it was enclosed.[121] The practice of hunting lions by trapping them in pits with dogs, spears, and nets was as ancient as the Babylonian epic of Gilgamesh itself, a sport recorded also in Ezekiel's description of the capture of the lion cubs.[122] Petrarch's image was that of a mountainous pass or cul-de-sac, such as the valley of the Sorgue of Avignon, into which the beast was driven, rather than that of a pit dug in the ground. The fate of the lioness was nevertheless the same: capture.

Petrarch's poetic enclosure of the lioness in stone recalled the imprisonment of Judah's kings in the palace of Babylon. In Petrarch's verse the noble beast bore a captivatingly human appearance, an iconographical detail that resonated with the bestial image envisioned by another prophet of Babylonian Captivity. In a dream at Nebuchadnezzar's palace during that exile, Daniel saw a beast like a lioness (*leaena*, Vg.) with eagles' wings. As its plumage was plucked before his very eyes, the lioness was elevated and made to stand upright like a man, and it was given a human mind. This apocalyptic creature symbolized prophetically the Babylonian empire, particularly Nebuchadnezzar himself (Dan. 7:1–4).[123]

Petrarch's variant on the lioness of Judah was the Roman Church, hounded into Babylonian captivity by the dogs of war. Its harriers—one black, one white—which tore viciously at its body from either side symbolized the divisive papal (Guelph, *bianci*) and imperial (Ghibelline, *neri*) parties in Italian politics. A feud between the "white" and "black" factions of a Pistoian family had fomented similar hostilities in Florence at the turn of the century that also divided the Guelphs of that city. This civil strife provoked the expulsion in 1302 of the disaffected "whites," who allied with the Ghibellines.[124] Among the expatriates was Ser Petracco, who escaped with his family to Arezzo, where the poet Francesco Petrarca was born, and then to Incisa, to Pisa, and to Babylon itself.[125] The Church had been pursued to exile there, hounded to exhaustion by the dogs of war, which then devoured its body.

II

>Then on the deep sea I saw a ship with ropes of silk and sails of gold, all fashioned of ivory and ebony;
>and the sea was calm and the breeze gentle and the sky such as when no cloud veils it, and the ship was laden with rich, virtuous wares.
>Then a sudden tempest from the East so shook the air and the waters that the ship struck a rock. Oh what heavy grief! A brief hour struck down and a small space hides those high riches second to no others.

This second portent imitated the poetic dirge for Tyre that composed the twenty-seventh chapter of Ezekiel. The prophet compared that prosperous and regal city to a gallant merchant vessel, constructed and outfitted with the finest materials and piloted and manned by noble and skilled mariners (Ezek. 27:1–11). An interpolated trade list, detailing the wares with which the nations of the compass bartered for Tyre's merchandise, emphasized its commercial power and wealth (vv. 12–25a). Its crew, however, rowed the splendid vessel, overloaded with these riches, from secure harbors onto the high seas. There a treacherous tempest raised by an east wind wrecked it, so that the rare cargo sank and all hands perished (vv. 25b–28). The terrified cries of the drowning men were echoed by the shocked grief of the traders, who lamented the destruction of the proud and prestigious emporium of Tyre (vv. 29–34).[126] Petrarch's description of the lavish ship and luxurious cargo on the high seas, its sudden wreck in a tempest from the east, and his ensuing lament for its loss paralleled this prophetic allegory. The navigation of the ship of the Church through perilous waters to be crowned with garlands on its prow in the port of salvation had been a patristic commonplace.[127] Here it was destroyed. Petrarch expressed fear for the shipwreck of the Church in the first epistle of *Liber sine nomine,* where he portrayed the pope as its helmsman, who, overconfident of calm weather and unreliable sightings, steered the holy craft too close to the shore. Intoxicated, the pope pitched headlong into sleep, while the overladen hold of the vessel burst open, spewing men and cargo into the water. Petrarch himself, fearing lest the storm drive him into the clutches of pirates or dash him on the reefs, beseeched God to steer the errant vessel, as he cast about for a plank on which to swim to dry land.[128]

No such rescue appeared in this vision. Petrarch preserved from Ezekiel's dirge the significant detail of the east wind, symbolically Yahweh's agent of destruction (Ps. 48:7, Is. 27:8, Ezek. 17:10, 19:12, Jer. 18:17, Hos. 13:15, John 4:8). He introduced the detail of the rock on which the ship shattered its hull, as implied in the verb *contero* (Ezek. 27:26 Vg), which means "to grind, pound, or pulverize," and as suggestive of the very etymology of "Tyre" itself (cf. Ezek. 26:4, 14). The navigation of the ship onto the "high seas" alluded to Babylon, for Petrarch's phrase was equivalent to the designation of that capital in ancient mythology. The primordial deep that claimed the ship of state in Ezekiel's prophecy (Ezek. 27:26, cf. 26:19) was the mythological "many waters." This phrase denoted the chaos of the primeval sea against which Yahweh had triumphed in his decisive victories as the Creator brooding over the watery abyss (Gen. 1:2) and as the deliverer of Israel from inundation in the Sea of Reeds (Ex. 14:21–29). In scripture Babylon was situated on these "many waters" (Jer. 51:13, Rev. 17:15). It was, therefore, a monument of the insurgent cosmic elements hostile to Yahweh and disastrous to men.[129] Its very etiology from the tower of Babel as the city of "confusion" repeated the primordial chaos. Now in Petrarch's vision the bark of Peter was recklessly steered onto its high seas to destruction.

The divine agency of the east wind in stirring up these turbulent waters provided Petrarch with the imaginative transition to his third and fourth portents, for the east wind also uprooted plants (Ezek. 17:10, 19:12) and dried up fountains (Hos. 13:15).

III

In a young grove were flowering the holy boughs of a laurel, youthful and straight, that seemed one of the trees of Eden,
   and from its shade came forth such sweet songs of divers birds and so much other delight that it had me rapt from the world.
   And as I gazed on it fixedly the sky around was changed and, dark to sight, struck with lightning and suddenly tore up by the roots that happy plant, whereat my life is sorrowful, for such shade is never regained.

This third portent was inspired by the parable of the cedar in the thirty-first chapter of Ezekiel that prophesied the defeat of the relief column sent by the pharoah Hophra to aid Israel in the final desperate months of its struggle against its Babylonian captor, Nebuchadnezzar, during the siege of Jerusalem (587 B.C.). Paralleling the metaphor of the magnificent ship for the beauty, wealth, and power of Tyre, was this image of the magnificent tree for the same attributes of Egypt. Ezekiel compared that nation to a mighty cedar, fair and lush in foliage, abundantly watered, and towering to such a height that its crown protruded into the clouds. Its strong boughs provided leafy bowers for the birds of the air; its ample shade sheltered the beasts and people of the land. Exquisite in its stately beauty, it rivaled all the trees of Eden, to their envy (Ezek. 31:1–9). For its pride, as symbolized in its height, it was hewn down by foreign power. As the splendid tree, crashing in its fall into the mountains, valleys, and streams, descended to the underworld in death, the birds and beasts preyed on its ruined branches. The deep that had once watered it mourned; the other trees of the forest fainted; the nations quaked at the sound of its fall. The prophet concluded with a warning of divine judgment on all trees that envied its greatness (vv. 10–18).

This mythopoeic cedar of Lebanon was identical to the great

world-tree, which extended from the zones of high heaven to the primal deep and was situated at the navel or center of the earth. As a common ancient symbol of inexhaustible life in diverse mythologies—Mesopotamian, Teutonic, Indian, Chinese, and Arctic—it represented the cosmos as a haven for aerial and terrestrial creatures and as a garden for the gods. In Ezekiel's prophecy this tree, which in the traditional mythologies survived all catastrophes, was felled by the judgment of Yahweh. The Lord delivered Egypt to his instrument, the ruler of Babylon, who executed sentence on its wicked pride and laid it low, so that the nations once under its sway fled and cursed it. The symbolic warning served notice to all rulers who indulged ambitions of world-empire or who aspired to be worshiped as gods that they existed only by divine permission. Yahweh could snap their power by death, as he had uprooted the trunk of the massive cedar.[130]

This third portent also resonated with the parable of the vine in the nineteenth chapter of Ezekiel. In a predictive lamentation on the ruin and exile of Israel's royal house, the prophet had compared the queen mother to a vigorous vine planted by a watercourse. Fruitful and luxuriant, it bore stout branches fit for sceptres, emblems of the kingly succession, and it grew so tall that it was conspicuous for its height and its trailing boughs. The vine was then furiously uprooted and thrown to the ground. An east wind dried it up, blowing off its fruit and withering its strong branches. A fire consumed it. Transplanted to an arid wilderness, a fire bursting from its own branches burned its shoots (Ezek. 19:10–13). The vine was a particular sign in scripture for the fullness of blessing in the messianic age (Gen. 49:11), an image perpetuated in the gospel parables of the vineyard. Fruitful and luxuriant (Hos. 10:1), it was an honorable plant worthy of kingship (Ju. 9:12–13), and a metaphor for the beloved of Yahweh (Is. 5:1–5, Song 7:13, 8:11–12). Ezekiel's prophecy of its uprooting from the fertile soil and its transplantation to the wilderness, where the once lush foliage became mere brushwood fit for burning, also concerned Nebuchadnezzar's siege of Jerusalem in 587 B.C. and the deportation to Babylon of Judah's king, Zedekiah. Like the parables of the lioness and the ship, it was poetically a funereal lament (*qinâ*), as its final verse emphasized.[131]

Substituting his own symbol of the laurel for the scriptural cedar, Petrarch similarly detailed its planting in fertile soil; its flourishing boughs, so young and straight that it seemed a paradisiacal tree; its shade, which harbored diverse song birds. The sudden agent of its destruction was neither the political force that felled the cedar nor the east wind that uprooted the vine, however, although the fire that consumed the branches was imitated. Lightning was the punishment. This was also a cosmic agent of Yahweh's power (e.g., Ex. 19:16, 20:18), and, as the universal weapon of the sky-god, it was a common omen in classical literature. Petrarch had employed it in *Africa* as revelatory of the heavenly realms and as symbolic of Jupiter's justice and punishment.[132] In classical and medieval lore the laurel tree alone was immune from this bolt.[133] Petrarch had praised in his coronation speech this extraordinary privilege, arguing that since the thunderbolt of temporal diurnity that consumed human labor and fame was not feared by the brave bough, the laurel crown was rightly bestowed on those whose glory did not fear the devastation of the ages.[134] In this portent his security was devastated, as the poet's rapturous gaze upon the laurel, imitating the prophet's admiring vision of the cedar and the vine, was altered under a darkening sky. Like the lamentation of Ezekiel, Petrarch's verse expressed his grief at the demise of the happy plant, struck by lightning and uprooted, its shade forever lost.

The dessication of the cedar and the vine in the prophecies of Ezekiel provided Petrarch with a further imaginative transition to the fourth portent. In the prophetic parable of the cedar, the roots of that mythopoeic tree were fed by the abundant waters of the cosmic deep, whose rivers flowed about its plantation and streamed to the other trees of the forest (Ezek. 31:4, 7b). Upon the descent of the tree to the underworld, the deep mourned for it, restraining its rivers and checking its streams, so that the entire forest fainted in gloom for lack of watering (v. 15). Then cast also into the pit, all the trees of Eden, the fairest and the best, all that drank that water, were comforted in the netherworld (vv. 16b, 18b). In the parable of the vine, the east wind that uprooted it also dried it up. It was thus stripped bare of its fruit, and its strong stem withered; then its refuse was blown to a futile transplantation in a dry and thirsty desert (Ezek. 19:12–13). Petrarch's fourth portent also prophesied the desiccation of a water-source.

IV

A clear fountain in that same wood welled from a stone, and fresh and sweet waters it scattered forth, gently murmuring;
   to that lovely, hidden, shady, and dark seat neither shepherds came nor kine, but nymphs and muses, singing to that burden.

> There I seated myself, and when I took most sweetness from that harmony and that sight, then I saw a chasm open and carry away with it the fountain and the place, whereat I still grieve, and I am stricken with fear by the very memory.

Although like the metaphors of the beast, the ship, and the tree, water was a universal and polysemous symbol in ancient and medieval cultures, Petrarch's location of the fountain in the very same woods—Eden—as the laurel of his third portent specified a scriptural inspiration. This was the final vision of Ezekiel, that of the temple spring and the river of paradise in the forty-seventh chapter. The prophet, guided by a divine messenger, saw a spring issuing from beneath the terrace of the Jerusalem temple and trickling eastward. As the brook flowed it increased miraculously in depth and volume into such a broad, swift stream that it irrigated the barren desert of Judah and freshened the saline waters of the Dead Sea. Its promise of life to a society threatened by droughts was detailed in an abundance of food from the river's swarming fish and from the fertile trees along its watered banks (Ezek. 47:1–12). The stream thus revived the paradisiacal river that had flowed primordially (Gen. 2:4–10), symbolizing the transformation of Israel after its Babylonian exile into a new Eden.

This oracle, which dated from the Babylonian Captivity following the siege of Jerusalem, envisioned a restored theocracy in which the temple of that city would be the source of Israel's blessings (cf. Ps. 46:4). The image of regenerative waters flowing from Yahweh's sanctuary recurred in later prophecies of the post-exilic restoration of Jerusalem: the fountain welling from Yahweh's house to water the mythical valley (Joel 3:18) and flowing in the time of salvation to cleanse the people from sin (Zech. 13:1, 14:8).[135] It was also the climax of the New Testament book of Revelation, from whose final chapter Petrarch also tapped his crystalline fountain. In its celebrated vision of the new heaven and the new earth, the Apocalypticist was transported to a mountain from whose height he saw the holy city of Jerusalem descending like a bride from heaven (Rev. 21). Through the middle of that city coursed the crystal-clear river of the water of life that flowed from the throne of God and of the Lamb, who slaked the thirst of the righteous (22:1–2a; 21:6b, 22:7b). On either bank of this river grew the tree of life, which bore monthly fruit and medicinal leaves (22:2b). In this prophecy the Lamb himself replaced the temple as the unique source of the water of life (cf. 7:17, Ps. 36:7), which flowed primordially in the garden of Eden (Gen. 2:10–14) and now watered the fruitful and healing tree of the eschatological city.[136]

Petrarch's metaphor of the fountain springing from a stone also repeated the symbol of the water flowing from the rock Moses had struck during the sojourn of the Israelites in the wilderness (Ex. 17:6). That miraculous sign that quenched the thirst of the parched and disbelieving people became typological for Christ, as the supernatural rock from whom the forefathers in faith had drunk (1 Cor. 10:4). Christ revealed himself to the Samaritan woman at the well as the living water from whom they had drunk, a bottomless spring welling up to eternal life and satisfying the thirst of all men (John 4:11, 14). At the feast of Tabernacles he promised the thirsty who would believe in him a river of living water springing from his own heart (John 7:37). Petrarch's metaphor also had an ecclesial connotation, in the derivation of the Church from the rock who was Peter, according to the saying of Christ (Matt. 16:18), which was commonly argued to be the establishment of the Petrine primacy and hence the papacy.

In Ezekiel's vision the spring welling from the Jerusalem temple had issued in a flood of new life and hope at the return of Yahweh's glory after the Babylonian exile (Ezek. 47:1–12, cf. 43:1–12). In Petrarch's portent this symbol of regeneration was destroyed. He prophesied the devastation of any life or hope for a new Jerusalem by an earthquake. In Hebrew symbolism an earthquake signaled Yahweh's advent as warrior, ruler, or judge, as during the celebrated theophany on Sinai (Ex. 19:18). While in Ezekiel's prophecy of divine combat against Gog it retained this traditional heraldic function (Ezek. 38: 19–23), in the book of Revelation the earthquake became an instrument of the judgment and fall of Babylon (Rev. 16:17–21, cf. 11:13). This Apocalyptic image imitated the Sibylline Oracles, which paraphrased and expanded Ezekiel's prophecy on Gog by reflecting the Roman attitude toward earthquakes as omens of divine displeasure. The earthquake was a standard expression in those oracles of God's judgment on the cities, and Babylon was specifically predicted to be leveled by one. In the Apocalyptic vision, however, the divine intervention signaled by the cosmic earthquake would also vindicate the people of God through the resurrection and ascension of its witnesses (Rev. 11:12–13).[137.]

Petrarch experienced no such consolation. The stream that had transformed the barren landscape of Ezekiel's vision into a forest of trees so fruitful that they were harvested monthly (Ezek. 47:7, 12) was now swallowed up in his fourth portent into the bowels of the earth. With the disappearance of the fountain went the verdant woods and the lofty laurel it had watered, and the poet at the site who depended upon its inspiration. With the descent of the fountain to the underworld, the living water of Christ himself, which had sustained the Israelites in the desert and had since flowed from the rock of Peter, the papacy, symbolically vanished. Petrarch envisioned that the Church that streamed spiritually from the temple of the new Jerusalem and its Lamb would not return there to Rome from its Babylonian captivity, but would instead descend catastrophically to death. This vision grieved and frightened him, as he testified. The jubilant prophecies of Ezekiel and the Apocalypticist were reversed into an oracle of doom. The desiccation of the streams that had once gladdened the city of God so grieved and frightened Petrarch that he disregarded the psalmist's injunction not to fear though the earth should change, shake, and tremble with the tumult of roaring waters (Ps. 46:1–4).

V

A wondrous phoenix, both its wings clothed with purple and its head with gold, I saw in the forest, proud and alone,
and at first I thought it a form celestial and immortal, until it came to the uprooted laurel and to the spring that the earth steals away.
Everything flies to its end; for, seeing the leaves scattered on the earth and the trunk broken and that living water dry, it turned its beak on itself as if in scorn, and in an instant disappeared, whereat my heart burned with pity and love.

Ezekiel's prophecy of the trees whose leaves never withered because they were fed by the stream of the Jerusalem temple (Ezek. 47:12, cf. Ps. 1:3) was fulfilled in the Apocalyptic vision of the tree of life as vivified by the water of life streaming from Christ in the heavenly Jerusalem. Like the groves that flourished in the desert of Judah, the heavenly tree of life yielded abundant fruit and medicinal leaves (Rev. 22:1–2).[138] Petrarch's fifth portent elaborated the fate of this arboreal symbol, already struck by the lightning-bolt of divine justice in the third portent. Petrarch's juxtaposition of the third and fourth portents—the destruction of the tree and the desiccation of the fountain—was symbolically coherent. In the fifth portent he prophesied a devastation extending from the laurel's aerial branches to its underground roots, binding heaven and hell in catastrophe. In this portent the poet introduced to his private bucolic scene another witness and mourner: a phoenix, who in his proud, solitary flight spied the uprooted tree and the arid spring. Observing the leaves of the laurel scattered, its trunk broken, and its water supply exhausted, the celestial bird bit himself scornfully and vanished.

This portent, substituting classical for biblical imagery, imitated the parable of the cedar and the eagles in the seventeenth chapter of Ezekiel. In that fable adopted from Wisdom literature, a great and richly plumaged eagle pucked the highest twig from the cedar of Lebanon and carried it in its beak to a commercial land, where it planted it in a mercantile city. Next it planted some native seed in a fertile nursery by abundant waters, where it sprouted into a vine, inclining its branches toward the eagle while its roots grew beneath it. The vine then twisted toward another great eagle, however. For this act it was uprooted, its fruit was plucked off, and its leaves withered (Ezek. 19:1–10). Ezekiel interpreted the prized cedar as the house of David, whose uppermost branch, which the eagle stole, was its heir, Jehoiachin. The preying eagle represented Nebuchadnezzar, who deported the young king into Babylonian exile during the first siege of Jerusalem (597 B.C.). The vine was his scion, Zedekiah, who was enthroned by Nebuchadnezzar in favorable circumstances and who depended obediently on him for sustenance. The second great eagle represented the pharaoh, either Psammeticus II or Hophra, with whom Zedekiah conspired for political independence. For this defection from his Babylonian lord in breach of covenant Ezekiel prophesied the king's death in Babylon and the failure of Egyptian military support for Israel in the second siege of Jerusalem (vv. 11–21). In an oracular sequel Yahweh himself promised to pluck a slip from the crown of the cedar and plant the tender shoot on the highest mountain in Israel. There he would foster its growth into such a noble tree that birds would roost in its sheltering branches and the entire forest would acknowledge that the Lord alone governed the course of history (vv. 22–24). This oracle prophesied "the Branch," a scion from David's royal lineage, the Messiah who would reign on Zion, bringing peace to the earth (cf. Is. 11:1, Jer. 23:5, Zech. 3:8, 6:12). This allegory became the foundation for the gospel parable of the kingdom of God as a mustard seed that developed into the greatest tree, so that all the birds nested in its shady branches (Matt. 13:31–32, Mk. 4:30–32, Lk. 13:18–19).[139]

In biblical symbolism the eagle was the king of birds; in Ezekiel's fable it specified the royal power of the Babylonian empire. The prophet's description of it as broad in wingspan, with long pinions and full plumage of brightly colored feathers was paralleled in Petrarch's portrayal of the phoenix as cloaked on both wings with purple plumage and hooded with gold. Petrarch's substitution of the eagle with the phoenix, also a proud and noble bird, replaced biblical with classical imagery, as the laurel had supplanted the cedar in the third and fourth portents. Petrarch's substitution was supported by Herodotus's account of the phoenix as purple and gold in plumage and as in outline and bulk very much like an eagle.[140] The royal and solar associations of both the eagle and the phoenix prompted such common comparisons of the birds and interlacings of their traditions.[141] It was appropriate for Petrarch to introduce the phoenix to his Eden, for the province of that bird in classical mythology was the Elysian Fields or the Isles of the Blessed. Christian literature elaborated this glorious theme, as in Lactantius's poetic description of its abode in a sacred grove, resplendent with eternal foliage, at whose center was a living spring of clear, gentle, and sweet water in abundance.[142] It was to such a site that the phoenix flew in Petrarch's verse, only to portend the ruin of paradise.

The portent resonated with the fable of the phoenix in the bestiary of Pierre de Bauvais, the most notable of the French examples, and in the *Image du monde* of Gauthier, or Gossouin, de Metz. These described the phoenix as flying to a mountain called "Liban" where it found a high tree and an excellent fountain. The version of the *Physiologus* from which the principal Latin bestiaries developed similarly told of the Indian phoenix flying to the frankincense tree (*in lignis libani*), where it filled its wings with spices. These allusions to the prophetic cedar of Lebanon were explicated in the earliest Latin drawing in a bestiary of a phoenix, which portrayed that bird as nesting in a tree labeled *cedrus libansi*.[143] Such identification of the phoenix's abode as Lebanon derived from the prophetic imagery of scripture, which associated that location with its fragrant, imperishable cedars with the eschatological bliss of paradise (Hos. 14:5–8, Ezek. 27:22–24). In rabbinical and Christian exegesis the cedars of Lebanon symbolized a realized eschatology, the Jerusalem temple and the Church. This theological symbol was thus fitting for the phoenix as the bird of immortality.[144] The biblical and bestiary traditions, together with classical descriptions of the phoenix as very similar to the eagle, supported Petrarch's variation on Ezekiel's imagery.

There was no apparent precedent, however, for his description of the phoenix biting itself and vanishing. It was rather the pelican that pierced its own breast with its beak, either to feed its young with its blood or to sprinkle it upon them to restore them to life. This was a common medieval allegory for the crucified Christ from whose pierced side flowed the blood of salvation that nourished the living and resurrected the dead. Certain motifs associated with the pelican did appear in the fifth portent, indicating Petrarch's poetic license in ascribing its manner to the phoenix. These were notably the pelican's solitude, its inhabiting of wasted locales, and its unselfish sacrifice. Its representation of charity (*pietas et amor*)[145] was replicated precisely in Petrarch's response to the voluntary death of the phoenix (*pietà et amor*). The phoenix was described in the bestiaries as striking its beak on a rock, however, and so was the eagle. In these fables the ancient phoenix ignited its funereal pyre by striking its beak on a stone. Consumed in the conflagration, it was then reborn from its own ashes, a tale symbolic of the resurrection of Christ.[146] The growth of the eagle's beak to such proportions that it could not eat was legendary. Upon being struck against a rock, the beak would be broken, enabling the eagle to stave off starvation. This rock upon which the eagle struck its beak was interpreted allegorically as Christ. There was also a motif of resurrection in lore about the eagle. Like the senescent phoenix it was said to seek a fountain and then to fly above it into the region of the sun. There its heavy wings were burned and the mist shrouding its eyes was consumed. Descending, it plunged three times into a fountain where it was wholly renewed. This was interpreted as an allegory of a man burdened and dulled by sin. He was exhorted to raise the eyes of his heart to Christ as "the sun of righteousness" and to be baptized in spiritual waters, just as the eagle soared to gaze at the physical sun and then plunged for its rebirth into a physical fountain.[147]

In Petrarch's portent the phoenix flew to the cedar of Lebanon, here the laurel, and to the fountain, as was its legendary custom. Observing the desiccation of the tree from whose twigs it used to build its pyre and of the fountain into whose waters it descended, both for its resurrection, it struck its beak against itself and vanished. This phoenix symbolized Christ, as he was commonly portrayed in patristic and medieval literature and art. In Petrarch's verse he struck his beak against himself, the true Rock, and vanished in the fire thus ignited in his heart. At this spiritual vision the poet's own heart burned with piety (*pietà*) and love. It was also consumed with pity (*pietà*), however, for Christ had been dashed against the Petrine rock of the papacy. The phoenix had discovered Eden made desolate by the removal to Avignon.

VI

Finally I saw walking thoughtful amid the flowers and the grass a Lady so joyous and beautiful that I never think of it without burning and trembling,

humble in herself, but proud against Love; and she wore a white garment so woven that it appeared gold and snow together,

but her highest parts were wrapped in a dark mist. Pierced then in the heel by a little snake, as a plucked flower languishes she departed happy, not merely confident: ah, nothing but weeping endures in the world!

Song, you may well say: "These six visions have given my lord a sweet desire for death."

This sixth portent imitated the oracle of the death of the prophet's wife in the twenty-fourth chapter of Ezekiel. Climaxing the initial phase of his mission, the pericope related Ezekiel's last utterance just before the news of the fall of Jerusalem to Babylon reached the hostages already deported during the earlier siege. The prophet was abruptly informed by Yahweh that the delight of his eyes, his wife, would suddenly be snatched from him in death. He was then forbidden any external expression of grief at this event, specifically the customary lamentation and weeping, the ceremonial baring of head and feet, and the funereal feast (Ezek. 24:15–18). This prohibition of mourning, which permitted the prophet only silent groans of desolation, was to serve as a sign to the nation. Ezekiel's symbolic inaction anticipated the paralysis of the influential elders who were captive in Babylon before the immense suffering about to befall the remaining citizens in Jerusalem. Just as the prophet was deprived of the delight of his eyes, his wife, so would the captives be deprived of the delight of theirs. The invading army of Nebuchadnezzar would profane the temple and slay the youths of the nation, thus destroying any hope of reunion for the captives. The prophet's obedience to this grievous injunction underscored his office as a messenger of divine judgment, one who personally shared in the suffering of Israel (vv. 19–27).[148]

Petrarch paralleled the death of the prophet's wife with that of Eurydice,[149] in classical mythology the wife of Orpheus. Medieval allegorizations of Orpheus as Christ[150] allowed Petrarch the license of identifying Eurydice, his spouse, as the Church. Such nuptial imagery, a commonplace of ecclesiology, was fostered by the Pauline injunction that husbands were to love their wives as Christ loved the Church (Eph. 6:25). It was explicated and elaborated by the Apocalyptic vision of the new Jerusalem descending from heaven as the bride of the Lamb (Rev. 21:9–22:5), a metaphor itself derived from the oracles of Ezekiel (Ezek. 40–48). This opposition of Jerusalem the bride to Babylon the whore was adapted by reformers, as in Petrarch's metric epistles to the exiled popes that confronted these symbolic women. Such allegorization of the papacy and Rome as husband and wife varied the scriptural roles of Christ and the Church in their mystical marriage.

In Petrarch's sixth portent the ecclesial bride, bitten by a snake in the grass, succumbed to death, just as the Church had perished in her other guises as the lioness of Judah, the ship of Tyre, the cedar of Lebanon, and the fountain sprung from a rock. All of these figures Petrarch adapted from the oracles of Ezekiel, the prophet of the Babylonian Captivity, to symbolize the destruction of the Church in its repetition of Israel's political exile. The effectiveness of Ezekiel's dirges had depended on their allusions to the collection of aphorisms traditionally misnamed "Jacob's blessing" (Gen. 49:1–28a).[151] In that patriarchal testament on the twelve tribes of Israel, the imagery of Petrarch's visionary poem was catalogued: Judah was like a regal lioness (v. 9); Zebulun, a harbor for ships (v. 13); Dan, a serpent in the path who bit the heels of raiders (vv. 17, 19); Joseph, a fruitful bough by a spring (v. 22). Just as the prophet Ezekiel had proclaimed the reversal of these promises through the Babylonian Captivity of Israel, so the prophet Petrarch announced them for the Church.

Petrarch's definitive composition of this song in October 1368[152] was not fortuitous. It coincided with the solemn entry on the nineteenth of that month of Charles IV into Rome. "Nothing," it has been judged, "could have been more nicely calculated to bring home to Petrarch the impracticability of his grandiose schemes for an Italy reborn." In May he had twice met with the emperor as a mediator for Milan, whose Visconti had patronized the poet as enthusiastically as they ruthlessly controlled territory. Petrarch's ideal of civic, national, and imperial renewal, which he successively invested in Robert of Naples, Cola di Rienzo, and Charles IV, now foundered in ambiguity. The poet had importuned the emperor to hasten to Rome to compose the Italian disorder. "Enter victoriously and undaunted!" he had insisted. "Move rapidly and cross the Alpine passes amidst the inhabitants' rejoicing. Rome summons her bridegroom, Italy summons her deliverer and desires to be trampled by your feet."

After a decade Charles IV had finally heeded Petrarch's persistent exhortations. Yet he was now intervening, with a formidable army, as the declared enemy of the Visconti dynasty, to which Petrarch was obligated for patronage.[153] The pope, allied with Joanna of Naples and twelve Tuscan communes against Ambrogio Visconti and the leaders of the *condottieri,* had requested the emperor's assistance. Of all the imperial lineage Charles was the most subject to papal policy and ideals, so much so as to earn the epithet "the priests' emperor." This incursion was in fulfillment of a vow he had sworn in 1355 at his coronation in Rome to defend the papal rights against the Visconti. Although his primary objective was the companies, he changed plans when Mantua was attacked by the Visconti. His army was joined by the papal and Neapolitan forces in hostility to Milan. The emperor nevertheless made overtures of peace. The Visconti promised through messengers to obey. Barnabò Visconti absolved some papal debts, agreed to respect the rights of the clergy in his territories, to return sites captured from Mantua, to join the league against the companies, to serve the emperor while in Italy with five hundred troops, and to renounce private alliances with papal subjects. Charles IV in turn reinstated the Visconti as imperial vicars and enjoined the Gonzaghi and della Scala to respect the treaty. Although the pope was dissatisfied with the agreement, the emperor continued his journey, and together they entered Rome triumphantly, with the emperor reviving the ancient etiquette of holding the stirrup by which the pope mounted his horse. The subsequent alliance of the pope, the emperor, Barnabò Visconti, and the Tuscan cities succeeded in defeating the companies at Arezzo on 15 June 1369. But the Visconti shortly after again hired the companies against the pope. He returned to Avignon, prompted by the discontent of the French cardinals at Rome and by the threat of an English invasion of France.[154]

This political scene was the context of Petrarch's climactic portent in which the Church in the guise of Eurydice was bitten in the heel by a snake in the grass. Whether the poet envisioned this agent to be the emperor who entered Rome, the pope who soon quit it, or perhaps the Visconti, whose emblem was a snake, the victim's demise was certain. Like Orpheus mourning the death of his spouse, Petrarch memorialized his grief in the poetic lament of Rime 323. The scriptural signs he appropriated from the prophet Ezekiel conveyed political import from their historical association with the sieges of Jerusalem and the Babylonian Captivity of its nation. They were, moreover, specifically royal symbols. The lion, the eagle, and the cedar, which Petrarch paralleled with the lioness, the phoenix, and the laurel, were regents of the animal, avian, and arboreal realms. Tyre was a queenly city and its ship had kings for oarsmen.[155] The advent of the phoenix, substituting in the fifth portent for the Israelite and the Roman eagle, especially signaled an imperial omen. As sharing the sky with the very gods, birds had been revered since antiquity for celestial and divinatory qualities. Avian flight, cry, and behavior were universal auspices, and prophecy was associated with drinking the blood of birds of prey. As the confidant of Apollo, the phoenix was singularly associated with prophecy.[156] In classical literature the advent of the phoenix on earth always presaged an important turn in universal history, such as the subjection of Egypt to Persia or the eight hundredth anniversary of the founding of Rome. It coincided particularly with the inauguration of a new political ruler, such as that of the Roman emperor Tiberius. Initiating a return to the Golden Age, the presence of the phoenix at imperial triumphs ensured a paradisiacal reign, like that of the Elysian Fields or the Isles of the Blessed that were the provenance of that bird.[157] Just as the phoenix had appeared auspiciously in legend to celebrate the founding and perpetuity of Rome, so it now appeared ominously in Petrarch's portent to lament the ruin of that city. Eden was wasted. The tree from which the phoenix used to gather aromatic branches for its resurrectional pyre was withered, its leaves scattered. The fountain into which it traditionally plunged for rebirth was desiccated. At this profanation the phoenix contemptuously sacrificed its life and vanished, without bequeathing to the nation either peace or progeny.

This imperial omen, devastating Petrarch's hopes for the inauguration at Rome of a new Golden Age, suggests that the snake in the grass of the final portent may have been the emperor himself. Although Petrarch had as late as 1361 assured Charles IV that his Bohemian birth was no impediment to claiming an Italian hegemony,[158] mistrust developed. The once effusive letters and enthusiastic meetings dwindled to utter silence, as the emperor triumphantly entered the city in which each, poet and Caesar, had been crowned a citizen. Such a vision of the German emperor or nation as a scourge of the Church was common among the French and Italian adherents of Joachim of Fiore, even until the sack of Rome in 1527. Applying politically the implications of that prophet's third estate, that of the Spirit, they identified the cosmic evil that afflicted the Church in its final tribulation as the Hohenstaufen rule.[159] In Joachim's complex interpretation of history, the Germans, to whom the Roman imperium had been transferred, played a significant role. Extrapolating from the Apocalypic symbol of the sealed book (Rev. 5:1), he developed a parallel pattern of seven seals and seven openings that corresponded to the eras of conflict in Israelite and Christian history.[160] Just as under the sixth seal the Babylonians had oppressed the Jews, so under the sixth opening the Germans persecuted the Christians. For inflicting on the Church the investiture controversy, the emperor Henry IV was paralleled with Nebuchadnezzar. He was, moreover, censured as the fifth head of an apocalyptic dragon breathing tribulation and schism. Although the German nation had been entrusted with the Roman rule for the exercise of peace, because of its prideful transgressions it had now inherited its scriptural condemnation as the new Babylon. When the angel of the sixth seal poured his phial of wrath into the Euphrates, it was prophesied to dry up, allowing the infidel hordes to cross over and seize the German territories. This act was already presaged in the disaster that had befallen the army of Frederick Barbarossa. In Joachim's scheme the fall of the new Babylon, as ushering in the final Sabbath, was the collapse of the Roman empire caused by the Germans.[161] While Petrarch's visionary sequence reversed this hope by predicting a perpetual Babylon, it was political prophecy and not merely romantic reverie. It incited the poet to crave death rather than exile, for, with the end of "the sun of righteousness," Babylon would indeed be "no light anywhere . . . but only gloom on all sides . . . a night of eternal darkness, I may add, devoid of stars, in which dawn never comes, and where deeds, moreover, are performed in deep and perpetual shadows."[162]

4

Wounded Lovers

The laurel wreath, Petrarch confidently declaimed from the Capitoline, was immune to natural flux, verdant amid the decay of time, staunch against the bolt of judgment.[1] It was not, however, exempt from human design, that of the laureate or of the crowd who sought and spurned him. The ruin of Petrarch's political ideal was the ruin of his poetic inspiration. The six portents of Babylonian captivity also presaged self-defeat. As with the prophet Ezekiel, his personal tragedy was indivisible from the national fate. The lioness, the ship, the laurel, the fountain, the phoenix, and the wife of his visions, all of which perished ominously, symbolized the failure of his poetry to incite virtue through the knowledge of truth veiled in fiction.

As he protested, no beast grazing in any wood was ever crueler than she for whom the poet sighed. Love impelled him to pursue in solitude the alluring voice but scattered footprints of that wandering wild creature who fled capture. It had a human visage in angelic form but the heart of a tiger or a bear. Within its eyes it held the tears of sorrow and death, so that its gaze must be avoided. Petrarch incautiously spied it naked at high noon, in full Apolline light, and for that blasphemous gaze was metamorphosed like Actaeon into a hounded stag. In that transformation into the object of his chase, the poet became the loneliest of howling beasts: "I have become a beast of the woods, remembering her beautiful face and her holy works."[2] Like the tormented captured beast of his first portent, the ship that sank in the second also symbolized the failure of his vatic vocation. The craft of poetry was a commonplace of Roman invention. To set its sails was to compose, by voyaging in a great ship on the sea of epic or by navigating in a small boat on the river of lyric, until the sails were furled again on entering port, the completion of the poem. In piloting his craft the poet as sailor relied on experience against the dangerous winds and tides, or the cliffs and monsters that intruded upon his course. This was a popular medieval metaphor,[3] and it pervaded *Rime sparse* as an image of Petrarch's art.[4] The destruction of the laurel by lightning in the third portent was an obvious symbol of the devastation of his poetic fame and glory. The fourth portent, in which bucolic scene the poet uniquely participated, also presaged the failure of his art in the desiccation of the fountain. Since springs issued from the lower depths, the realm of the dead, they were chthonic powers. The ancient association of prophecy and divination with secret knowledge of the underworld extended mantic powers to springs. Spirits and dream-visions were summoned from the deep.[5] At Delphi the Pythia drank from the Castalian springs before uttering the oracles of Apollo, and perhaps because she composed these sometimes in verse, or perhaps because the Muses haunted the temple precincts, the Castalian springs became a sacred font of poetic as well as prophetic inspiration.[6] It was the desiccation of this source that Petrarch envisioned, and his own descent to the underworld through the cleft rent by the catastrophic earthquake.

Versions of the phoenix myth, whether of its regeneration from suicidal ashes or from natural decay, universally associated its death and resurrection with the sun. In Egyptian lore the phoenix symbolized the total renewal of the solar year, which was associated with the rising of the Nile. As consecrated to the sun, the phoenix was depicted in Graeco-Roman cultures as feathered in the gold and red colors of the sunrise, its omniscient eyes glowing with a supernatural beauty. A nimbus about its head, often radiated, symbolized the sun at its zenith: Apollo beaming light to the planets. In Jewish apocalyptic literature the phoenix was the escort of the sun on its daily journey across the celestial vault. As derived from the oriental myth of the cosmic cock, the phoenix flew just ahead of the solar chariot. With its outspread wings it caught the burning rays of the sun, lest the creatures on earth below be scorched by its intensity. In Christian poetry this tradition was preserved and celebrated in Lactantius's *De ave phoenice,* which described the restorative immersion of the phoenix's charred body in a sacred spring each dawn. It then ascended to the top of the tree of life, where it summoned the new day with a beautiful hymn. The phoenix was thus lauded as "the venerable priest of the grove of the sun and the sole initiate of the secrets of Phoebus."[7] In the context of these traditions of solar and even sacral symbolism of the phoenix, its contemptuous suicide in Petrarch's fifth portent presaged the sunset of his Apolline light.[8]

In his sixth portent a snake bit the heel of a woman modeled on

Eurydice, the wife of the lyricist Orpheus, who charmed her and all Nature with his poetry. To the Ovidian features of her nuptial stroll through the meadow where she carelessly trod on the serpent,[9] Petrarch added the topic of *effictio*, the description of a beautiful woman from head to toe.[10] Her head was wreathed in an obscuring cloud, her body clad in a dazzling garment, but her bare heel was vulnerable to the bite of the tempter. This portrayal encompassed medieval allegorizations of Eurydice as either profound judgment or base concupiscence.[11] Petrarch's figure was poetry itself, whose sublime thought pierced heaven while its lowly form was pierced by hell. The cloud that enveloped its highest parts and the garment that robed its body were synonymous with allegory in his poetics. The image of the head thrust through the clouds also resonated, however, with the scriptural metaphors of the cedars of Lebanon and of the tower of Babel itself, which were destroyed for their hubris in piercing heaven with their height. The part of the lady not veiled in allegory, the bare flesh, was prone to evil, and she perished like the fading flowers of the field. The lamenting poet desired to pursue her in death, as Orpheus had sought Eurydice even in the underworld. Petrarch understood that in espousing poetry he was wedding himself to a temporal reality: language. Yet he rejected the argument that dialectical knowledge, such as scholastic theologians preferred, was firm, immutable, and eternal. "What knowledge is without words?" he rejoined, citing the famous verses of Horace's *Ars poetica:* "Many terms that have fallen out of use shall be born again, and those shall fall that are now in repute, if Usage so will it, in whose hands lies the judgement, the right, and the rule of speech."[12] He aspired to demonstrate that, although temporal, and thus variable and evanescent like Daphne fleeing, poetry still participated in the eternal, like Daphne transfixed. The symbol he invented to surmount the portent of poetic demise was the apotheosis of Laura, in which poetic truth personified triumphed over death. It was thus that Petrarch incorporated the poet's vision into the beatific vision of God.

For Petrarch eloquence was a force for moral persuasion, an active philosophy, not an aesthetic perfection. Poetry was defined by rhetoric.[13] The initial task of rhetoric, invention, classically involved seeking out the subject with talent and ingenuity, or nature and genius.[14] Petrarch asserted that his Laura was "all that Art, Wit [genius], and Nature and Heaven can do in this life."[15] She was thus the perfect temporal invention. Of his genius Petrarch confessed that in his youth it was slight and that he did not place much confidence in it. His fresh steps faltered, "afraid of the high undertaking." Yet genius and force could not avail him against the constraint of poetic inspiration, and so, compelled by Love, in the shade of the laurel his feeble genius flowered. So increased his troubles. His aspiration was Nature's highest flight on a pinion of genius, so elevating him that like a sun "'among brilliant wits [geniuses] his name shines.'" Petrarch was ultimately constrained to confess, however, that "'he flies to fall who mounts too high, nor can a man well do what the heavens deny him.'" Heaven was to prove adamant to his genius. The truth he desired to view naked, like Actaeon spying at high noon on Artemis, took revenge for his audacity. When "thunderstruck and dead lay my hope that was mounting too high," he was transformed into a swan, like the mythological Cygnus, who grieved when Phaeton lost control while driving the chariot of the sun and was blasted with Jupiter's judgmental bolt. "Neither my wit [genius] nor my tongue can equal the truth," he stated. Moreover, he said, no human genius could add to the virtuous forms that adorned its celestial garments. No human genius could display on any page the honor, piety, and virtue of poetry, which ideally showed "the straight way to go to Heaven." It was vainly, then, that he strove to paint in song its extreme beauties, for he was able to hatch in with his pen only a few shaded areas. As he acknowledged, "But when I come to her divine part, which was a bright, brief sun to the world, there fails my daring, my wit [genius], and my art."[16]

Celebrating his privileged ecstatic vision, the poet regretted that his weak mortal eyes were unable to tolerate the sight of other celestial, immortal forms. While the sun is omniscient, as *Africa* piously acknowledged,[17] his poems, which only reflected that Apolline source, were mere fragments of the truth, scattered refractions of a singular light: *rime sparse*.

> I knew (so much did Heaven open up my eyes, so much did eagerness and Love raise up my wings) things new and full of grace, but mortal, which all the stars showered on one subject.
>
> Those many other high celestial and immortal forms, so strange and so wondrous, because they were not accommodated to my intellect, my weak sight could not endure.
>
> Thus whatever I spoke or wrote about her, who now before God returns my prayers in exchange for praises, was a little drop from infinite depths

for one's style does not extend beyond one's wit [genius], and though one has his eyes fixed on the sun, the brighter it is the less he sees.[18]

And, he confessed, "my wit [genius (was)] overcome by the excess of light."[19] In vain has Love a thousand times engaged "wit [genius], time, pens, papers, inks," he declared. "Poetry has not yet reached the summit, I know it in myself and anyone knows it who up to now has spoken or written of love." So he advised, "he who knows how to think, let him esteem the silent truth which surpasses every style, and then let him sigh, 'Therefore blessed the eyes that saw her alive!' "[20]

The lady of whom Petrarch sang as the symbol of poetic truth, he lauded as a gift of the provident and artful Creator who fashioned the universe with remarkable command. In admiration and thanksgiving he praised God. Again he acknowledged poetically, "All things with which the world is beauteous come forth good from the hand of the eternal Workman." He thus refuted Augustinus's allegation that poetry did not elevate his soul to verity and virtue. Countering the saint's charge that the poet was enraptured by mere appearance and not by true reality, Petrarch declared that his lady was to be honored not only for her beautiful visage but also for her "holy works." Heaven itself honored her, he stated, "in whom virtue and courtesy dwell."[21]

It was in imitation of the divine paradigm of creation that Petrarch strove to create artfully and providentially. Yet his struggle for a language to express his insight—to give shape to the idea—testified to his humanity. What God accomplished by sheer will, the singular *fiat*, Petrarch labored for with sighs. While the pious, compassionate glance of Lady Poetry could transport him to the state of primal innocence, her disdainful look could petrify him, so that burdened with original sin he could only invoke its consequence: death. The fault was not in poetry, he explained, but in human craft, which necessarily fails to express the ideal, like Apollo's foiled designs on Daphne. Petrarch distinguished his artifice from the art of the Creator:

> but I, who do not discern so far within, am dazzled by the beauty that I see about me, and if I ever return to the true splendor, my eye cannot stay still, it is so weakened by its very own fault, and not by that day when I turned toward her angelic beauty: "In the sweet time of my first age."[22]

The aspiration to see was not at fault, only the flaw in the eye. Bidding Love to kiss the fair form, he ruefully repeated the observation of Christ on the somnolent disciples who failed to watch during his agony in Gethsemane: The spirit is willing but the flesh is weak (Matt. 26:41).[23]

Augustinus had warned Franciscus that eloquence was the pursuit of the impossible, a veritable Daphne who would allure but elude him. Lecturing him on the poverty of language, the "saint" had chided, "How ashamed you should be to have spent so much time in pursuing something which cannot be attained."[24] Petrarch was not ignorant of the evasion and elusion of language, however, as he declared even in praising the eloquence that Augustinus deprecated. He wrote:

> I consider it a great accomplishment to express great concepts with words and to reveal with artistically combined words the beauty hidden in the mind. If I am not mistaken, that is precisely the highest purpose of eloquence. Though the human spirit aspires toward it, often it halts overwhelmed in the middle of the road. I would like now to tell you something that will impress you; the concept is clearly in my mind, yet I am incapable of expressing what I wish to convey to you. How astonishingly feeble is the language of mortals![25]

Petrarch moralized about the vice of cupidity, how it served as its own punishment by tormenting him whether its excessive desire failed or succeeded. He advised contentment with one's allotted genius and moderation in the pursuit of goals. Yet boasting that grace had almost liberated him from the throes of cupidity, Petrarch confessed that there remained "one implacable passion that holds me which so far I have neither been able or willing to check, for I flatter myself that the desire for noble things is not dishonorable." The passion? "I am unable to satisfy my thirst for books." This cupidity was not only directed toward the possession of books, which was the subject of this particular remark, but toward the production of them. While Petrarch professed that genius should not be compelled to ascend where it cannot, for otherwise, "while we long for the impossible, we neglect the possible," it was the very pursuit of the impossible that he boldly essayed. Although he acknowledged that "one must indeed be mad to attempt excellence in something which one will probably not achieve," that was precisely his affliction: madness, poetic raving. Confessing that his aspirations would exhaust the talents of Demosthenes, Homer, Cicero, and Vergil, he declared that "mortal tongue cannot reach her divine state." Yet Petrarch was driven to aspire there: "Love drives and draws his tongue, not by choice but by destiny."[26]

Petrarch had discovered in himself the "strange pleasure that in human minds [geniuses] is often found, to love whatever strange thing brings the thickest crowd of sighs! And I am one of those whom weeping pleases." With the failure to achieve his ideal, he admitted that "dry is the vein of my accustomed wit [genius]." His genius could not avail against death, for death had "scattered the fire." Yet in reviewing his poetry he still hoped: "May my wit [genius] not displease her, may she not despise my praises." So he implored Love to extend his hand to his weary genius, that he might at least praise the heavenly state of poetry to which his ideal had flown like the soul of Scipio himself.[27] The description of the vivid image of the laurel that initially captivated him had proved beyond his genius. "No wit [genius] or style can ever describe it," he decided. Although it escaped invention, Petrarch attempted to preserve it in another category of rhetoric, memory. "But often I return to it with memory," he disclosed. Annually the ancient wounds of love were renewed, "the new season that year by year renews on that day my ancient wounds." Seven years, ten, eleven, fourteen, fifteen, sixteen, seventeen, twenty, and twenty-one anniversaries are all recorded.[28] At first glance his ideal was most beautiful:

> I never saw the sun rise so fair when the sky is most free of mist, nor after a rain the heavenly arc diversify itself through the air with so many colors,
>
> as, on the day when I took on my burden of love, I saw her face flaming transform itself, which—and I am sparing of words—no mortal thing can equal.[29]

Yet even in remembering the inaugural vision the poet was defeated:

> At times, ashamed that I do not speak in rhyme, Lady, about your beauty, I recall the time when I first saw you, such that there will never be another who pleases me;
>
> but I find a weight that is not for my arms, a work not to be polished with my file; therefore my wit [genius], judging its strength, becomes all frozen in its workings.
>
> Many times already have I opened my lips to speak, but then my voice has remained within my breast: but what sound could ever rise so high?
>
> Many times have I begun to write verses, but my pen and my hand and my intellect have been vanquished in the first assault.[30]

Petrarch nevertheless could not abandon "the first laurel, for still its sweet shade turns away from my heart any less beautiful pleasure."

Although he had explored woods and hills, he had never since discovered a tree so honored by the supernal light that it did not change seasonally.

> Therefore, more and more firm from season to season, following where I heard myself called from Heaven and guided by a mild and clear light, I have come back always devoted to the first branches.[31]

The laurel, which Love once planted in the poet's heart through a gaping wound in his side, was now transplanted to heaven.

> The world was full of its perfect honors when God, to adorn Heaven with her, took her back to Himself, and she was a thing fit for Him.[32]

She was now the honor of heaven, which she beautified and brightened with her presence. Her beatitude consoled the poet, "seeing that she has come so near to Him whom in her life she had always in her heart." Petrarch no longer desired to envision her with an external corporeal eye, for that would recall her from heaven to hell. Rather, "more beautiful than ever I see her with my internal eye, risen in flight with the angels to her and my eternal Lord." She who inspired the poet now delighted the heavenly king. She awakened "among the elect spirits, where the soul internalizes itself in her Maker." Indeed, the heavenly citizens marveled at her arrival there, for never had ascended from the straying earth "so lovely a soul [a vestment so adorned]."[33] More astonishingly still, the Lord himself confirmed their saintly admiration with his divine judgment. When Petrarch prayed for the grace to praise her unexcelled virtue and beauty, the Lord responded:

> there has never been a form equal to hers, not since the day when Adam first opened his eyes; and let this now suffice: weeping I say it, and do you weeping write.[34]

While Petrarch remained a citizen of the woods, poetry had become a citizen of heaven. Poetry, of whose perfection the world had proved unworthy, was content to have exchanged her earthly abode for a heavenly one, for she was "equal to the most perfect souls." Yet "still from time to time she turns back, looking to see if I am following her, and seems to wait; and so I raise all of my desires and thoughts toward Heaven, for I hear her even pray that I may hasten," he recorded.[35]

Gloriously enthroned in heaven, the poet's lady might now see on the face of the omniscient Creator "my love and that pure faith for which I poured out so many tears and so much ink." Thus might she know that the poet's heart revered her on earth as in heaven, only desiring the inspirational sunlight of her eyes. He prayed to be united with her.[36] Indeed, he wished to be rapt there in the very triumphal chariot in which he beheld his beloved laurel personified:

> Then I saw them in a triumphal chariot, and my Laurel with her holy, retiring manner sitting to the side and sweetly singing.[37]

Petrarch desired to share in this celestial triumph, for he had ever sought through poetry the beatific vision of God:[38]

> For Rachel have I served and not for Leah, nor could I live with another; and I would endure, if Heaven called us, going off with her on the chariot of Elijah.[39]

Rachel and Leah, as the Old Testament prototypes of the New Testament characters Mary and Martha (Gen. 29:16–17; Luke 10:38–42), symbolized in medieval spiritual literature the contemplative and the active lives. As the far-sighted, patient, beautiful woman, Rachel was moralistically contrasted with the near-sighted, busy, yet fruitful Leah.[40] Petrarch thus allied his poetic aspiration with the contemplative ideal.[41] The laurel of which he sang was ultimately the crown of the saints, as he gazed toward "heaven where now she triumphs adorned with the laurel that her unvanquished chastity has merited."[42] It was specifically in the chariot of Elijah that the poet sought to ascend to a rapturous triumph. With this metaphor Petrarch indicated his prophetic vocation.

In his meditation *De vita solitaria* Petrarch had lauded Elijah as the model of the solitary prophet. He had recounted his wondrous deeds, particularly how he was seized up to heaven from the wilderness in a flaming chariot.[43] The biblical description of this vortiginous rapture in "a chariot of fire and horses of fire" (2 Kings 2:11) is very suggestive of the iconography of that other prophet whom Petrarch revered as the source of his poetic genius: Apollo the charioteer, who daily drives the quadriga of the burning sun across the heavens. This similarity did not escape ancient Christian theologians. Speculating on spiritual ascension, they compared Elijah's rapture to the human mind taken up in a chariot of fire, the Spirit itself, and transported through the air to the glories of heaven. This Christian theme of apotheosis, conceived as a rapture on the chariot of Elijah, originated in Mithraism. Its initial application was to Roman emperors, precisely in relation to the solar cult Augustus established when he adopted Apollo as his personal god. From the beginning of the Roman empire, the emperor was depicted as transported in a chariot drawn by winged horses, as interpreted in this oracle to Julian: "Then a vehicle of dazzling flame will bear you to Olympus; and you will reach the eternal abode in ethereal light." This chariot of Apollo as Helios, the solar deity, was adopted in Judaic and Christian art for the conveyance of souls to heaven, as in the famous mosaic beneath the Vatican. As interpreted in conjunction with the other mosaics of deliverance in that hypogeum, the Apolline figure of Christ not only depicted "the sun of righteousness," it also prefigured the eschatological hope of Christians to rise with him. Such artistic assimilation of the chariots of Apollo (Helios) and Elijah as vehicles of spiritual ascent was confirmed by literary texts that, playing on their names Ἠλίας and Ἥλιος, compared the prophet with the sun. A notable example that Petrarch knew was this verse from the pen of the Christian poet Sedulius:

> Elias, shining in name and merit, is worthy to shed his light on the pathways of Heaven: by the change of one letter his name in Greek becomes "sun."[44]

Was not a vision of "the pathways of Heaven" the hieratic prayer of Vergil to the Muses?[45] And had not Petrarch in imitation espoused poetry against asceticism as the most sublime and direct course there?[46]

The traditional metaphor of Elijah's chariot, which Petrarch adopted as a model of spiritual ascension, served also for him to recapitulate his Apolline vocation as an inspired prophet. He would be enraptured like Elijah in a fiery chariot to a celestial triumph, where he would be crowned with the imperishable laurel of the saints. Like Apollo he would drive toward that apotheosis the very quadriga of the sun, whose rays illumined him with poetic truth. He would play the roles not only of these two prophets, but of one who was famously identified in his own apocalyptic age with both of those enlightened spirits: Francis of Assisi.

In his *Rime sparse* Petrarch paralleled the celebrated birth of Laura, his poetic symbol, with that of St. Francis. Lauding the town of Assisi, Dante had written in the *Divina commedia:*

> From this slope, where most it breaks its steepness, a sun rose on the world.⁴⁷

In imitation Petrarch wrote of Laura:

> And now from a small village He has given us a sun, such that Nature is thanked and the place where so beautiful a lady was born to the world.⁴⁸

He thus resounded the simile with which the papal bull of canonization, *Mira circa nos* (1228), had saluted Francis, "just as a sun shining in the church of God." The first biography of the saint had praised him as a new light sent from heaven to earth to banish the universal gloom of darkness. This theme was developed in the prologue of the *Legenda maior* by Bonaventure, who declared of Francis that God "set him up as a light for believers so that by bearing witness to the light he might prepare for the Lord a way of light and peace into the hearts of the faithful."

> Shining with the splendor of his life and teaching, like the morning star in the midst of clouds, by his resplendent rays he guided into the light those sitting in darkness and the shadow of death, and like the rainbow shining among clouds of glory he made manifest in himself the sign of the Lord's covenant.

The first liturgy to honor Francis extended this solar imagery:

> Thou of our arduous service the triumphal car and charioteer; in the sight of the friars a fiery quadriga rapt thee transformed in solar splendor; on thee radiating with signs on thee announcing the future has rested the cloven spirit of prophets.

The twin prophets were Elijah and Elisha, but it was with the fiery charioteer Elijah that Francis was especially associated. As Bonaventure expounded his praise:

> And filled with the spirit of prophecy, he was also assigned an angelic ministry and was totally aflame with Seraphic fire. Like a hierarchic man he was lifted up in a fiery chariot, as will be seen quite clearly in the course of his life; therefore it can be reasonably proved that he came in the spirit and power of Elijah.⁴⁹

The scriptural verse "Then the prophet Elijah arose like a fire, and his word burned like a torch" (Sir. 48:1) inspired an entire class of sermons lauding Francis as a type of that prophet:

> Among all the other saints of the New Testament who were like Elijah, blessed Francis was to such a degree that it truly seems possible to say concerning him what is said about John the Baptist, that he undoubtedly came in the spirit and power of Elijah. For just as Elijah will have come to convert the hearts of fathers toward sons and the hearts of sons toward fathers, so Francis came to announce peace, as the angel of true peace; and just as Elijah has been rapt to heaven in a fiery chariot so the soul of Francis has been seen rapt to heaven as a certain solar or luciform ball.[50]

Bonaventure's *Legenda maior* recorded the origin of this belief in an episode from the early history of the Franciscan Order:

> At about midnight while some of the friars were resting and others continued to pray, behold, a fiery chariot of wonderful brilliance entered through the door of the house and turned here and there three times through the house. A globe of light rested above it which shone like the sun and lit up the night. Those who were awake were dumbfounded, and those who were sleeping woke up terrified. They felt the brightness light up their hearts no less than their bodies, and the conscience of each was laid bare to the others by the strength of that marvellous light. As they looked into each other's hearts, they all realized together that their holy father, who was absent physically, was present in spirit (1 Cor. 5:3), transfigured in this image. And they realized that by supernatural power the Lord had shown him to them in this glowing chariot of fire (2 Kings 2:11), radiant with heavenly splendor and inflamed with burning ardor so that they might follow him like true Israelites (John 1:47). Like a second Elijah, God had made him a chariot and charioteer for spiritual men (2 Kings 2:12).[51]

From this association of Francis with the solar prophet Elijah, there developed an identification of him as the Apocalyptic angel of the sixth seal who ascended from the sun (Rev. 6:2a). As Bonaventure continued in praise:

> And so not without reason
> is he considered to be symbolized by the image of the
> Angel who descends from the sunrise
> bearing the seal of the living God,
> in the true prophecy of that other friend of the
> Bridegroom, John the Apostle and Evangelist.

> For "when the sixth seal was opened,"
> John says in the Apocalypse,
> "I saw another Angel
> ascending from the rising of the sun,
> having the seal of the living God."[52]

Identifying this very seal as the stigmata of Francis, the Franciscan literature of the thirteenth and fourteenth centuries commonly hailed him as the Apocalyptic angel of the sixth seal. In the Joachimite literature he was particularly revered as the initiator of the third state, the age of the Holy Spirit in which Babylon would be defeated.[53]

Petrarch shared his unusual name, Francesco, which according to the hagiography signified the spread of the saint's fame.[54] That fame originated in an espousal of Lady Poverty as a devout imitation of the nakedness of Christ crucified. As Dante celebrated this holy marriage:

> Their harmony and joyous semblance made love and wonder and tender looks the cause of holy thoughts.[55]

Petrarch numbered Francis with "those outstanding despisers of worldly goods," and in reviewing the examples of the saints as masters of the flesh he declared "no man more distinguished than Francis."[56] In *De vita solitaria* he praised Francis as the prime exemplar of solitude in its triple manifestations of place, time, and mind. It was particularly the saint's singular ability to contemplate eternal verities while still in commerce, even in collision, with men that impressed Petrarch. "He travelled through wildernesses, he often passed the night in half-ruined temples, by day and among crowds he was often snatched away from the perception of present objects and, while his body was thrust hither and thither, in collision with men, his mind remained fixed on heavenly thoughts." Petrarch ascribed this sublime security to an extremely fervent love of Christ and to a body marvelously submissive to the spirit. Thus Francis, while a votary of solitude, accepted a post in populous places instead, so that he might guard the safety of the many offspring of his marriage to poverty.[57]

Poverty was a condition of the contemplative life to which Petrarch as a poet aspired. He considered the love of poverty, together with scorning pleasures and not fearing death, as the three most magnificent acts of virtue. Such poverty need not mean penury, external want, he explained. An interior poverty that contemned wealth while daily amid its circumstances was no less meritorious than indigence. Indeed, Petrarch considered it the mark of a more noble mind to scoff at the sight of gold than to shun its sight, just as victory over an enemy at hand was more glorious than the avoidance of one in approach. He admired those who, intent on study, "esteem an ingenuous poverty" and who "not so much hate wealth as place little value upon it. Gold neither frightens nor attracts them." He counted himself since youth among those who were striving toward this virtue and were making some progress.[58] The mob, however, bent on cheap gain, he portrayed as mocking his effort: "Philosophy, you go poor and naked!"[59] Against sophistry he affirmed that poverty was the necessary condition of philosophy: "Philosophers, if you do not know, spurn money: you cannot make philosophy venal. For who sells what he does not have?"[60] He composed an epistolary dream in which the anxiety prompted by base greed for a pile of ancient gold coins discovered in a field robbed him of his true spiritual values. The moral, he concluded, was that "wealth brings more harm than good to ambitious mortals."[61] And so for himself he averred, "Some long for riches, I seek poverty—not abject, squalid, sad, and full of fear, but tranquil, peaceful, and honorable."[62] Petrarch described himself poetically as a "mendicant" seeking buried treasure. He even dared to appropriate to himself the epithet of St. Francis, *poverello,* while he graced his beloved with the epithet of St. Clare, *poverella.*[63] Who was she?

O poor little song, how inelegant you are![64]

It was for poetry, Petrarch affirmed, that he had "exchanged Arno for Sorgue and slavish riches for free poverty."[65] This deprecating portrait reflected the "courtly" convention of the poet as a mere beggar before his lady. It derived ultimately, however, from the Platonic doctrine that Love is the child of Poverty, and thus himself a mendicant.[66]

Not only prophecy and poverty attracted Petrarch to Francis, but also poetry and passion. Here, unlike Augustinus, was finally a saint who was a poet, to whom creation was a source of consolation rather than censure. Francis's perspective on creation inspired an influential theology of the personal experience of God, especially through affective meditation on the incarnation of the babe in the crèche and the man on the cross, but also through intellectual perception of his vestiges in the universe and his image impressed on natural human powers as transformed by grace.[67] It was thus by praising the exquisite creature

Laura, as the personification of poetic truth, that Petrarch dared to claim that he was a contemplative. It was thus that he boldly expected spiritual ascent in the very chariot of Elijah. As he paralleled the birth of Laura with the birth of Francis, he praised divine providence for the creation and incarnation, in which holy acts he sought to share:

> He who showed infinite providence and art in His marvelous workmanship, who created this and the other hemisphere, and Jove more mild than Mars,
>
> who, coming to earth to illuminate the pages that for many years had hidden the truth, took John from the nets and Peter, and gave them a portion of the Kingdom of Heaven;
>
> He, when He was born, did not bestow Himself on Rome, but rather on Judea, and so beyond all other states it pleased Him always to exalt humility.
>
> And now from a small village He has given us a sun, such that Nature is thanked and the place where so beautiful a lady was born to the world.[68]

Francis, who himself praised the sun famously in his canticle, provided Petrarch with an exemplar for his poetic aspirations. Although the saint had never advocated erudition for his Order, within twenty-five years of his death it had achieved the status of one of the most learned institutions. With the blessing of the illustrious Bonaventure, who was confident that not only the heart but also the mind could participate in God, Franciscans lectured in theology at the universities of Oxford and Paris. Provisions were admitted to the Rule for study even by average friars, and Franciscan convents soon sheltered libraries that could have incited a humanist like Petrarch to envy.[69] Petrarch deplored the exquisite explorations into God that the dialectical method of Franciscan theologians invented: yet the intensely affective piety that engendered nominalist reservations about the cognitive faculty also promoted an emotional, spontaneous Franciscan poetry that he could approve. An effusion celebrated the saint's memory: metrical biographies, liturgical sequences and anthems, lyrics of religious love, praises and songs, allegories and homilies in verse.[70] This was fitting tribute, for Francis himself sang like a troubadour. As his biographer reported:

> When the sweetest melody of spirit would bubble up in him, he would give exterior expression to it in French, and the breath of the divine whisper which his ear perceived in secret would burst forth in French in a song of joy. At times, as we saw with our own eyes, he would pick up a stick from the ground and putting it over his left arm, would draw

across it, as across a violin, a little bow bent by means of a string; and going through the motions of playing he would sing in French about his Lord. This whole ecstasy of joy would often end in tears and his song of gladness would be dissolved in compassion for the passion of Christ. Then the saint would bring forth continual sighs, and amid deep groanings, he would be raised up to heaven, forgetful of the lower things he held in his hand.[71]

It was not toward heaven, however, but into the world that Francis commissioned his friars in this spirit.

> His heart was then full of so much sweetness and consolation that he wanted Brother Pacificus, who in the world had been the king of poets and the most courtly master of song, to go through the world with a few pious and spiritual friars to preach and sing the praises of God. The best preacher would deliver the sermon, then all would sing the "Praises of the Lord," as true jongleurs of God. At the end of the song, the preacher would say to the people: "We are the jongleurs of God, and the only reward we want is to see you lead a truly penitent life."[72]

In Petrarch's promotion of repentance his poetic symbol waned from the salute to the rising sun that had expressed his matutinal hopes. Although he aspired toward his sun like a butterfly seeking the light, it fatally vanquished his desire, like that of the simple insect who flies into someone's eyes and dies while inflicting pain. "So bright is her face with celestial light that your sight cannot rest on it," Fortune had advised him. In gazing on that countenance with yearning, his power of sight was indeed extinguished, leaving him blinded like "a nocturnal bird in the sun."[73] The poet confessed: "As the sun dazzles him who looks on it fixedly, thus desire, which keeps no proportion with itself, is lost in an object too immense."[74] The death of the lady extinguished the sun that used to dazzle him. The sun was eclipsed. It fell from the sky; rather it rose to heaven, returning to "the highest Sun." Amid celestial rejoicing in her radiance, she was there "bright and happy in the Light that rains salvation and life." At her loss the poet burned more than the sand of Ethiopia under the hottest sun.[75] Now it was his fidelity to her memory that shone. "Brighter than the sun is my faithfulness to my lady and to the world," he affirmed. "And if my rhymes have any power, among noble intellects your name will be consecrated to eternal memory."[76]

Yet the resolution of Petrarch's poetics transcended the conventional translation of its ideal from earth to heaven in the triumph of Laura and the categorical shift of its rhetoric from invention to memory in an annual recollection. Eloquence had been defined by Augustinus as the pursuit of the unattainable, and the saint had scolded the poet for wasting time on it when language was such a poor vehicle of truth.[77] In his Apolline guise of pursuing the desirably alluring but chastely elusive truth the poetic laurel symbolized, Petrarch was embodying the ideal orator. As Cicero had declaimed, perfect eloquence was an ideal not sensorily perceived but intellectually and imaginatively apprehended. It was comparable to Plato's ideas and to the ideas in the mind of the artist.[78] While Petrarch acknowledged and lamented in himself the vanity of the poetic pursuit of this ideal, he also acknowledged and lamented the equal futility of a flight from poetry. Confessing this to Augustinus, Franciscus cited Vergil's figure of Dido:

> Even as a hind, smitten by an arrow, which, all unwary, amid the Cretan woods, a shepherd hunting with darts has pierced from afar, leaving in her the winged steel, unknowing: she in flight ranges the Dictaean woods and glades, but fast to her side clings the deadly shaft.

"I am," he said, "even as that deer. I have fled, but I bear everywhere my wound within me."[79]

The source of this wound Petrarch described in poetic conceit as darts shot by Love from Laura's eyes.[80] "Your weapons were those eyes from which came forth arrows lit with invisible fire, and they feared reason but little, for no human defense avails against Heaven."[81] This sweet glance inflicted a wound that only love could heal. Petrarch judged it incurable, however.[82] This was the supreme adynaton of the vision of the sixth of April: "Every impossible thing will happen before another than she or Death heals the wound that Love made in my heart with her lovely eyes."[83] The shaft pierced his inward parts deeply, penetrating to his heart. He both hated and loved the wound, which he called cruel and bitter, yet contenting and sweet, indeed bittersweet. It was through this wound that his heart overflowed with eternal tears, the tears that watered his poetry, although he deemed it just that Love should rather wash the wounds of his soul.[84]

Although classically the laurel had therapeutic qualities,[85] there was no cure to be discovered in grasping poetically at its branches, only exacerbation of the wound. The desire that impelled the poet was "only to come to the laurel, whence one gathers bitter fruit that, being tasted, afflicts one's wounds more than it comforts them."[86] The fruit, as Petrarch announced in the initial poem of *Rime sparse,* was shame, repentance, and the knowledge of the evanescence of worldly pleasures. The sylvan citizen exited the woods he had so swiftly entered in pursuit of that bough, both limping and lamenting "the wounds I received in that wood thick with thorns; on account of them it is my lot to come out lame, and I entered with so swift a course." He prayed to the Apolline Christ:

> Full of snares and thorns is the course that I must complete, where a light, free foot would be in need, one whole in every place. But you, Lord, who have all pity's [piety's] praise, let your sun vanquish this my strange shadow.[87]

The imagery of wound and thorn, sun and shade, converged in Christ, who is crucified Savior and the sun of righteousness. Both attributes were Apolline. It was precisely as the wounded one that Christ healed others, a venerable tradition Petrarch repeated in his exhortation to "recall the wounds with which our wounds were healed."[88] Apollo too was the god of medicine.[89] These medicinal and solar aspects of Christ were united in the prophetic verse that informed Petrarch's poetics: "But for you who fear my name the sun of righteousness shall rise, with healing in its wings" (Mal. 4:2).

The wounding of the poet in the side[90] imitated the driving of the spear into the side of the crucified Christ, from which gash had flowed blood and water (John 19:34). Petrarch's wound extended to his very heart, and from it too flowed water, "eternal tears." Yet the poet had twice been transfixed, once by love, once by piety:

> That high lord before whom one cannot hide or flee or make any defense had kindled my mind to sweet pleasure with a burning arrow of love;
>
> and, although the first blow was bitter and mortal in itself, to advance his undertaking he took a dart of pity [piety]; and from both sides he pierces and assails my heart.
>
> One wound burns and pours forth smoke and flame; the other, tears, which sorrow distills through my eyes on account of your suffering state.
>
> Nor in spite of those two fountains does any spark decrease of the fire that inflames me; rather my pity [piety] increases my desire.[91]

This poem revealed Petrarch's wonder at the wounded Christ, whose inescapable glance of love inflamed him with passion and inflicted him with sorrow: the burning and the weeping that pervaded his verse. The poet was inspired to his art not only by love of the truth to which it aesthetically aspires, but also by piety, in Vergil's sense of a ritual and relational conformity of man and God that included familial affection and reverence and extended to patriotic loyalty to the state.[92] It was to heal the wounded Italian people that Petrarch sustained his own amorous wounds, in poetic imitation of the crucified Christ.

Petrarch believed emphatically that Christ was undergoing a second crucifixion in Rome.[93] He traced the decline of the state from dignity to infamy directly to the removal of the papacy to Avignon with an arrogance of power. "What at the outset had been a wound capable of treatment has finally grown putrid," he complained, "for, I confess, the ugly sore had begun to fester even before our own time, as we know from our forefathers. . . . Now it's coming to a head, and all the pus is bursting forth in our day." The only remedy was to implore Christ for justice.[94] This entreaty became a prophetic mission for the poet Petrarch. "In the way of wounded lovers," he wrote, "the more desperately we love the more hopefully we complain."[95] And so he portrayed a wounded Roman matron who bared to her Christian husband a breast lacerated with a thousand sores, pitiful wounds as numerous as the city's violated temples and citadels.[96] In "Spirto gentil" he pleaded for the oppressed Roman throng crying for relief and evoked this miserable scene: "The terrified poor people show you their wounds by thousands and thousands, which would make Hannibal, not to speak of anyone else, pity them."[97] Again, he lamented, in his outstanding political poem, "Italia mia":

> My Italy, although speech does not aid those mortal wounds of which in your lovely body I see so many, I wish at least my sighs to be such as Tiber and Arno hope for, and Po where I now sit sorrowful and sad.

Immediately he begged God, whose pity had occasioned the incarnation of Christ, to regard these wounds mercifully and to soften the hearts that war had hardened, so that peace might be restored.[98] His own sighs—his poems—breathed forth to heaven and to Italy.

The epic *Africa*, designed to inspire Italy's repentance through self-knowledge of its past glory, probed a mass of wounds: the wounds of Scipio's father and of his slain Roman comrades; the self-inflicted wound of Lucretia, whose violated chastity had inspired republican liberty; the amorous wound of Massinissa for Sophonisba; the wounds of the Roman and Carthaginian armies, remembered, revealed, and realized; and crucifixion as the fate of Hannibal and of those Roman soldiers who had unpatriotically deserted their posts.[99] It was Scipio's dream-vision of his wounded father that motivated the epic:

> Then lo, from the calm welkin high above,
> clad in a cloud, appeared to him the shade
> and visage of his noble sire, who there
> displayed to his beloved son his heart
> and breast and flank, transfixed by countless spears.

Urging the son to brandish the fallen arms again for Rome, the father stated:

> "The task shall fall
> to you, my son, and all the honor too
> which by the waging of a righteous war
> will make you equal to the gods. I swear
> by these most justly sacred wounds, through which
> I paid the debt I owed the fatherland
> and which laid open to my martial soul
> the way to Heaven—solemnly I swear
> that as the foeman pierced my limbs and while
> my soul took flight, no other balm I found
> save that I knew that in my house survived
> a glorious avenger. And this hope
> at once allayed the fears that filled by heart
> and made more sweet the bitterness of death."

The wounds upon which the father swore his hope and honor moved the son:

> As thus his father spoke, young Scipio gazed
> with mournful eyes upon him, marking all
> the dreadful wounds that scarred him head to heel;
> his filial heart was stirred and a rich flood
> of tears gushed forth. Permitting not his sire
> further discourse, he broke in with these words:
> "Alas, what see I here? Say, father, who
> has pierced your bosom with so cruel a thrust?
> What impious hand has dared to violate
> that brow, by all revered? I pray, disclose
> these things to me; for naught else have I ears."

The son's pious lamentation moved the father:

> Then did his father in affectionate
> embrace enfold him, comforting his woe
> with exhortations and these solemn words:

> "I pray you put aside your tears and grief
> untimely and ill suited to this place.
> If looking on these wounds of mine so sorely
> troubles your heart, if you would care to learn
> what ills shall yet befall the fatherland,
> then heed me, for I purpose to reveal
> in brief discourse much matter you should hear."[100]

Petrarch intended this poetic display of the wounds of the elder Scipio to move the sons of Rome to its defense in filial piety. He justified this patriotic proposal by an appeal to the wounds of another father, "whose guiltless flesh we see scarred by five gaping wounds."[101] This was the invocation of *Africa* to the Apolline Christ, the "all-highest Father," whose victory over death established Rome as the seat of church and state.[102] In pondering the dream-vision of his wounded father, Scipio thus imitated the plea of Christ from the cross to his own Father. His cry, "Forgive your maddened land that knows not what it does,"[103] echoed the narrative of another passion: "And Jesus said, 'Father, forgive them; for they know not what they do'" (Luke 23: 34).[104] It was in the service of knowledge, Delphic wisdom, that Petrarch essayed his poetry. In acknowledging his own failures to shoulder the prophetic yoke, he prayed thus to the Apolline Christ by the same Vergilian invocation that had introduced *Africa:*

> Father of Heaven, after the lost days, after the nights spent raving with that fierce desire that was lit in my heart when I looked on those gestures so lovely to my hurt,
>
> let it please you at last that with your light I may return to a different life and to more beautiful undertakings, so that, having spread his nets in vain, my harsh adversary may be disarmed.
>
> Now turns, my Lord, the eleventh year that I have been subject to the pitiless yoke that which is always most fierce to the most submissive:
>
> have mercy on my unworthy pain, lead my wandering thoughts back to a better place, remind them that today you were on the Cross.[105]

Petrarch looked for enlightenment toward the cross, just as light beamed from the Apolline symbol of the carbuncle in his epic palace of truth. The palace of Syphax, whose glorious description embellished *Africa*,[106] was studded with rare glowing gems, illumined by one at the apex of its vaulted roof:

> A great carbuncle, placed
> in the mid-point, with splendor like the sun's

> effulgence, banished every shadow. Well
> you might have deemed its lustre could avail
> to generate the day and banish night—
> true image of our Phoebus.[107]

The association of the carbuncle with the sun, and hence by allusion with Apollo, was suggested by its self-luminous quality.[108] As a reflector of eternal light it was in medieval allegory, as in Jean de Meun's *Roman de la Rose*, a natural mirror of God.[109] Such allegory was surpassed by the ordinary Christian symbolism of the carbuncle, however. The deep red color of this garnet signified blood and suffering, so that the stone was symbolic of Christ's passion, and also of martyrdom. Medieval crosses were set with five carbuncles to represent the wounds of the crucified Christ.[110] Thus the edifice of truth in Petrarch's national epic adumbrated symbolically at its apex the passion of Christ.

In the initial sonnet of enamorment Petrarch dated his vocation by the pathetic fallacy of a solar eclipse of shame at the crucifixion of the Creator:

> It was the day when the sun's rays
> turned pale with grief for his
> Maker when I was taken [seized] . . .
> . . . .
> . . . and so my
> misfortunes began in the midst of the universal woe.[111]

Petrarch likened his quest for the manifestation of the ideal form in singular appearances to a pilgrimage for the veneration of Veronica's veil:

> The little white-haired pale old man leaves the sweet place where he has filled out his age and his fear-stricken little family, who watch their dear father disappear;
>
> thence dragging his ancient flanks through the last days of his life, as much as he can he helps himself with good will, broken by the years and tired by the road;
>
> and he comes to Rome, following his desire, to gaze on the likeness of Him whom he hopes to see again up there in Heaven.
>
> Thus, alas, at times I go searching in others, Lady, as much as is possible for your longed-for true form.[112]

This image of Christ was no carbuncle but rather the vernicle, the most venerated relic at the vacant See of St. Peter in Rome. According to legend a pious woman had wiped the face of Christ as he struggled up Calvary under the weight of his cross. In gratitude he had left on her cloth a perfect likeness of his face. Dante in the empyrean had compared his own vision of St. Bernard, as the personification of contemplation, with a pilgrim's sight of Veronica's veil:

> As is he who comes perchance from Croatia to look on our Veronica, and whose old hunger is not sated, but says in thought so long as it is shown, "My Lord Jesus Christ, true God, was then your semblance like to this?" such was I, gazing on the living charity of him who, in this world, in contemplation tasted of that peace.[113]

As a pilgrim to Rome during the jubilee year, Petrarch himself anticipated such a fortunate viewing of the vernicle, the most popular image for indulgence in the fourteenth century.[114] In his poetry he did not merely imitate the rapturous wonder of the pilgrim, however. He did gaze on the very veil, the image of Christ crucified, precisely in searching for a glimpse of the true poetic form he desired. In his struggle for perfection, personal and poetic, the example of Christ struggling up Calvary chastised him:

> I go on thinking and in thought pity for myself assails me, so strong that it often leads me to a weeping different from my accustomed one: for, seeing every day the end coming near, a thousand times I have asked God for those wings with which our intellect raises itself from this mortal prison to Heaven.

Such prayer did not avail him. Unlike Christ, who fell on the way under the weight of the cross and was assisted by Veronica, Petrarch was "able to stand": "But until now no prayer or sigh or weeping of mine has helped me; and that is just, for he who, able to stand, has fallen along the way deserves to lie on the ground against his will." He hoped, nevertheless, while trembling at his human frailty and buffeted by contrary counsels, in the embrace of the crucified Christ: "Those merciful arms in which I trust I see still open."[115] The divine passion consoled and strengthened him: "Nor do I fear the threats of death, which the King suffered with worse pain in order to make me constant and strong in following Him."[116] He could even boldly summon death, for: "He who was not stingy of His blood, who broke with His foot the Tartarean gates, with His death seems to strengthen me."[117]

Petrarch professed this piety in a lengthy letter of consolation to his patron Cardinal Colonna:

> Yet for a learned and religious man in dealing with all the hardships and griefs which cannot be avoided in this moral life it is an admittedly much sweeter, more pleasant, and more worthy medicine to recall the hardships and griefs that Christ suffered for us. Likewise it is appropriate to recall the wounds with which our wounds were healed, and that we were snatched from the danger of an eternal death; to recall the nails and the spear and the most precious blood in which our filth was cleansed as in a bath and through which we were reborn and were mildly warned to spurn earthly burdens with a lofty mind and to fear nothing except the punishment of eternal damnation with its infinite sufferings.[118]

It was with the very passion and death of Christ that Petrarch associated his own suffering as a poet and finally the ruin of his aspiration. As the inscription on the flyleaf of his manuscript of Vergil recorded this death:

> The laurel, illustrious through its own virtues, and long famed through my verses, first appeared to my eyes in my youth, in the year of our Lord 1327, on the sixth day of April, in the church of St. Clare in Avignon, at matins; and in the same city, also on the sixth day of April, at the same first hour, but in the year 1348, that light was withdrawn from the light of day, while I, as it chanced, was in Verona, unaware of my fate. The rumor reached me in Parma, in the same year, on the morning of the 19th day of May, in a letter from my Ludovicus. Its chaste and lovely form was laid to rest at vesper time, on the same day on which it died, in the place of the Brothers Minor.[119]

Perhaps this notice did memorialize Laura de Noves or another noble woman who succumbed to the greatest natural disaster in European history, the second pandemic of *Y. pestis*. In its virulent strains of bubonic, pneumonic, and septicemic plague, it had traveled from the Gobi desert by commercial routes and ecological chains to the port of Marseilles, which it reached in January 1348.[120] It then coursed the fifty miles up the Rhône river to Avignon, whose congestion guaranteed its rapid dissemination and an excessive mortality. Although the figures are preposterous, in the initial three days 1,800 were reported dead. The constant daily total was said to be 400; in sum, 150,000 in that city alone reputedly died.[121] Each parish except Saint-Etienne had its own modest cemetery adjoining the church, and outside the ancient walls of the city was a cemetery that received the bodies of the paupers from the nearby hospices.[122] When these filled, the putrefying corpses were dumped into the Rhône until pits could be dug for the mass burials of "herded souls," as one witness reported. The pope himself purchased a large field that was consecrated as a cemetery, and in the six weeks from 13 March, 11,000 corpses were said to have been interred in that single graveyard alone: half the estimated actual population of Avignon. Fear of contagion prompted a scandalous desertion of the sick even by their intimate family. Those who did not die of pestilence perished from neglect; in despair, many were even buried alive. Others—Jews—were burnt for allegedly poisoning the wells. Those who had not fled to the environs of the city processed about in sackcloth and ashes lamenting and flagellating themselves in penitence for a pest whose origin the rude populace could only ascribe to an enraged deity. By 27 April, 62,000 were reported buried in Avignon. According to a contemporaneous chronicle, on that last day of March and the first two days of April, more than 450 died daily. Although the tallies are hyperbolic, if "Laura" succumbed on the sixth of April, she died during the peak of the plague.[123]

In Parma, where Petrarch was then in attendance as a canon of the cathedral, an estimated 40,000 died.[124] The poet recorded his shock:

> Funerals meet my terrified eyes, wherever I turn them,
> Horror piles upon horror, the churches crowded with coffins,
> Echo to loud lamentations, while countless bodies unburied,
> Noble and peasant alike, all lie in the open, unhonored.[125]

It is fantastic to suppose that amid so horrific a scene, which by the extravagant tallies reported 150,000 dead in Avignon, the precise hours of one woman's death and burial would have been recorded. Compounding this rarity is the fabulous coincidence of her death on the same day, and at the same hour, in the same city as the poet first envisioned her. Petrarch's inscription may have memorialized a human victim, but he wrote "laurel" not "Laura." The death of the laurel, the evergreen symbol of eternity legendarily immune from the judgment of Zeus, was an adynaton, a hyperbolic impossibility. The semantics of Petrarch's memorial allows the deposition of a corpse (*corpus*) in a grave (*locum*). The faithful were indeed permitted to use Franciscan churches as burial places, although the practice was a particular grievance of the secular clergy, who resented it as an encroachment on their pastoral rights.[126] In the fourteenth century letters of fraternity, which united a lay person to the Order as a "co-brother" or "co-sister" were common. Among the privileges of these documents, the right to be buried in the habit of a Friar Minor was granted to notable and distinguished persons.[127] It may be that like other wealthy nobles Laura was borne to her grave there in the custom the plague enforced—without candles and without mourners, by hired ruffians who were lavishly rewarded for a service families shunned.[128]

Petrarch's semantics equally allows for the deposit of a body of writings (*corpus*) in the Franciscan place (*locum*). His immediate reference to the soul's ascent to heaven in imitation of Scipio Africanus suggests that Ludwig's letter may have conveyed that in Petrarch's absence he had left a manuscript, perhaps *Africa,* in the Franciscan convent as a precaution against its loss or destruction during the plague. The reputation of that particular Franciscan convent suggests a rhetorical reference, however. Founded in 1227, it was a famous fortress of the Conventual movement, which represented the majority of the Order in the conflicts over absolute poverty. During the curial investigations that commanded the Spiritual leaders to Avignon, they shunned the place, choosing to live rather in the hermitage of St. Lazare in the vicinity and in an abandoned church near Malaucène. It was in the same Franciscan convent in Avignon that John XXII had imprisoned the band of Spirituals who upon his election importuned him for a hearing of their grievances. When the pope, in a more conciliatory manner, tried to persuade their leader, Ubertino da Casale, to spend several nights in the convent as a gesture of solidarity with the Conventuals, the reformer ironically stated his contempt for their laxity: "If I stayed with them for one day only I should need neither yours nor anyone else's provision in this life."[129]

Symbolically the Franciscan convent in Avignon, in which Petrarch's laurel was buried, represented the antithesis of the church of St. Clare, in which he had initially envisioned it. Like Francis, Clare of Assisi had renounced her familial luxury for the privations of poverty, both individual and corporate. She wrested from Innocent III the "privilege of poverty," the special right of owning nothing at all, and she remained tenacious to that principle in great penury and austerity. Although later the papacy opposed this policy and some foundations of her Order were required to accept gifts of property, the convents of the Claresses were, in contradiction to those of the Conventuals, bastions of the original Franciscan ideal of utter abnegation.[130] They were also, like all foundations of religious women in that era, strict enclosures. Unlike the male Friars Minor, who were itinerant, their female counterparts were governed by rigid rules concerning silence, the use of the parlor, and of the grille. The door to the cloister was secured by double iron locks with bolts and bars, and guarded by the portress. "And by no means," stated the Rule of St. Clare, "shall it be opened to anyone who wishes to enter, except to those who have been granted permission by the Supreme Pontiff or by our Lord Cardinal." With such permission the bishop was allowed to celebrate Mass within the enclosure, as for the blessing of an abbess or the consecration of a nun. The entry of other males, however, such as workmen or pallbearers, was strictly regulated by the prudence of the abbess. Even the chaplain, who was not admitted to the convent without a companion, was required to remain in an open place, only being allowed within the enclosure to administer the sacraments of the sick.[131]

The grille that separated the cloister from its environs was covered by a wooden door, which was usually secured by two iron locks, bolts, and bars. It was kept open during the recitation of the Divine Office, however,[132] and so perhaps Petrarch was an interloper at the psalms of the Claresses on 6 April 1327, when and where he noticed Laura at matins. It must have been the convent of Claresses that Petrarch indicated, for there was no other "church of St. Clare" in Avignon. The seven parishes of that city were Saint-Pierre, Saint-Didier, Notre-Dame-le-Principale, Saint-Geniès, Saint-Symphorien, Saint-Etienne, and Saint-Agricol.[133] Petrarch's location of the vision of Laura in the church of St. Clare was more probably symbolic than factual, however, an imitation of Dante's vision of Beatrice in the church of the Holy Trinity of Florence. In both cases the poets did not so much see these women, if ever they did, as envision "beatitude" and the "laurel."

The association of St. Clare with Petrarch's poetic vocation was Apolline. While Francesco meant "fame," Chiara from the Latin *clarus* meant "clear," also "bright, shining, brilliant," like the very sun. According to legend the saint was so christened because her mother's prayer for a safe childbirth was greeted with this celestial voice: "Fear not, woman, for you shall bring forth without danger a light which shall greatly illumine the world."[134] The papal bull of her canonization, *Clara claris praeclara,* glorified the metaphor: "O Clare, endowed with so many titles of clarity! Clear even before your conversion, clearer in your manner of living, exceedingly clear in your enclosed life, and brilliant in splendor after the course of your mortal life. In Clare, a clear mirror is given to the entire world."[135] Apollo's epithet "Delian," referring to his birthplace at Delos, where he slew the monster Python, also meant "clear." There was, moreover, a famous Apolline sanctuary in Asia Minor at Claros, which name is phonetically suggestive of *clarus*.[136]

When the clarity of vision that marked Petrarch's vatic vocation failed, he reported his ideal as put to rest in the Franciscan "place." This need not refer to a physical site such as lodgings or a grave. The noun *locus* was also the term for a rhetorical topic, from which all poetry was invented. The rhetorical "place" or topic so famous to the Franciscan Order was the wounds of Christ. Devotion to Christ crucified was the singular medieval piety promoted by the Franciscan movement. The passion was not the monopoly of that Order, but it was its particular mark. Once, when the young ascetic Francis of Assisi was praying fervently with total absorption in God, there appeared to him Christ crucified. At this vision his soul so melted that whenever he recalled this internal impression he would weep and groan. The evangelical invitation "If any man would come after me, let him deny himself and take up his cross and follow me" (Matt. 16:24) became his personal precept. In imitation of the nudity of Christ crucified, he mortified his own flesh, nursed the rotting flesh of lepers, and embraced absolute poverty as his only lady. The wounds of love Francis experienced spiritually were manifested corporeally when he received the stigmata. As he was praying on Mt. Alverno near the feast of the exaltation of the holy cross, an angelic man descended. He was in the sublime image of a seraph who bore between his fiery, dazzling wings a crucified man who inflamed Francis internally and signed him externally. In joy and terror Francis was transformed wholly into an image of the crucified Christ: in the midst of his hands and feet round, black nailheads appeared, while on his right side a gash exuded fresh blood, as if it had been transfixed by a lance.[137] Petrarch's own wonder at "that amazing proof of the holy stigmata of Christ, or the limbs that gave evidence of the wound of his mind"[138] repeated Franciscan hagiography, which regarded the external signs as an exterior manifestation of Francis's interior state.[139]

Meditation on Christ crucified, as a major motif of fourteenth-century piety, literature, and art, ranged from sentimentality to mysticism. Its vivid realism was embraced with an emotional intensity that could become physical brutality. The fascination with the passion seems to have been a beautiful horror that was cathartic in a century of ugly horrors. It was an enormously popular devotion.[140] The Colonna family, into whose service Petrarch entered and whose patronage he enjoyed, was one exemplar of this universal piety. Early in the thirteenth century Giovanni Colonna shipped from the east the column (*colonna*) at which Christ had been scourged during his passion, and erected it in S. Prassede, Rome, for veneration. It was he who influenced Innocent III to accept the Franciscans officially, and he increasingly involved his family in the development of the Order.[141] Outstanding in Franciscan piety was Margherita Colonna (c. 1255–80), sister of the Roman senator Giovanni and the cardinal Giacomo, who was venerated in the Colonna territories as a saint. The hagiography narrated holy conversations between Margherita and Giacomo modeled on that of Monica and Augustine at Ostia. In these they were aroused to ecstasy by discussing whether Thomas the doubting apostle had indeed put his finger in Christ's wounds at the invitation: "'Put your finger here, and see my hands; and put out your hand, and place it in my side; do not be faithless, but believing'" (John 20:27). Later in a vision or dream Margherita heard the sound of the apostle's cry at the sight of Christ's wounds. Later still she herself had a vision of the crucified that left her ill. Renouncing marriage, she garbed herself as a Claress and tended the sick, especially the leprous, in typical Franciscan ministry.[142]

This realism in Franciscan meditation on the wounds of Christ as the very apertures to mystical ecstasy was vividly displayed in a letter of Bonaventure to a Poor Clare:

> Draw near, dear handmaiden, with loving feet to Jesus wounded, to Jesus crowned with thorns, to Jesus fastened to the gibbet of the cross; and be not content, as the blessed apostle Thomas was, merely to see in his hands the print of the nails or to thrust your hand into his side; but rather go right in, through the opening in his side, to the very heart of Jesus where, transformed by the most burning love for Christ, held by the nails of divine love, pierced by the lance of profound charity, and wounded by the sword of deep compassion, you will know no other wish or desire or hope of consolation except to die with Christ upon the cross, so that you can say with St. Paul: "I am crucified with Christ.... I live; yet not I, but Christ liveth in me."[143]

St. Clare, whose rule these women obeyed, was herself devoted to the wounds of Christ. Her exhortations to novices to bewail the crucifixion were punctuated with tears. She frequently recited a prayer on the five wounds of Christ and also the Office of the Cross that St. Francis had composed. Her affective meditation on the passion enraptured her into such ecstasy that she herself seemed "crucified with Christ." By the sign of the cross Clare reputedly worked many miracles of healing. As the legend by her contemporaneous biographer recounted her fervent love: "Deep and full of tenderness was her lament over the Passion of the Lord. His holy wounds were for her at times a source of sorrowful affections, at others a reason to flee sweeter joys. The tears of the suffering Christ inebriated her, and her memory often recalled to her Him whom love had impressed so deeply on her heart."[144] Like Francis, his female counterpart was celebrated in verse, in hymn, and in liturgy,[145] and her rare chaste beauty was painted among the saints of Assisi by the very artist who legendarily portrayed Petrarch's Laura, Simone Martini.[146]

It was in the church of St. Clare in Avignon, Petrarch declared, that he had been wounded by Love as rays of light darted from Laura's eyes. He thus located the inaugural vision of his vatic vocation in the church of the poor, humble, chaste servant Clare in repudiation of the greedy, arrogant, meretricious papal court of that same city. The symbolic dating of the vision to the liturgy of Good Friday allied his vocation with the passion of Christ. The incisive image of the Avignon papacy whose repentance Petrarch prophetically implored was not that of the tawdry harlot or the abandoned flock, nor of the shipwreck, the labyrinth, or the inferno (all of which he also evoked),[147] but rather the visage of the crucified Christ, with whom and for whom the poet pleaded. He indicted the rebellious papal court as "swollen with the blood of Christ." He imputed to it the hailing of Judas Iscariot, who betrayed Christ with a kiss, and the mockery of the Jews who vested him with a purple cloak, crowned him with thorns, spat, and jeered. "In a savage judgment," he wrote, "they decreed that he was neither God nor king, and deserved neither divine nor human honours, but rather that he was 'guilty of death' [Matt. 26:26], a blasphemer who merited blows and execution. What else, I ask," Petrarch reflected on Avignon,

> goes on daily among these enemies of Christ, these Pharisees of our own time? Day and night they exalt Christ's name with the highest praises, they vest him in purple and gold, they deck him with gems, they salute him and prostrate themselves before him in worship, and meanwhile they buy him and sell him, hold an auction on him, crown

him with thorns of base wealth as though with his eyes thus veiled he will not see, befoul him with spittle from the filthiest mouths, taunt him with their viperous hissing, and wound him with the lance of their poisonous deeds. With all their strength they drag him again and again to Calvary—scoffed at, naked, helpless, scourged—and to blasphemous applause they nail him once again to the cross.[148]

Considering the wounds of Christ, Petrarch prayed: "Then turning again and again to the crucified one who is my delight, with mournful voice and tearful eyes I cry out: Oh good Jesus, you are too indulgent. What can this be? 'Arise! why do you sleep? Arise! Do not cast us off forever! Why do you hide your face? Why do you forget our affliction and our oppression?'" (Ps. 43:23). The poet begged his protector to regard the sufferings of the faithful and to revenge the deeds the enemy perpetrated against them in his holy name, or at least to assuage them before evil prevailed. Considering the divine indifference and hesitation, Petrarch wondered whether the Lord failed to see the evil, or if he had converted the love that had prompted his death on the cross into hatred, or whether he persisted in vision and love but had lost the strength to succor men. Without his omnipotence, the poet lamented, there was no hope. It would not be divine to fear the strength of the enemy or to destroy the faithful in mercy toward the wicked. Mindful of creation and of providence, Petrarch curtailed his quarrel with the silent crucifix and pleaded for Christ's advent. "Come, our one hope, and as we say in our daily prayer, 'make haste to help us.' Destroy the world's many evils, we pray, or else destroy the world itself."[149]

This apostrophe to Christ crucified, which composed the seventh letter of his *Liber sine nomine,* Petrarch expanded in the lamentation of the twelfth: "Woe to your people, oh Christ Jesus, woe to your people, oh Christ! Oh fount of mercies, let us come before you to bewail our misfortunes. In the way of wounded lovers, the more desperately we love the more hopefully we complain." The complaint, he expounded, was not that of men but of worms, nor that of arrogant accusers but of humble petitioners. Petrarch protested to Christ about the shame of the faithful, insolently mocked by their enemies as proof of abandonment by God. He pondered the indulgence, neglect, hatred, even cruel dalliance with which the Savior seemed to regard the sufferings of the people. Let anger, however justly deserved, yield to mercy, he pleaded in lengthy prayer.[150] Again in the seventeenth letter he cried out: "You, oh Christ, you who can change things, you from whom all empires on earth, in heaven, or in hell are held at your will, you who, even in silence, hear this complaint which is not just my own but is made especially on behalf of all your people, hearken to us if it is just, we pray." Petrarch justified his complaint of oppression under a harsh, ignorant, and detestable papacy by appealing to the scriptural verse, "Thou hast made us like sheep for the slaughter" (Ps. 44:11a). "What have we who used to be lords of nations been turned into, if not sheep to be eaten? If only we were merely sheep to be sheared, or milked—but no, we are sheep to be eaten. We let ourselves be chewed, consumed, devoured," he protested. Yet he blamed the torpor of the people themselves for this, since the devouring lions despised the people only superficially while they feared them profoundly, he believed.[151]

This pastoral imagery was again prophetic, as especially derived from Ezekiel's oracle against the false shepherds of Israel (Ezek. 34: 1–16, cf. Jer. 23:1–4), to which Christ had contrasted his own role as the good shepherd (John 10:1–18). The prophet castigated the shepherds for exploiting the flock while so neglecting its care as to allow it to be scattered and devoured by wild beasts, the foreign nations. For this dereliction of duty he pronounced Yahweh's climactic rejection of Israel's political leaders and his promise of a rescue and rest for the populace that would restore them to their own land.[152] Such representation of sovereign and subject by the metaphor of shepherd and flock was familiar throughout the ancient Near East, as in the introduction to the celebrated Babylonian code of law, where Hammurabi described himself as the shepherd of men who supplied their pasture and water and destroyed the wicked who would prey on the weak.[153] Now Petrarch, surveying a similar scene, appropriated this pastoral motif. It sustained his *Carmen bucolicum,* the covert parallel to his *Liber sine nomine.* The sixth and seventh eclogues attacked the Avignon papacy under the allegories of the good shepherd (St. Peter) reproaching the roguish pastor (Clement VI) for the ravagement of the pasturage and flock, and of the pope and his Babylonian whore inspecting the curial remnant of a plague-stricken flock.[154]

Petrarch regarded the plague as an apocalyptic sign whose misfortunes exceeded anything in all the centuries since Noah's ark. Lamenting this extraordinary vengeance of God, he demanded:

> How [will] posterity [be able to] believe that there was once a time without floods, without fire either from heaven or from earth, without wars, or other visible disaster, in which not only this or that part of the

world, but almost all of it remained without a dweller? When was anything similar either seen or heard? In what chronicles did anyone ever read that dwellings were emptied, cities abandoned, countrysides filthy, fields laden with bodies and a dreadful and vast solitude filled the earth? Consult the historians: they are silent; question the scientists: they are stupefied; ask the philosophers: they shrug their shoulders, they wrinkle their brows and they order silence by holding their finger to their lips."[155]

Yet the plague was perhaps not the sole disaster behind the symbolic burial of Laura in the Franciscan grave or the reposal of the laurel in the wounds of Christ. The plague was not the only momentous visitor to Avignon that month. On 13 March 1348 Joanna, queen of Naples, to whose territory Avignon belonged, entered the city. She had fled her Italian capital in January before a rapidly advancing Hungarian army intent on invasion and, like the very pest, had journeyed by ship to Provence. On 20 March she was solemnly received at the papal court; on 27 March the pope authorized her to marry her lover, Louis, prince of Taranto. As early as April she negotiated with Clement VI for the sale of Avignon to the papacy, a transaction settled on 9 June for 80,000 gold florins. A receipt detailing the disposition of the papal money was recorded in Naples on 10 July, and on the 23d of that month the pope formally took possession of Avignon. Charles IV ratified the sale in November.[156] Meanwhile, by 27 April the pope had since fled the infested city for the castle of Stella, two leagues distant.[157]

It was the rumor of these negotiations in April 1348 for the sale of Avignon to the papacy that killed Petrarch's cherished ideal of Roman restoration and Italian peace. With that political finality the inspiration for his patriotic epic waned. His correspondence recorded the demise of *Africa*. To an inquirer he sighed that he anticipated its conclusion with difficulty; the adynaton of counting sand or stars would be easier. "For me indeed it would be simpler to count the sands of the sea and the stars of the heavens than all the obstacles envious fortune has put in the way of my labors. I myself await its end, uncertain as to whether I [have] spent sleepless nights utterly in vain or whether at least some joy, though late, is reserved for me for my labor." In exhaustion he reflected on the ambitious undertaking: "I started my *Africa* with such great energy and effort that now, as I try to apply the file to what I started, I seem to shudder at my boldness and at the great framework I laid." To yet another inquirer he promised the first glimpse of the manuscript, "if ever it does see the light," and he explained that "it is being delayed by the owner's laziness and by fortune's countless obstacles." He intended to retard its public appearance until it had matured with age and improved with revision. While he confided that his genius "daily undergoes extraordinary change," he considered, nevertheless, that "unless I am mistaken I have now become whatever was destined for me from above, although until the last day I shall not desist from pressing forward as much as I am able."[158]

The epic *Africa,* whose success or failure Petrarch believed would alone resolve the question of his fame, long inspired his dedication to poetry. Yet the initial ardor that had impelled his ascent of the Capitoline had diminished. He had undertaken *Africa,* he said, "with a spirit that burned more than Africa ever does during the dog days," but the work had now long weighed heavily upon him. Nevertheless, he believed that it alone would "either lessen or quench the thirst in my heart, if there is any hope for that." Again to an inquirer he declined to share the manuscript, offering these excuses:

> My Scipio is not fully developed in the poem, and my *Africa,* which I have long possessed and cultivated with greater toil than I thought possible, has still not been given its final hoeing. I have not yet broken down its useless clods with my rake; I have not yet evened off with a harrow the mounds of my uncultivated fields; my pruner has not yet checked the growth of the overgrown vine leaves or my sickle its thorny hedges. Therefore do as you please with everything else I possess, but for this work alone you must have patience. Allow me, while there is still time, before making you the possessor of African land, to review it and revise it a little to the extent that my tired and fragile talent [genius] will permit.

Whether or not Petrarch, who termed himself its "solicitous cultivator,"[159] did patiently tend to these tasks is uncertain. Those were his final explicit intentions about the completion of *Africa.* Ultimately, like Vergil judging his *Aeneid,* he wanted it burned.

Of the difficulties besetting a poet, Petrarch had cited three in his coronation speech: lack of inspiration, the adversity of fortune, and the disdain of men.[160] It was adverse fortune, he emphasized, that obstructed the composition of *Africa.* Just as fame, idealized as the woman Laura, had incited him to his arduous labor, so fortune, realized as the woman Joanna, discouraged it. Petrarch consistently portrayed Joanna in his *Liber sine nomine* as Semiramis, the legendary Assyrian queen who had founded ancient Babylon.[161] Depicting Avignon as its infernal Western counterpart, populated with reincarnations of the nefarious cast of old, he identified Joanna as "Semiramis with her quiver." "I see," he observed, "how this imitation Semiramis covers her head with a man's crown, and with what artifice she dazzles the eyes of all bystanders; and how, defiled by incestuous embraces, she tramples men underfoot."[162] This portrayal reflected the popular belief that an adulterous Joanna had conspired in the murder of her husband, Andrew of Hungary, on the verge of his coronation as her consort in the kingdom of Naples.[163]

Petrarch had known Joanna since 1343, when, upon the death of King Robert, he had served as papal envoy to ascertain the state of the Neapolitan court. She was then a minor, and with her consort, Prince Andrew, was governed by a regency that had usurped power. Petrarch was horrified at the degradation of the court, which so contrasted with its splendor at his original visit for the poetic examination. Already upon the death of King Robert, Petrarch had voiced "fear that those other presentiments of mine may also come true, presentiments which my distressed mind, always a too certain prophet of evils, now suggests to me." As he elaborated his fear: "I am really alarmed about the youthfulness of the young queen, and of the new king, about the age and intent of the other queen, about the talents and ways of the courtiers. I wish that I could be a lying prophet about these things, but I see two lambs entrusted to the care of a multitude of wolves, and I see a kingdom without a king."[164]

Upon his diplomatic arrival at the Neapolitan court, Petrarch's alarm exploded: "Alas, what a shame, what a monster! May God remove this kind of plague from Italian skies! I thought that Christ was despised at Memphis, Babylon, and Mecca." The provoker of this anger was a Friar Robert, ostentatiously and arrogantly of the Spiritual band of Franciscans, for which that court was a famous haven, yet hypocritically wealthy and influential. It was he, Petrarch discovered, who treacherously controlled the kingdom.[165] Upon the assassination of Andrew of Hungary, reputedly by Joanna, the poet proved that he had been no lying prophet in his outcry to the Apolline Christ: "But you, oh Christ, sun of justice [righteousness], who see all and illumine the universe with your eternal rays, why did you suffer this cloud of infamy to lie upon our lands when you could so easily (unless these transgressions of men are obstacles for you) have broken through the offensive vapors of hatred hardened by the misty cold of the night with the glowing brilliance of your love?"

This apostrophe to Christ as the prophesied "sun of righteousness" was also reflected in Petrarch's prophetic office, as he regretted that his presentiment of the deed could not avert its inexorable fatality. As he enumerated its portents: "Disturbing clouds shaded serious faces; stubborn winds pressed upon disturbed hearts; glowing eyes flashed; mouths thundered and uttered menaces; it was almost as though ungodly hands were hurling lightning. The seas of the royal court were sometimes swollen with anger; at times a horrible glow and clashing of waves resounded and foul birds and strange portents seemed widely to encompass your shores." These dire omens of evil intimidated their witnesses, reducing them to public silence and private whispers, he recalled. "In short," he wrote, evoking the classical omen of judgment, "minds were benumbed by the eyes as if struck by the dreadful light of a close thunderbolt."

In this electric atmosphere Petrarch alone dared to speak out. "Unless I am mistaken," he declared, "no one feared more openly than I and grieved more freely. No one looked more closely at those portents of the court, and struck out more obstinately either with his tongue or with his pen. Alas, how great and how evident is the truth of Proverbs! 'Let him who wishes to be a truthful prophet prophesy evil.'" Petrarch stated that his own prophecy was as accurate as a dart. "Who therefore among those who hold these views," he asked, "should be surprised that just as a spear hurled within a crowd of people cannot stray, the same holds for a prophecy released amid such an accumulation of evils, thus would the prophecy strike the truth?" He recalled how, near the death of King Robert, "I either orally when I was present or through letters when I was absent, and not long after his death, again orally, revealed not without visible disturbance what I felt and what I feared would be coming as if I were certain of the future. For I saw the foundation of the kingdom being shaken from the top, and I saw before my eyes the serious misfortunes befalling the collapsing kingdom."

He admitted that, amid these gloomy conjectures, he did not foresee that the initial fall of the kingdom of Naples would be that of the innocent head of Andrew. Yet he did recall his having prophesied about a lamb among wolves. "Would that my prediction had been less true!" he regretted. At the climax of an ensuing condemnation of

Naples for this vulpine crime, Petrarch pleaded with Christ, the sun of righteousness, for just vengeance. He mentioned a presentiment of evil multiplied, which he did not describe "in order to avoid once again being more correct than I wish to be or appearing to be a prophet of doom."[166] Now, in exchange for papal approval of a marriage that might consolidate and control Naples again, Joanna had sold Avignon, establishing the new Babylon. The papacy now legally owned the territory it had appropriated and could settle there forever, mindless of Rome.

Petrarch sought consolation in another woman, whose prayers might persuade "the sun of righteousness," as his poetry had failed to. The final poem of his *Rime sparse,* numbered 366, was projected beyond the calendar year with its inexorable solar revolution toward eternity. It addressed the Apocalyptic woman who writhed in labor with her portentous son (Rev. 12:1–6):[167]

> Beautiful Virgin who, clothed with the sun and crowned with the stars, so pleased the highest Sun that in you He hid His light: love drives me to speak words of you, but I do not know how to begin without your help and His who loving placed Himself in you.

The Marian invocations progressed with luminous imagery. As wise, the Virgin carried "the brightest lamp"; as pure, she "lightens this life and adorns the other," worthy to be hailed as the "shining noble window of Heaven"; as full of every grace, she bore "the Sun of justice [righteousness], who makes bright the world though it is full of dark and thick errors."[168]

Rarely in theology or in art before the fourteenth century was the Apocalyptic woman thus identified with the Virgin. The iconographical type developed from the Madonna of humility, so named because she was depicted in a revolutionary pose for a sacred personage: seated on the ground. The earliest extant example of this dethronement is a fresco by Simone Martini, the very portraitist of "Laura," executed between 1339 and 1343 in the tympanum of the Roman portal of Notre-Dame-des-Doms, precisely the cathedral of Avignon. There in a semicircular lunette was an elegant Madonna seated on the ground before the cloth of honor held by two angels. In her lap was the Christ Child, who uncommonly bore this inscribed scroll: "Ego Sum Lux Mundi" (I am the light of the world). Another example by Martini, now lost, promoted a Simonesque type celebrated throughout Europe as a devotional image. This combined the Madonna of humility with the ancient type of the lactating Virgin.[169]

The iconography of the Apocalyptic woman thus comprised important elements of Petrarch's poetry: Laura as the young matron seated on the grass in *Rime sparse*,[170] the adynaton of the lactating Virgin in *Africa*,[171] and the Apolline Christ as radiating the aesthetic light of this inspiration. This concluding poem to the Virgin was no sop. Petrarch composed it from meditation on Martini's fresco in the ecclesiastical see of the detested city, Avignon. Although the Madonna's pose has been considered unprecedented for a sacred personage in classical or medieval art, the ancient cult of the Magna Mater, who was painted importantly in *Africa*,[172] suggests differently. Cybele, when seated, was enthroned; but Attis, her consort, was seated or recumbent on the ground. A local Gaulish example is the depiction of Attis in his Phrygian cap seated half-recumbent on the ground between two trees, from a "House of Attis" discovered with the sanctuary of Bona Dei at St-Rémy-de-Provence.[173] His posture is similar to that of Jesse's in Christian iconography. Martini had allegorized that prophecy as the frontispiece of Petrarch's manuscript of Vergil, substituting the poet for Jesse.[174] Is not his Madonna of humility in the fresco a natural development of that type? The shoot (*virga*) that was to grow from the stump of Jesse (Is. 11:1) was traditionally identified as the Virgin (*virgo*), who bore as the fruit of her womb the Christ Child. Martini's concept of the Madonna as seated on the ground is coherent with this prophetic iconography and with its emphasis on the humble origins of the Messiah.

The Madonna of humility is seated on the ground because she is that tree. On the frontispiece is the same tree, which Vergil prophesies, the laurel. Martini's "lofty concept," as Petrarch phrased and praised it in *Rime sparse,* was the symbolic laurel. This laurel of the frontispiece and of the fresco is the famous "portrait of Laura," lost for centuries because assumed to be the actual portrait of an illicitly loved matron of Avignon.[175] It is symbolic rather, and its human archetype is the Madonna of humility. Petrarch's salute to the "Beautiful Virgin" is thus an appropriate conclusion to *Rime sparse,* which began with an invocation to Apollo. In the medieval *Ovide moralisé* Apollo was Christ as the light of the world who illumines everyone and is master of every art. For love of humanity he joined himself in the incarnation to Mary, just as Apollo desired to unite with Daphne. She was a symbolic laurel.[176]

Poetic truth had been in its personification as Laura "angelic," angelic in form and in quality.[177] An angel, however, was but the intermediate being between the human and divine orders. Through the adynaton of the virgin mother, Petrarch sought Christ, in whom the human and the divine had been united in incarnation. He petitioned from that source of illumination upon a darkened humanity the righteousness of repentance, as he gathered up the fragments of his poetic soul—rhymes, leaves, tears, and hopes—rendering himself and his scattered sheep repentant unto God.[178] Failing the advent of justice upon a world still unripe for final judgment, he sought repose. As Petrarch had once expressed this longing in a consideration of the hasty journey of life: "The goal is not the threshold of death but of eternal life, truly hidden because of our sins yet revealed by the blood of Christ and opened by His wounds. Oh, would that we be allowed to sleep there in peace, would that after lengthy and countless labors we may finally rest in Him who in a most unique manner provided us with a hope that could not be false, coming as it did from Him!"[179]

Petrarch's prophetic summons of the Avignon papacy to repentance was established in his personal conversion, which he acknowledged as a call from a gracious God. Encumbered by sin and by habit, the poet feared failure and so prayed for divine guidance of his frail nature.[180] He recalled the friendship of Christ, who once delivered man and now invited him to share his glory. And so Petrarch prayed for an ecstatic repose in him:

> I am so weary under the ancient bundle of my sins and bitter habit that I am much afraid I shall fail on the way and fall into the hands of my enemy.
>
> True, a great Friend did come to free me, in His highest and ineffable graciousness; then He flew out of my sight so that I strive in vain to see Him.
>
> But His voice still resounds down here: "O you who labor, here is the way; come to me, if the pass is not blocked by another."
>
> What grace, what love, or what destiny will give me wings like a dove, that I may rest and lift myself up from the earth?[181]

It was in the final poem, however, where Petrarch did rest in prayer after the 365 days of his creation, that the mysticism that was a literary convention in his claims of poetic rapture became a personal aspiration. There he addressed "mother, daughter, and bride, O glorious

Virgin, Lady of that King who has loosed our bonds and made the world free and happy, in whose holy wounds I pray you to quiet my heart, O true bringer of happiness."[182]

In that act of seeking entry into the wounds of Christ that loosed his adamantine chains, Petrarch imagined the mystical response that justified his poetry against the ascetical carping of a mock Augustine.[183] In union with the wounds of the Savior he had sought forgiveness for the wounds of sin in a conversion that was merely purgative. Petrarch also sought mystical consolation for the wounds of love. The natal genius identified by medieval moralizers as concupiscence was here elevated toward a love that was not carnal but spiritual. So it was in poetic imitation of the divine passion[184] of an Apolline Christ, suspended on the cross like the psalmist's lyre on a tree in Babylon, that Petrarch in his genius invented his books: the prophetic labors of love.[185]

Epilogue

A humanist circle of prominent literary, religious, and political figures who disputed daily in the Florentine convent of Santo Spirito voiced their expectation of a universal renewal by quoting the Babylonian sonnets of Petrarch.[1] Thus was the poet honored as a prophet in his own town and in his own time, reversing his rueful self-judgment: "If I had stayed in the cave where Apollo became a prophet, Florence would perhaps have her poet today."[2] Two centuries later the Protestant apologist Johannes Wolf could still embrace Petrarch in the awesome company of such visionaries as Hildegard of Bingen, Joachim of Fiore, Dante, Catherine of Siena, Nicholas of Cusa, and Nostradamus.[3] At the climax of the Renaissance, however, a tormented monk who had been advised by his confessor to seek refuge in the wounds of Christ (as did Petrarch), preferred certitude to mysticism and so rejected poetry as a theological method, spurning the allegorizers of Ovid who supposed that Apollo might in pentimento be Christ.[4] This fundamentalism—which exalted plain words and naked truth, buttressed by the prevailing scholastic denigrations of rhetoric—discredited poetical theology, save among the remnant who resisted the doctrine that God represented only clear and distinct ideas, and so should his purveyors. Theologians abandoned Petrarch to those scholars who dealt with the ambiguities of life and of language: historians and literary critics. With the historiographical designation of Petrarch as the herald of modernity,[5] his sacred charism was resolutely replaced by secular virtue. The secularization of Petrarch depreciated and dismissed his assertions of divine inspiration and prophetic vocation. While acknowledging that he professed a belief in the spiritual endowment of the poet, it has been asserted that in fact he believed that this gift functioned naturally and sought natural truth within natural limits. Never, it has been said, did Petrarch allow in poets oracular, prophetic gifts.[6]

A stumbling-block to the serious regard of Petrarch as a poetic theologian has been his own avowal of that devil concupiscence, which hounded him toward the laurel and enlimed him on its branches. Yet the adamantine chains of love and fame that bound him to poetry are only shackles within the context of the asceticism the mock Augustine articulated. To evaluate the religious significance or commitment of Petrarch's poetics by that norm is to capitulate to the very standard he endeavored to supplant with a spirituality of the secular. Just before his death Petrarch sent to Luigi Marsili, the friar who presided over that admiring Florentine circle, his personal copy of Augustine's *Confessions*. It was good, he considered, that the volume that had accompanied him through so many vagrant labors should secure a home.[7] While this gesture genuinely sought to acknowledge the enlightening influence of Augustine,[8] it also suggests where Petrarch thought such counsel finally belonged. Petrarch, although a tonsured cleric,[9] shared the religious aspirations of those who had by choice or by circumstance eschewed the elitism of the monastery.[10] These were aspirations that the intinerant evangelism of the Franciscan and other movements fostered by preaching the gospel as a social ideal. The cloistered discipline thus intruded upon the political, economic, and domestic areas, leavening the laity with the expectation of sanctity and salvation while yet in a secular state. The idea would explode into the assertion of the humanist Erasmus that one could be a monk in the world, and, moreover, that "all can be theologians," whether weavers, farmers, tailors, travelers, masons, prostitutes, pimps, Turks, or mere women.[11]

Petrarch, who was but a harbinger of this popularization of the discipline of theology, was considerably more reserved. Although he complained of being a lonely bird on the rooftop,[12] he preened himself on that lofty position. Appealing to his divinely endowed genius, he trenchantly defended the rarity of the poetic vocation against the crowds of poetasters who would usurp the holy title and privilege of theologian.[13] Talents he affirmed as gifts of God, liberally or sparingly bestowed by his will, and to be accepted without impious questioning.[14] Although he thus defended the exclusivity of the theological vocation, his elitism was definitively shifted from the ecclesiastical enclave to the civic square.

The ideal Petrarch prophetically espoused, as a Vergil and Ezekiel revived, as a worthy bearer of the name Francesco in imitation of that true contemplative even in commerce with men, failed in the restoration of the papacy to Rome, which he had established as his goal. The revival of the Roman question, its universal hegemony, he believed to be the single method for "the restitution of the public order and the beginning of the golden age."[15] To this renewal he committed the energy of his genius in the conviction that:

> There is nothing in the world that cannot be done by verses; they know how to enchant asps with their notes, not to speak of adorning the frost with new flowers.[16]

Petrarch's poetics foundered, however, on political facts and fortunes that proved beyond the lure or grasp of his rhetorical persuasion. Even as he prophesied, it was fortune who usurped the superior stance as "the sad and certain prophetess of my losses."[17] While the poet maintained that "no nature is so rough that it is not soothed by the sweetness of customs and words," the papal nature eluded his voice, like Daphne foiling Apollo. The elder Africanus, he noted, had pacified with speech the barbarian king Syphax, who was unaccustomed to Roman ways, and also Hasdrubal, a ferocious enemy of Rome.[18] Yet Petrarch could not persuade the pope to Roman residence or manner. His poetic method, he was constrained to acknowledge, was inadequate, "the weak sounds of Apollo's lyre amid the trumpets of Mars."[19]

Petrarch maintained that "what is grasped without mental stretching is without value or merit," and he believed that for such exercise the discovery of truth through poetry would be the more gratifying. "I prefer being understood and approved by the few," he declared, "than to be understood by all and approved by no one."[20] The few who understood and approved, however, were neither popes nor politicians who shared his patriotic vision. His poetic futility reduced him to public shame. As he complained, so extinguished was the celestial light that shapes virtuous human life that the mob ridiculed his desire for the laurel as a strange thing.[21] He was mocked like the prophets; in their common phrase he was "the talk of the town" (Job 30:9, Lam. 3:14, Ps. 69:12).[22] He was like Ezekiel the Babylonian captive, the poet of love songs gossiped about at city walls and household doors but spurned for his holy counsel (Ezek. 33:30–33; epigraph).

> I never wish to sing again as I used to, for I was not understood, wherefore I was scorned, and one can be miserable in a pleasant place.
>
> Always to be sighing helps nothing. . . .
>
> I entrusted things to Saint Peter, now no more, no, understand me who can, for I understand myself. . . .

> Perhaps not everyone who can read can understand, and he who sets up the net does not always catch, and he who is too subtle breaks his own neck.[23]

Christ, who also spoke in parables, had failed to gather a city to himself: "O Jerusalem, Jerusalem, killing the prophets and stoning those who are sent to you! How often would I have gathered your children together as a hen gathers her brood under her wings, and you would not!" (Lk. 13:34). Petrarch's devotion to the crucified Savior was the recourse of a humanist who imitated the divine risk of inventing truth through a language of persuasion liable to the historical contingency of the creative act and of its audience. His prayer for the repose of his amorous wounds in the wounds of the Savior was not a pious ornament to his poetry but its spiritual conclusion. This was his "golden martyrdom."[24] It was an affective act, however, not an intellectual system. It was mystical in intention, but inchoate. Only from the example and experiment of many other such authors would Erasmus finally formulate a humanist theology that was securely established cognitively, by relating their collective choice of rhetorical method to the epistemological doctrine of the Logos.[25] Petrarch also appropriated literature for the expression of his identity as a poetic theologian, particularly seeking in ancient texts the authorization his scholastic contemporaries denied him. Had not Homer and Ennius prophesied his advent?[26] Were not the pages of Plato and Cicero compatible with those of Christ?[27] Vergil's ideal of the poet as a sacred seer enlightened by an Apolline inspiration about national destiny especially furnished him with a role and a reason for his art. With his native genius thus divinely endowed and sanctioned, he could aspire to ascend Parnassus, confident that its peak pierced heaven.

Petrarch's impetus was not elaborated in any formal treatise on poetics, such as would engage later humanists, intent on examining and defending their profession. It was stated in his coronation speech and in certain verses and letters. Its supreme articulation was his poetry itself, for despite every criticism and monition, and every experience of failure that confirmed them, Petrarch persisted in the art. To the reputed vision of a holy monk who claimed to read on the face of Christ a stern judgment against his poetry, and who thus urged him to repent of it,[28] Petrarch countered with a vision of Christ, "the sun of righteousness," whose radiant visage was the source of his illumination. Yet beyond these apologetics, pagan and Christian, which he marshaled by exemplar and metaphor to justify his vocation, there remains the deed of the text, the poetry he summoned by sheer conviction of conscience to witness to his holy gift. Like all valid prophetic verse, it engages men in the act of interpretation, as in Petrarch's enduring challenge of Delphic wisdom:

Understand me who can, for I understand myself.[29]

Notes

INTRODUCTION

1. See Richard Kieckhefer, *Unquiet Souls: Fourteenth-Century Saints and Their Religious Milieu* (Chicago: University of Chicago Press, 1984), pp. 122–49; for context, Donald Weinstein and Rudolph M. Bell, *Saints and Society: The Two Worlds of Western Christendom, 1000–1700* (Chicago: University of Chicago Press, 1982); for background, Thomas N. Tentler, *Sin and Confession on the Eve of the Reformation* (Princeton: Princeton University Press, 1977).

2. Thomas M. Greene, *The Light in Troy: Imitation and Discovery in Renaissance Poetry* (New Haven: Yale University Press, 1982), pp. 114–15, but with serious qualification, for which see p. 5 above; Nancy J. Vickers, "Remembering Dante: Petrarch's 'Chiare, fresche et dolci acque,'" *Modern Language Notes*, 96 (1981), 11; Giuseppe Mazzotta, "The *Canzoniere* and the Language of the Self," *Studies in Philology*, 75 (1978), 271–96.

3. Robert M. Durling, "Petrarch's 'Giovene donna sotto un verde lauro,'" *Modern Language Notes*, 86 (1971), 1–20. He does acknowledge that the language is at least "ambiguous," so that it cannot be cancelled by theological condemnation (pp. 19–20).

4. John Freccero, "The Fig Tree and the Laurel: Petrarch's Poetics," *Diacritics*, 5 (1975), 34–40; rpt. in *Literary Theory / Renaissance Texts*, ed. Patricia Parker and David Quint (Baltimore: Johns Hopkins University Press, 1986), pp. 20–32. This is speculation, undocumented in the texts of Augustine or in the scholarship on his symbolism and semiotics. For the symbol of the fig tree as erotic, not semiotic, the classic research is that of Vinzenz Bucheit, "Augustinus unter dem Feigenbaum (zu Conf. VIII)," *Vigiliae Christianae*, 22 (1968), 257–71; and see also such related studies as Leo C. Ferrari, "The Arboreal Polarization in Augustine's Confessions," *Revue des études augustiniennes*, 25 (1979), 35–46. For my research, which adduces further evidence and locates the fig tree in the garden of the Plotinian exegesis of the myth of Eros, see "Augustine in the Garden of Zeus: Lust, Love, and Language," *Harvard Theological Review* 83 (1990), 117–39; and for my interpretation of the entire text, "The Prudential Augustine: The Virtuous Structure and Sense of His *Confessions*," *Recherches augustiniennes*, 22 (1987), 129–50. The issue of his semiotics will be discussed shortly.

5. The magisterial revisionist work is Charles Trinkaus, *In Our Image and Likeness: Humanity and Divinity in Italian Humanist Thought* (2 vols.; Chi-

cago: University of Chicago Press, 1970); and see such books as Salvatore I. Camporeale, *Lorenzo Valla: Umanesimo e teologia* (Florence: Istituto Nazionale di Studi sul Rinascimento, 1972); John W. O'Malley, *Praise and Blame in Renaissance Rome: Rhetoric, Doctrine, and Reform in the Sacred Orators of the Papal Court, c. 1450–1521* (Durham, N.C.: Duke University Press, 1979).

6. See, e.g., Robert Hollander, "Dante *Theologus-Poeta*," *Dante Studies*, 94 (1976), 91–136; Dennis John Costa, "Dante as a Poet-Theologian," *Dante Studies*, 89 (1971), 61–72.

7. The standard work on this classical genre is Theodore C. Burgess, *Epideictic Literature* (Chicago: University of Chicago Press, 1902). For my analysis of one of the texts about Gherardo as epideictic (the epistolary ascent of Mont Ventoux, *Ep. fam.* 4.1) see my hermeneutics, "A Likely Story: The Autobiographical as Epideictic," *Journal of the American Academy of Religion*, 52 (1989), 23–51, esp. 28–33.

8. See, e.g., C. Karl Galinsky, *The Herakles Theme: The Adaptations of the Hero in Literature from Homer to the Twentieth Century* (Oxford: Basil Blackwell, 1972), and Theodore E. Mommsen, "Petrarch and the Story of the Choice of Hercules," *Journal of the Warburg and Courtauld Institutes*, 16 (1953), 178–92; Mia Irene Gerhardt, *Two Wayfarers: Some Medieval Stories on the Theme of Good and Evil* (Utrecht, 1964); Heino Gehrts, *Das Märchen und das Opfer: Untersuchungen zum europäischen Brudermärchen* (Bonn: Bouvier, 1967).

9. The hierarchy at the charterhouse of Montrieux descended from the prior to the priest, the monk, the subdeacon, the convert, the novice, the donate or renderer, the prebendary, and the workman. The *donatus* or *redditus*, very distinctly from the *monachus*, did not live in the monastery there but in the lower house. He wore garb similar to that of the *convertus*, but not the beard, and was addressed not as *frater* but as *burdon*, or mule, to designate his obedient domestic service. He was a layman pledged by civil contract, not religious vow. There was at the charterhouse only one position for a clerical renderer, whose status was something like that of the choir religious but without religious profession or constraint of cloister. Raymond Boyer, *La Chartreuse de Montrieux aux XIIe et XIIIe siècles* (2 vols.; Marseilles: Jeanne Laffitte for the Centre National de la Recherche Scientifique, Paris, 1980), 1: 191–246, and for Gherardo as a clerical renderer, 151–52.

10. See Ernest H. Wilkins, "Petrarch's Ecclesiastical Career," in *Studies in the Life and Works of Petrarch* (Cambridge, Mass.: Mediaeval Academy of America, 1955), pp. 3–32.

11. Reference is to the conversion of the poetry of *fin' amors* into a Christian allegory by John V. Fleming, *Reason and the Lover* (Princeton: Princeton University Press, 1984); *The Roman de la Rose: A Study in Allegory and Iconography* (Princeton: Princeton University Press, 1969); D. W. Robertson, *A Preface to Chaucer: Studies in Medieval Perspectives* (Princeton: Princeton University Press, 1962). This conversion has been rejected by virtually every other critic of the text. For the difference between medieval and modern irony, see Simon Gaunt, *The Troubadours and Irony* (Cambridge: Cambridge University Press, 1989), pp. 5–38.

12. Boyle, "Augustine in the Garden of Zeus."

13. The landmark book was Prosper Alfaric, *L'Evolution intellectuelle de saint Augustin* (Paris: E. Nourry, 1918), which argued for his conversion not to Christianity but to Neoplatonism. Although this argument has been modified by that of conversion to a Neoplatonized Christianity, through Ambrose and other authors (see, e.g., the research of Pierre Courcelle, *Recherches sur les Confessions de saint Augustin*, rev. ed. [Paris: E. de Boccard, 1968]), the scholarship readily accepts a variety of non-Christian influences and elements in the thought of Augustine.

14. Robert J. O'Connell, *Art and the Christian Intelligence in St. Augustine* (Cambridge, Mass.: Harvard University Press, 1978), pp. 143-72.

15. The best orientation to the subject is Marcia Colish, *The Stoic Tradition from Antiquity to the Early Middle Ages* (2 vols.; Leiden: E. J. Brill, 1985), 2: 142-238, esp. 181-98. The following bibliography on Augustine's semiotics as Stoic includes several other items that may be of interest to critics: Christopher Kirwan, *Augustine* (London and New York: Routledge, 1989), pp. 35-59; M. F. Burnyeat, "Wittgenstein and Augustine *de Magistro*," *Proceedings of the Aristotelian Society*, suppl. vol., 61 (1987), 1-24; Tzvetan Todorov, "A propos de la conception augustinienne du signe," *Revue des études augustiniennes*, 31 (1985), 209-14; G. Watson, "St. Augustine's Theory of Language," *Maynooth Review*, 6 (1982), 4-20; Hans Ruef, *Augustin über Semiotik und Sprache: sprachtheoretische Analysen zu Augustins Schrift De dialectica mit einer deutschen Übersetzung* (Bern: K. J. Wyss Erben, 1981); Marc Baratin, "Les Origines stoïciennes de la théorie augustinienne du signe," *Revue des études latines*, 59 (1981), 260-68; T. Adamik, "Zur Terminologie und Funktion von Augustinus' Zeichentheorie," [Magyar Tudományos Akadémia, Budapest] *Acta Antiqua*, 29 (1981), 403-16; Guy Bouchard, "La Conception augustinienne du signe selon Tzvetan Todorov," *Recherches augustiniennes*, 15 (1980), 305-46; Robert H. Ayers, *Language, Logic, and Reason in the Church Fathers: A Study of Tertullian, Augustine and Aquinas* (Hildesheim: Georg Olms, 1979), pp. 61-81; Louis G. Kelly, "Saint Augustine and Saussurean Linguistics," *Augustinian Studies*, 6 (1975), 45-64; Jean Collart, "Saint Augustin grammairien dans le *De magistro*," *Revue des études augustiniennes*, 17 (1971), 279-92; Raffaele Simone, "Semiologia agostiniana," *Cultura*, 7 (1969), 88-117; B. Darrell Jackson, "The Theory of Signs in St. Augustine's De Doctrina Christiana," *Revue des études augustiniennes*, 15 (1969), 9-49, rpt. in *Augustine: A Collection of Critical Essays*, ed. R. A. Markus (London: Macmillan, 1972), pp. 92-137; Alfred Schindler, *Wort und Analogie in Augustins Trinitätslehre* (Tübingen: Mohr, 1965); Ulrich Duchrow, *Sprachverständnis und biblischen Hören bei Augustin* (Tübingen: J. C. B. Mohr, 1965), esp. pp. 42-63; Georges Bavaud, "Un Thème augustinien: Le Mystère de l'Incarnation à la lumière de la distinction entre le verbe intérieur et le verbe proféré," *Revue des études augustiniennes*, 9 (1963), 95-101; Markus, "St. Augustine on Signs," *Phronesis*, 2 (1957), 60-83, rpt. in *Augustine*, ed. idem, pp. 61-91.

16. *Pace* Freccero, "The Fig Tree and the Laurel," 37, 38.

17. Boyle, "Stoic Luther: Paradoxical Sin and Necessity," *Archiv für Re-*

formationsgeschichte, 73 (1982), 69–93; related, "The Stoic Paradox of James 2.10," *New Testament Studies*, 31 (1985), 611–17; "The Chimera and the Spirit: Luther's Grammar of the Will," in *The Martin Luther Quincentennial*, ed. Gerhard Dünnhaupt (Detroit: Wayne State University Press for *Michigan Germanic Studies*, 1985), pp. 17–31; for his anti-rhetoric, *Rhetoric and Reform: Erasmus' Civil Dispute with Luther* (Cambridge, Mass.: Harvard University Press, 1983); for dualism in the history of religions as background, "Luther's Rider-Gods: From the Steppe to the Tower," *Journal of Religious History*, 13 (1985), 260–82; related, "Erasmus and the 'Modern' Question: Was He Semi-Pelagian?" *Archiv für Reformationsgeschichte*, 75 (1984), 59–77.

18. Durling, "Petrarch's 'Giovene donna sotto un verde lauro,'" and idem, trans. and ed., *Petrarch's Lyric Poems: The Rime Sparse and Other Lyrics* (Cambridge, Mass.: Harvard University Press, 1976), p. 88.

19. Greene, *The Light in Troy*, p. 115, who also notes that both Durling and Freccero recognize "phantasm" as a secondary meaning. The lexical sense of *eidolon* is also noted by Mazzotta, "Antiquity and the New Arts in Petrarch," *Romanic Review*, 79 (1988), 40.

20. See David C. Lindberg, *Theories of Vision from Al-Kindi to Kepler* (Chicago: University of Chicago Press, 1976), pp. 1–3, 23, 113, 161.

21. James S. Ackerman, "Leonardo's Eye," *Journal of the Warburg and Courtauld Institutes*, 41 (1978), 114–15, 123, 124, 144.

22. David E. Hahm, "Early Hellenistic Theories of Vision and the Perception of Colour," in *Studies in Perception: Interrelations in the History of Philosophy and Science*, ed. Peter K. Maehammer and Robert G. Turnbull (Columbus: Ohio State University Press, 1978), pp. 62, 75 n.53.

23. Michael V. Wedin, *Mind and Imagination in Aristotle* (New Haven: Yale University Press, 1988), pp. 178–79.

24. See Durling, "Petrarch's 'Giovene donna sotto un verde lauro,'" 12–16, and *Petrarch's Lyric Poems*, p. 88n. with reference to Ps. 118:127 Vg.

25. See Michael Baxandall, *Painting and Experience in Fifteenth Century Italy: A Primer in the Social History of Pictorial Style*, 2d ed. (Oxford: Oxford University Press, 1988), pp. 81–82.

26. Ibid., pp. 138–39, 83, 15–16.

27. Abbot Suger, *Abbot Suger on the Abbey Church of St-Denis and Its Art Treasures*, p. 23 (not in Baxandall).

28. Petrarch, *De remediis utiusque fortunae* 1.40–41, in *Operum* (Basel, 1554; rpt., 3 vols.; Ridgewood, N.J.: Gregg, 1965), 1: 50–52.

29. Baxandall, *Giotto and the Orators: Humanist Observers of Painting in Italy and the Discovery of Pictorial Composition, 1350–1450* (Oxford: Clarendon, 1971), pp. 51–65.

30. Petrarch, *Rime sparse* 30.27, ed. Durling, p. 89.

31. Michael Camille, *The Gothic Idol: Idolatry and Image-making in Medieval Art* (Cambridge: Cambridge University Press, 1989), pp. 50, 57, 19–20, 57–72, 103.

32. Ibid., pp. 298–316 with reference to the Robertsonian school, for which see n. 11 above.

33. Donald R. Howard, *The Three Temptations: Medieval Man in Search of the World* (Princeton: Princeton University Press, 1966), p. 27.

34. Ovid, *Heroides* 13.153–62.

35. Dante, *Purgatorio* 10.31–36.

36. Camille, *The Gothic Idol*, pp. 36, 42.

37. Baxandall, *Giotto and the Orators*, p. 51, with reference to Petrarch, *Ep. sen.* 4.3 and *Ep. fam.* 16.11.

38. G. Zanker, "Enargeia in the Ancient Criticism of Poetry," *Rheinisches Museum für Philologie*, 124 (1981), 297–311; Heinrich Lausberg, *Handbuch der literarischen Rhetorik: Eine Grundlegung der Literaturwissenschaft* (2 vols.; Munich: Max Hueber, 1960), 1: pars. 810–19.

39. Terence Cave, "*Enargeia:* Erasmus and the Rhetoric of Presence in the Sixteenth Century," *L'Esprit créateur*, 16 (1976), 6.

40. Trinkaus, *The Poet as Philosopher: Petrarch and the Formation of Renaissance Consciousness* (New Haven: Yale University Press, 1976), pp. 26, 90–113; Ronald Witt, "Coluccio Salutati and the Conception of the *Poeta Theologus* in the Fourteenth Century," *Renaissance Quarterly*, 30 (1977), 539, 542–44.

41. Boyle, "Augustine in the Garden of Zeus."

42. Including a possibly new work, previously attributed to Francis of Assisi, but now "probably" to Petrarch by Cajetan Esser in his critical edition of Francis of Assisi, *Opuscula*, p. 37. The text is "Collatio," *Archivum Franciscanum Historicum*, 7 (1904), 527–29.

1. HAIL, TRUE APOLLO!

1. Ena Makin, "The Triumphal Route, with Particular Reference to the Flavian Triumph," *Journal of Roman Studies*, 11 (1921), 25–36.

2. Petrarch, *Africa* 2.404–9, ed. Nicola Festa, in Edizione Nazionale, vol. 1 (Florence: G. C. Sansoni, 1926), p. 276; trans., Thomas G. Bergin and Alice S. Wilson, *Petrarch's Africa* (New Haven: Yale University Press, 1977), p. 237. For Scipio's triumph and that of the poet Ennius, see *Africa* 9.398–402, ed. Festa, p. 276.

3. Petrarch, *Epistolae familiares* 4.6.7, ed. V. Rossi and U. Bosco, in Edizione Nazionale, vols. 10–13, *Le familiari* (4 vols.; Florence: G. C. Sansoni, 1933–42), 1: 171. See Ernest H. Wilkins, "The Coronation of Petrarch," in *The Making of the Canzoniere and Other Petrarchan Studies* (Rome: Storia e letteratura, 1951), pp. 66–68.

4. Wilkins, "The Coronation of Petrarch," pp. 31–32.

5. Aldo S. Bernardo, *Petrarch, Scipio and the "Africa": The Birth of Humanism's Dream* (Baltimore: Johns Hopkins University Press, 1962), pp. 170–79; David Groves, "Petrarch's Inability to Complete the 'Africa,'" *Parergon*, 12 (1975), 11–19.

6. Petrarch, *Posteritati*, in *Prose*, ed. G. Martellotti et al. (Milan: Riccardo Ricciardi, 1955), p. 16.

7. Ibid., p. 14; *Ep. fam.* 4.2, ed. Rossi, 1: 161–64; cf. 4.3, 164–67. Wilkins, "The Coronation of Petrarch," pp. 45–53. For the custom of oral

recital see Paul Zumthor, *La lettre et la voix: De la "Littérature" médiévale* (Paris: Seuil, 1987).
   8. Petrarch, *Africa* 1.38–70, ed. Festa, pp. 4–5.
   9. *Laurea et ciuitatis Romanae donatae Priuilegium,* in Petrarch, *Operum* (Basel, 1554; rpt., 3 vols.; Ridgewood, N.J.: Gregg, 1965), 3: 1254–56. Wilkins, "The Coronation of Petrarch," pp. 53–61.
   10. Bernardo, *Petrarch, Scipio and the "Africa."*
   11. Petrarch, *Posteritati,* in *Prose,* ed. Martellotti, pp. 14–16; *Rerum memorandarum libri* 1.37, ed. Giuseppe Billanovich, in Edizione Nazionale, vol. 5 (Florence: G. C. Sansoni, 1945), p. 41. Wilkins, "The Coronation of Petrarch," pp. 46–53.
   12. Petrarch, *Collatio laureationis,* ed. Carlo Godi, "La 'Collatio laureationis' del Petrarca," *Italia medioevale e umanistica,* 13 (1970), 13–27.
   13. Ibid., pp. 20–21. Petrarch cites Lactantius, *Divinae institutiones* 1.11, and Macrobius, *Commentariorum in somnium Scipionis* [libri] 2.10.11. For the concept of discovery through difficulty he is indebted to Augustine, *De doctrina christiana* 2.6.7–8, and to the sources he cites in a similar argument in *Invective contra medicum* 3, ed. Pier G. Ricci, (Rome: Storia e letteratura, 1950), pp. 69–70, and 1, p. 37. See also his *De secreto conflicto mearum curarum* 2, in *Prose,* ed. Martellotti, p. 104; and *Ep. fam.* 6.3.66, ed. Rossi, 2: 76.
   14. Petrarch, *Collatio laureationis,* ed. Godi, pp. 13–14; trans. Ernest H. Wilkins, "Petrarch's Coronation Oration," in his *Studies in the Life and Works of Petrarch* (Cambridge, Mass.: Mediaeval Academy of America, 1955), appendix, pp. 301–2. He cites Cicero, *Pro Archia,* 8.18, for which manuscript see Pierre de Nolhac, *Pétrarque et l'humanisme,* rev. ed. (2 vols.; Paris: Honoré Champion, 1907), 1: 221; Juvenal, *Saturae* 7.66–68; Lucan, *Bellum civile* 9.980. Petrarch also cited the Ciceronian passage in his *Invective contra medicum* 1, ed. Ricci, p. 33. For his estimate of this work see *Ep. fam.* 1.2.23, ed. Rossi, 1: 19.
   15. Petrarch, *Liber sine nomine,* praef. 5–11, ed. Paul Piur, *Petrarcas "Buch ohne Namen" und die papstliche Kurie: Ein Beitrag zur Geistesgeschichte der Frührenaissance* (Halle: Max Niemeyer, 1925), p. 163. The text is *Bucolicum carmen* 1, ed. Antonio Avena, *Il Bucolicum carmen e i suoi commenti inediti* (Padua: Società cooperativa tipografica, 1906), pp. 95–99. See also Nicholas Mann, "The Making of Petrarch's 'Bucolicum Carmen': A Contribution to the History of the Text," *Italia medioevale e umanistica,* 20 (1978), 130–37. For discussion see Giuseppe Mazzotta, "Humanism and Monastic Spirituality in Petrarch," *Stanford Literary Review,* 5 (1988), 64–66.
   16. Petrarch, *Ep. fam.* 10.4.1–9, ed. Rossi, 2: 301–3; trans. Aldo S. Bernardo, *Rerum familiarum libri I–VIII* (Albany: State University of New York Press, 1975), and *Rerum familiarum libri IX–XVI* (Baltimore: Johns Hopkins University Press, 1982), pp. 69, 70. Rev. 5:5, John 1:29, Ps. 22:6. Aristotle, *Metaphysica* 1.983b29, 1000a9. For the first pagan theologians as poets and philosophers see also Petrarch, *Invective contra medicum* 3, ed. Ricci, p. 71. See also Mazzotta, "Humanism and Monastic Spirituality in Petrarch," 66–69; A. J. Minnis, *Medieval Theory of Authorship: Scholastic Literary Attitudes in the Later Middle Ages* (London: Scolar, 1984), p. 216; Trinkaus, *The Poet as Philosopher,* pp. 102–3.

17. Petrarch, *Collatio laureationis,* ed. Godi, p. 13.
18. See Wilkins, "The Coronation of Petrarch," pp. 21-23.
19. Albertino Mussato, *Epistolae* 4, 7. See Ernst R. Curtius, *European Literature and the Latin Middle Ages,* trans. Willard R. Trask (New York: Pantheon, 1953), pp. 215-21; and for more recent accounts, Giorgio Ronioni, *Le origini delle dispute umanistiche sulla poesia (Mussato e Petrarca)* (Rome: Bulzone, 1976), and Concetta C. Greenfield, *Humanist and Scholastic Poetics, 1250-1500* (Lewisburg, Pa.: Bucknell University Press, 1981), pp. 79-94. Curtius's statement that Mussato's designation of poetry as theology is "in the line of established medieval tradition," p. 219, which is accepted by Greenfield, pp. 25-26, is questionable. His argument assumes that the concept, which was transmitted from Cicero, *De natura deorum* 3.21.53, to Lactantius, *De ira Dei* 11.8, to Isidore of Seville, *Etymologiae* 8.7.9, and thence to the medieval encyclopedists, was accepted theologically by those authors.
20. Lucan, *Bellum civile* 9.980.
21. Horace, *De arte poetica* 343.
22. Augustine, *De doctrina christiana* 1.3.3, 2.18.28, 2.39.58, 2.40.60-61, 2.52.63. See also Oliver O'Donovan, "*Usus* and *Fruitio* in Augustine, *De doctrina christiana* I," *Journal of Theological Studies,* 33 (1982), 361-97.
23. Augustine, *Retractationum* [libri] 1.3.
24. Petrarch, *Epistolae seniles* 1.5, in *Operum,* 2:823. Consider also: "Though salvation may not lie in literature, it still is and was for a great many men a way to salvation" (*Ep. fam.* 17.1.3, ed. Rossi, 3:221; trans. Bernardo, 3:1).
25. The most recent major studies of the text are Hans Baron, *Petrarch's "Secretum": Its Making and Its Meaning* (Cambridge, Mass.: Mediaeval Academy of America, 1985), and Francisco Rico, *Vida y obra de Petrarca,* vol. 1: *Lectura del "Secretum"* (Padua: Antenore, 1974); see also Bortolo Martinelli, "Sulla data del 'Secretum.' Nova et Vetera 1, 2," *Critica letteraria,* 13 (1985), 431-82, 645-93.
26. Petrarch, *Secretum* 1, in *Prose,* ed. Martellotti, pp. 36, 44; trans. William S. Draper, *Petrarch's Secret or The Soul's Conflict with Passion,* (London: Chatto & Windus, 1911), p. 14; see also p. 42.
27. Petrarch, *Secretum* 3, ed. Martellotti, p. 194; trans. Draper, p. 172. Ed. pp. 136, 144-50; trans. p. 124. Ed. pp. 148-50, 162-64.
28. Petrarch, *Secretum* 3, ed. Martellotti, pp. 22-24 and passim. See Pedro Lain-Entralgo, *The Therapy of the Word in Classical Antiquity,* ed. and trans. L. J. Rather and John M. Sharp (New Haven: Yale University Press, 1970).
29. Petrarch, *Secretum* 1-3, ed. Martellotti, pp. 26, 40, 114, 142, 148; 212; 144; trans. Draper, p. 121.
30. Petrarch, *Rime sparse,* in *Petrarch's Lyric Poems: The Rime sparse and Other Lyrics,* trans. and ed. Robert M. Durling (Cambridge, Mass.: Harvard University Press, 1976), 159.1, pp. 304-5; 126.55, p. 247; 279.6, p. 459, 309.3, p. 489; 28.2, p. 75. 192.4, pp. 338-39, 243.3, pp. 404-5; 268.34-36, p. 439. 72.2-3, pp. 162-63. 14.7, pp. 48-49. 341.9-10, pp. 538-39.
31. Petrarch, *Secretum* 3, ed. Martellotti, p. 214; trans. Draper, p. 192.
32. Petrarch, *Rime sparse,* ed. Durling, 167.14, pp. 312-13; 268.38-39,

pp. 438–39, 278.5, pp. 456–57, 301.13, pp. 480–81. 193.9, pp. 338–39; 280.12–14, p. 459; 285.13, p. 465. 278.5–6, pp. 456–57; 29.39–40, pp. 84–85.

33. Petrarch, *Ep. fam.* 3.12.8, ed. Rossi, 1:130; trans. Bernardo, 1:146.

34. Ibid. 1.12.3–5, ed. Rossi, 1:51–52; trans. Bernardo, 1:55.

35. Petrarch, *Rime sparse,* ed. Durling, 261.7–8, pp. 422–23; 29.40, pp. 84–85.

36. Ibid. 13.9–14, pp. 48–49.

37. Ibid. 333.13–14, pp. 530–31; 331.29–30, pp. 520–21, 91.7, pp. 194–95. 277.10–11, pp. 456–57; 286.9–14, pp. 464–65.

38. Petrarch, *Ep. sen.* 1.5, in *Operum,* 2: 823.

39. Petrarch, *Secretum* 1, ed. Martellotti, p. 34; trans. Draper, p. 13. Vergil, *Aeneid* 9.641.

40. *Secretum* 3, ed. Martellotti, p. 212; trans. Draper, pp. 189, 190.

41. See sources cited in n. 32 above.

42. For other studies see my "A Likely Story: The Autobiographical as Epideictic," *Journal of the American Academy of Religion,* 52 (1989), 28–33; Jill Robbins, "Petrarch Reading Augustine: 'The Ascent of Mont Ventoux,'" *Philological Quarterly,* 64 (1985), 533–53; Michael O'Connell, "Authority and the Truth of Experience in Petrarch's 'Ascent of Mont Ventoux,'" *Philological Quarterly,* 62 (1983), 507–20; Baron, *Petrarch's "Secretum,"* pp. 196–202; Thomas M. Greene, *The Light in Troy: Imitation and Discovery in Renaissance Poetry* (New Haven: Yale University Press, 1982), pp. 104–11; Carolyn Chiapelli, "The Motif of Confession in Petrarch's 'Mt. Ventoux,'" *Modern Language Notes,* 93 (1978), 131–36; Durling, "Il Petrarca, il Ventoso e la possibilità dell'allegoria," *Revue des études augustiniennes,* 23 (1977), 304–23, and "The Ascent of Mt. Ventoux and the Crisis of Allegory," *Italian Quarterly,* 18 (1974), 7–28; Dieter Kramers, "L'Ascension du Mont Ventoux," in *Actes du congrès international Francesco Petrarca* (Avignon, 1974), pp. 122–31, rpt. "Petrarcas Besteigung des Mont Ventoux," in *Sprachen der Lyrik: Festschrift für Hugo Friedrich zum 70. Geburtstag,* ed. Erich Köhler (Frankfurt: Vittorio Klostermann, 1975), pp. 487–97; Martinelli, "Del Petrarca e il Ventoso," in *Studi in onore di Alberto Chiari* (2 vols.; Brescia: Paideia, 1973), 2:767–834, rpt. "Petrarca e il Ventoso," in his *Petrarca e il Ventoso* (Rome: Minerva, 1977), pp. 149–215; Ph. de Vries, "Petrarca's brief over de bestijging van de Mont Ventoux (Familiarum rerum libri, IV, 1,)" *Tijdschrift voor Geschiedenis,* 83 (1970), 181–205; Giuseppe Billanovich, "Petrarca e il Ventoso," *Italia medioevale e umanistica,* 9 (1966), 389–401; Pierre Courcelle, "Pétrarque entre saint Augustin et les Augustins du XIVe siècle," *Studi petrarcheschi,* 7 (1959), 51–71.

43. Petrarch, *Ep. fam.* 4.1, ed. Rossi, 1: 153–61; trans. Bernardo, 1: 178. Augustine, *Confessionum libri tredecim* 8.12.29, 10.8.15. Although the composition of this fictional letter has been dated to 1352 or early 1353 (Billanovich, *Petrarca letterato,* vol. 1: *Lo scrittoio del Petrarca* [Rome: Storia e letteratura, 1947], pp. 193–98), Petrarch dated it 1336 to indicate the seminal importance of its tenets for his poetic career. The dating is challenged by Baron, *Petrarch's "Secretum,"* pp. 196–202, but his argument that Petrarch could not be a "liar"

is entirely off the mark, because the epistle is epideictic rhetoric. See my "A Likely Story," 23–51, esp. pp. 28–33.

44. Petrarch, *Ep. fam.* 4.1.26–32, ed. Rossi, 1: 158–60; trans. Bernardo, 1: 178.

45. Petrarch, *Rime sparse,* ed. Durling, 129, pp. 265–67; 10.7–8, p. 45. For this ascent and descent as the alternation of poetic theory and practice, see *Ep. fam.* 10.4.27, ed. Rossi, 2: 308. For other studies see Gabriel Lanyi, "The 129th Poem in Petrarch's Canzoniere: An Analysis," *Forum Italicum,* 13 (1979), 201–12; Pierre Antonetti, "Poésie et littérature dans la canzone: 'Di pensier in pensier . . . ,'" *Annales de la Faculté des lettres et sciences humaines d'Aix,* 38 (1964), 195–204.

46. Petrarch, *Ep. fam.* 4.1.32–33, ed. Rossi, 1: 160.

47. Petrarch, *Secretum* 3, ed. Martellotti, pp. 206–8; trans. Draper, pp. 184–85.

48. Petrarch, *Ep. fam.* 4.1.17, ed. Rossi, 1: 157. See also *Ep. fam.* 11.3.9–10, ed. Rossi, 2: 328.

49. Michael Baxandall, *Giotto and the Orators: Humanist Observers of Painting in Italy and the Discovery of Pictorial Composition, 1350–1450* (Oxford: Clarendon, 1971), pp. 15–17; Francesco Tateo, *Rhetorica e poetica fra Medioevo e Rinascimento* (Bari: Adriatica, 1960), pp. 82–92.

50. David Summers, *The Judgment of Sense: Renaissance Naturalism and the Rise of Aesthetics* (Cambridge: Cambridge University Press, 1987), p. 99.

51. Winthrop Wetherbee, *Platonism and Poetry in the Twelfth Century* (Princeton: Princeton University Press, 1972), pp. 94–104; idem, "The Theme of Imagination in Medieval Poetry and the Allegorical Figure 'Genius,'" *Medievalia et Humanistica,* 7 (1976), 45–64.

52. Mario Trovato, "The Semantic Value of *Ingegno* and Dante's *Ulysses* in the Light of the *Metalogicon,*" *Modern Philology,* 84 (1987), 258–66.

53. Martin Kemp, "From 'Mimesis' to 'Fantasia': The Quattrocento Vocabulary of Creation, Inspiration and Genius in the Visual Arts," *Viator,* 8 (1977), 384–86, noting Petrarch's citation of Cicero, *Pro Archia* 8.18, in *Invective contra medicum* 1.286–89, ed. Ricci, p. 33.

54. Jane Chance Nitzsche, *The Genius Figure in Antiquity and the Middle Ages* (New York: Columbia University Press, 1975), pp. 7–41. Horace, *Ep.* 2.2.187–89.

55. Nitzsche, *The Genius Figure,* pp. 42–136; Denise N. Baker, "The Priesthood of Genius: A Study of the Medieval Tradition," *Speculum,* 51 (1976), 277–91.

56. Nitzsche, *The Genius Figure,* pp. 107–14, 124–25, 129–30, 131–32, 135–36.

57. Petrarch, *Africa* 9.78–105, 133–289, ed. Festa, pp. 264, 266–76; trans. Bergin and Wilson, pp. 226, 231. For Ennius's vision in the *Africa* and in *Rime* 186, 187, see also Martellotti, "Stella diforme," in *Tra latino e volgare: Per Carlo Dionisotti,* ed. Gabriella B. Trezzini (2 vols.; Padua: Antenore, 1974), 2: 569–84. For Petrarch on Homer see Cesare F. Goffis, "L'epistola del Petrarca ad Omero," in *Il Petrarca ad Arquà: Atti del convegno di studi nel VI centario*

(1370–1374), ed. Billanovich and Giuseppe Frasso (Padua: Antenore, 1975), pp. 149–64; Roberto Weiss, "Notes on Petrarch and Homer," in his *Medieval and Humanist Greek: Collected Essays* (Padua: Antenore, 1978), pp. 150–65.

58. Petrarch, *Rime sparse*, ed. Durling, 360.39–40, p. 563.

59. Petrarch, *De vita solitaria* 1.6, in *Prose*, ed. Martellotti, p. 358; trans. Jacob Zeitlin, *The Life of Solitude*, (Urbana: University of Illinois Press, 1924), p. 151. See also John Daniel Cooke, "Euhemerism: A Mediaeval Interpretation of Classical Paganism," *Speculum*, 2 (1927), 396–410.

60. For Jupiter, see Nitzsche, *The Genius Figure*, pp. 24–26 and passim.

61. Petrarch, *Collatio laureationis*, ed. Godi, 319, 325; trans. Wilkins, pp. 306, 311. He cites Persius, *Saturae*, prol. 10.

62. Petrarch, *Africa* 9.18–22, ed. Festa, p. 261; trans. Bergin and Wilson, p. 223. 9.114, ed. p. 265; trans. p. 227.

63. *Ap.* Cicero, *De divinatione* 1.31.66; trans. William A. Falconer, in *De senectute, De amicitia, De divinatione* (New York: G. P. Putnam's Sons, 1923), p. 297. For madness and dreaming as due to the full force of Apollo's gilded arrow see Ennius, *ap.* Cicero, *Academica* 2.28.89; and for the interpretation of dreams through Apollo's oracle, *ap.* Cicero, *De div.* 1.21.42. Cf. also *ap.* Cicero, *De oratore* 1.45.199. See *The Tragedies of Ennius: The Fragments*, ed. H. D. Jocelyn (Cambridge: Cambridge University Press, 1969), pp. 75–76, 77–78, 74, 140, 81, 83. For a survey of Petrarch on Ennius see Werner Suerbaum, "Ennius bei Petrarca: Betrachtungen zu literarischen Ennius-Bildern," in *Ennius: Sept exposés suivis de discussions*, ed. Otto Skutsch (Geneva: Vand, 1971), pp. 293–347.

64. Petrarch, *Secretum* 3, ed. Martellotti, p. 214. The text is more forceful than Draper's translation, however: "Sed desiderium frenare non valeo."

65. Petrarch, *Secretum* 3, ed. Martellotti, p. 158; trans. Draper, p. 135; and ed. p. 174, citing Aristotle, *ap.* Seneca, *De tranquillitate animae* 17.10. See also Aristotle, *Problemata* 30.1, *Poetica* 17.35–37.

66. Petrarch, *Africa* 9.440, ed. Festa, p. 277; *Ep. fam.* 4.4.5, ed. Rossi, 1:168.

67. Petrarch, *Ep. fam.* 1.2.6–11, ed. Rossi, 1:16–17; 4.7.5, p. 172.

68. Petrarch, *Secretum* 2, ed. Martellotti, p. 90; trans. Draper, pp. 68–69.

69. Augustine, *De civitate Dei* 7.16; 6.5–10; 7.13. For Petrarch's purchase of this text see Wilkins, *Life of Petrarch* (Chicago: University of Chicago Press, 1961), pp. 6–7. Although Augustine refuses to identify Christ as the new Apollo, for some commonplaces of Christ as solar hero see Suzanne Poque, *Le Langage symbolique dans la prédication d'Augustin d'Hippone* (2 vols.; Paris: Etudes augustiniennes, 1984), 1:377–400. See also Jean Doignon, "Les Images virgiliennes d'Apollon et le vrai soleil d'Augustin à Cassiciacum," in *Présence de Virgile: Actes du colloque des 9, 11 et 12 décembre 1976* (Paris E.N.S., Tours), ed. R. Chevallier (Paris: Belles lettres, 1978), pp. 175–83.

70. Petrarch, *Africa* 7.710–14, 23–24, ed. Festa, p. 199; trans. Bergin and Wilson, pp. 166, 167.

71. Petrarch, *Bucolicum carmen* 1.65–68, ed. Avena, p. 97; trans. Thomas

G. Bergin, *Petrarch's Bucolicum carmen* (New Haven: Yale University Press, 1974), p. 9. Petrarch, *Ep. fam.* 10.4.30, ed. Rossi, 2: 308; my translation. *Ep. fam.* 24.12.16, ed. 4:257.

72. See Tatian, *Oratio ad Graecos* 12; Clement of Alexandria, *Protrepticus* 2.41.2, 2.11.2, 2.35.1. Petrarch, *Ep. fam.* 18.12.2, ed. Rossi, 3: 295–96; trans. Bernardo, 3: 63.

73. Origen, *Contra Celsum* 7.3–6; trans. Henry Chadwick, *Origen: Contra Celsum* (Cambridge: Cambridge University Press, 1953), p. 397. See also John Chrysostom, *In epistolam ad Corinthos 1, homiliae* 29.2. Origen, *Contra Celsum* 3.37; trans. p. 153. *Contra Celsum* 3.25; trans. pp. 143–44.

74. Lactantius, *Divinae institutiones* 4.27. See Petrarch's citation of 1.7.9 as documented in n. 72 above.

75. Gregory the Great, "De vita et miraculis venerabilis Benedicti Abbatis," 2.8.10–12. See Petrarch, *De vita solitaria* 2.6, ed. Martellotti, p. 452.

76. Origen, *Contra Celsum* 7.4.

77. Clement of Alexandria, *Protrepticus* 2.32.3–4.

78. Tatian, *Oratio ad Graecos* 8; trans. B. P. Pratten et al. in *The Writings of Tatian and Theophilus; and the Clementine Recognitions* (Edinburgh, 1867), p. 13. He argues that Apollo also failed to foresee that Zephyrus would slay his beloved Hyacinthus, and therefore was not omniscient in prophecy. This polemic was repeated by Theophilus, *Ad Autolycum* 1.9, and Athenagoras, *Legatio* 21.6. For the fathers of the Church on Daphne see also Yves F.-A. Giraud, *La Fable de Daphné: Essai sur un type de métamorphose végétale dans la littérature et dans les arts jusqu'à la fin du XVIIe siècle* (Geneva: Droz, 1968), pp. 87–89.

79. See Charles Witke, *Numen litterarum: The Old and the New in Latin Poetry from Constantine to Gregory the Great* (Leiden: E. J. Brill, 1971), pp. 42–65.

80. Paulinus of Nola, *Carmina* 10.19–49; trans. P. G. Walsh in *The Poems of St. Paulinus of Nola* (New York: Newman, 1975), pp. 58–59.

81. Ibid. 10.57–58; trans. p. 59.

82. Ibid. 10.134–35; trans. p. 62.

83. Ibid. 20.28–62. See Witke, *Numen litterarum*, pp. 89–94; and Jacques Fontaine, "Les Symbolismes de la cithare dans la poésie de Paulin de Nole," in *Romanitas et christianitas: Studia Iano Henrico Waszink A.D. VI Kal. Nov. A. MCMLXXIII XIII lustra complenti oblata*, ed. W. den Boer et al. (Amsterdam and London: North-Holland, 1973), pp. 123–43.

84. Witke, *Numen litterarum*, pp. 110, 117.

85. Paulinus, *Carmen* 10.110–16; trans. Walsh, p. 61.

86. For examples of such substitution see Witke, *Numen litterarum*, pp. 76, 80, 82, 94, 200.

87. Paulinus, *Carmen* 15.30–33; trans. Walsh, p. 83.

88. Prudentius, *Apotheosis* 402–5; trans. H. J. Thomson, in *Prudentius* (2 vols.; Cambridge, Mass.: Harvard University Press, 1949), 1: 151.

89. Prudentius, *Cathemerinon* 3.26–30; trans. Thomson, p. 21. He also introduced his *Psychomachia,* that allegorical personification of embattled vir-

tues and vices that so influenced medieval and Renaissance literature, by pitting pagan and Christian cultures against each other in confrontation. He rhetorically replaced the classical invocation of the heroic Aeneas, praying that Apollo might reveal the prophetic mysteries of the underworld, with the prayer of the Christian poet to Christ. Cf. *Aeneid* 6.56–65, *Psychomachia* 1–11. See Macklin Smith, *Prudentius' Psychomachia: A Reexamination* (Princeton: Princeton University Press, 1976), pp. 272–73, and for the argument that the poem is a sophisticated literary assault on Vergil, pp. 234–300.

90. Petrarch, "Laurea occidens" 311–18, in *Laurea occidens: Bucolicum carmen X,* ed. G. Martellotti (Rome: Storia e letteratura, 1968), p. 33; trans. Bergin, p. 173.

91. Dante, *Commedia: Paradiso* 1.13–36, trans. Charles S. Singleton (Princeton: Princeton University Press, 1975), vol. 1: *Text,* pp. 3–5.

92. Giovanni Pico della Mirandola, *Oratio de hominis dignitate,* ed. Garin, 1:320. For the continuation of the Apolline motif in Renaissance poetry see, e.g., Terence C. Cave, "Ronsard as Apollo: Myth, Poetry and Experience in a Renaissance Sonnet-Cycle," *Yale French Studies,* 47 (1972), 76–89.

93. John Milton, "Ode on the Morning of Christ's Nativity" 19. Cf. Prudentius, *Apotheosis* 435–43.

94. Petrarch, *De otio religioso* 1, in *Il "De otio religioso" di Francesco Petrarca,* ed. Giuseppe Rotondi (Vatican City: Biblioteca Apostolica Vaticana, 1958), p. 32, citing Lucan, *Bellum civile* 5.111–13; trans. J. D. Duff, *The Civil War* (New York: G. P. Putnam's Sons, 1928), p. 247. See also the loss of literature as even greater and more deplorable than the silence of the Delphic oracle in *Ep. fam.* 18.12.2, ed. Rossi, 3: 295.

95. Petrarch, *Africa* 1.1–18, ed. Festa, pp. 3–4; trans. Bergin and Wilson, p. 1. For other studies of the preface, see Giuseppe Velli, "Il proemio dell' 'Africa,'" *Italia medioevale e umanistica,* 8 (1965), 323–32; Enrico Carrara, "Sulla soglia dell' 'Africa,'" *Studi romanzi,* 21 (1931), 117–37, rpt. in his *Studi petrarcheschi ed altri scritti* (Turin: Bottega d'Erasmo, 1959), pp. 115–33.

96. Vergil, *Aeneid* 3.119.

97. Macrobius, *Saturnalia* 3.6.2–5, 9.

98. For the medieval allegories, see pp. 32–33.

99. Petrarch, *Rime sparse,* ed. Durling, pp. 92–93, 574–75. The poem numbered 34 in the final redaction stood first in the original form. Wilkins, "The Chronology of the *Canzoniere,*" in his *The Making of the "Canzoniere,"* p. 361.

100. Petrarch, *Ep. sen.* 1.5, in *Operum,* 2: 822.

101. See also Angelo Mazzocco, "The Antiquarianism of Francesco Petrarca," *Journal of Mediaeval and Renaissance Studies,* 7 (1977), 222.

102. Appendix II to Paulinus, *Carmina.*

103. For the classical background see Joseph Fontenrose, *Python: A Study of the Delphic Myth and Its Origins* (Berkeley: University of California Press, 1959).

104. See Lester K. Born, "Ovid and Allegory," *Speculum,* 9 (1934), 362–79; Giraud, *La Fable de Daphné,* pp. 83–152.

105. Arnulf of Orleans, *Allegoriae super Ovidii Metamorphosin* 1.8, 1.9; and

see 2.8, 6.14 for Apollo as a personification of wisdom. See also Giraud, *La Fable de Daphné,* pp. 95–97.

106. John of Garland, *Integumenta Ovidii* 91–96. See Giraud, *La Fable de Daphné,* pp. 97–98.

107. The text dates to between 1291 and 1328, more probably between 1316 and 1328. Joseph Engels, *Etudes sur l'Ovide moralisé* (Groningen-Batavia: J. B. Wolters, 1945), pp. 46–48, and for the author, pp. 48–62. See also Giraud, *La Fable de Daphné,* pp. 98–106.

108. For Boccaccio's allegory, see Giraud, *La Fable de Daphné,* pp. 115–22; for the tropological commentary, which Clement VIII condemned, by Dionigi da Borgo San Sepolcro see ibid., p. 124, and Wolfgang Stechow, *Apollo und Daphne* (Darmstadt: Wissenschaftliche Buchgesellschaft, 1965, rpt. of Leipzig and Berlin ed., 1932), p. 67.

109. Pierre de Bersuire, *Reductorium morale* 3215–60, and the version of Avignon, fol. XVI v. Giraud, *La Fable de Daphné,* pp. 107–12.

110. Petrarch, *Ep. fam.* 10.4.30, ed. Rossi, 2: 308.

111. Ibid., 2: 308–9; my translation.

112. Petrarch, *Ep. fam.* 17.1.15–22, ed. Rossi, 3:224–25.

113. Ibid. 6.2.4, ed. Rossi, 2: 55; trans. Bernardo, 1: 290. See also *Invective contra medicum* 4, ed. Ricci, p. 92.

114. Petrarch, *De sui ipsius et multorum ignorantia liber,* in *Prose,* ed. Martellotti, p. 714; *Ep. fam.* 5.17.3, ed. Rossi, 2: 38–39. Cf. n. 56.

115. See Nitzsche, *The Genius Figure,* pp. 30–34.

116. See n. 54.

117. Ibid., pp. 3–4.

118. Petrarch, *De vita solitaria,* 1.5, ed. Martellotti, p. 350; trans. Zeitlin, pp. 146, 147.

119. Petrarch, *Ep. fam.* 10.3.49, ed. Rossi, 2: 298; trans. Bernardo 2: 66. 22.2.15, ed. 4: 106; trans. 3: 213.

120. See n. 68.

121. André Grabar, *Early Christian Art: From the Rise of Christianity to the Death of Theodosius,* trans. Stuart Gilbert and James Emmons (New York: Odyssey, 1968), pp. 92–93.

122. Ibid., pp. 80–81 and pl. 74; B. M. A. Ghetti et al., *Esplorazioni sotto la confessione di S. Pietro in Vaticano* (2 vols.; Vatican City, 1951), 1: 38–42 and pls. 10–12; Jocelyn Toynbee and John W. Perkins, *The Shrine of St. Peter and the Vatican Excavations* (London: Longmans, Green, 1957), pp. 72–74, 116–17, pl. 32.

123. Adolphe N. Didron, *Christian Iconography: The History of Christian Art in the Middle Ages,* trans. E. J. Millington (2 vols.; New York: Frederick Ungar, 1965), 1: 35.

124. Jean Gagé, *Apollon romain: Essai sur le culte d'Apollon et le développement du "ritus Graecus" à Rome des origines à Auguste* (Paris: E. de Boccard, 1955), esp. pp. 426–27, 499–516, 540–41, 585–94, 673–74. Horace, *Carmen saeculare* 9–12; trans. C. E. Bennett, *The Odes and Epodes* (Cambridge, Mass.: Harvard University Press, 1964), p. 351.

125. Franz J. Dolger, *Sol Salutis: Gebet und Gesang im christlichen Altertum* (1925; rpt., Münster: Aschendorff, 1972), esp. pp. 336–79.

126. Dolger, *Die Sonne der Gerechtigkeit und der Schwarze: Eine Religionsgeschichtliche Studie zum Taufgelöbnis* (1918; rpt., Münster: Aschendorff, 1970), esp. pp. 100–141. Jerome, *Commentariorum in Amos prophetam libri III* 3.6.14, cited ibid., p. 2.

127. Ambrose, "Splendor paternae gloriae" 3.5, *Hymni* and passim. See also Dolger, *Sol Salutis,* pp. 379–410.

128. *Speculum perfectionis* 119, a compilation dating to 1318 but emanating from original reminiscences of Brother Leo and companions; trans. Hugh McKay in *The Little Flowers of St. Francis, The Mirror of Perfection, St. Bonaventure's Life of St. Francis* (New York: Dutton, 1910), p. 294.

129. Francis of Assisi, "Canticum fratris solis vel laudes creaturarum," 3–4; trans. Regis J. Armstrong and Ignatius C. Brady in *Francis and Clare: The Complete Works* (New York: Paulist, 1982), p. 38.

130. Petrarch, *Rime,* ed. Durling, 4.12, pp. 38–39, 325.59, p. 511, 9.10, p. 45, 218.1–4, p. 375, 225.1–2, p. 381, 208.9, pp. 362–63, 90.12, pp. 192–93, 135.58, pp. 276–77, 230.2, pp. 386–87. 325.69, p. 511. 291, p. 471. 127.19–28, p. 249, 29.57–58, pp. 84–85; 127.66–70, pp. 252–53, 50.44, p. 119, 23.115, p. 65, 135.52–60, p. 277, 216.9, p. 373, 222.5–7, p. 379, 223, p. 379. 146.7–8, pp. 292–93, 154.3–4, pp. 300–301, 348.1–3, pp. 544–45, 133.9, p. 271, 119.1–2, p. 227, 200.13–14, p. 347. 37.81–82, p. 101, 197.7–8, p. 343; 156.5–6, p. 303, 352.2, p. 549. 255.5–6, p. 417. 220.12–13, p. 377, 270.46, p. 447, 347.11, p. 545; 133.8, p. 271, 175.9, p. 321. 233.9, p. 391, 359.57–58, p. 559. 95.9–10, pp. 198–99. 219.10–11, pp. 374–75. 108.3–4, pp. 216–17; 173.1–4, p. 319. 73.15, p. 169; 30.21, p. 87, 127.45, p. 251, 133.2, p. 271. See also Cesare Galimberti, "Amate del sole (*R.V.F.,* XXXIV, CLXXXVIII, CCCLXVI)," in *Dal medioevo al Petrarca: Miscellanea di studi in onore di Vittore Branca* (2 vols.; Florence: Leo S. Olschki, 1983), 1: 427–34.

131. Petrarch, *Rime,* ed. Durling, 9.10–12, pp. 44–45.

132. Ibid. 4.5–6, pp. 38–39. 207.15, pp. 356–57; 175.9–14, pp. 320–21.

133. Petrarch, *Africa,* ed. Festa, 1.30, p. 8, 2.21, p. 23, 2.487–90, p. 48, 3.1–3, p. 51, 4.319, p. 96, 6.562–63, p. 155, 6.866, p. 167, 7.1051–52, p. 212, 8.1–3,8, p. 217, 8.462–64, p. 236, 8.1073–75, p. 259, 9.127–28, pp. 265–66, 9.291–96, p. 272, 9.309, p. 273. 1.21, p. 29, 9.325–29, p. 273. 5.19–22, p. 102, 5.562, p. 123. 5.477–87, p. 120. 5.692–93, p. 129. 5.770, p. 131. 4.51, p. 87, 4.95–100, p. 89, 7.753–61, p. 201, 7.954–55, p. 208.

134. Ibid. 2.185–89, ed. Festa, p. 36; trans. Bergin and Wilson, p. 29.

135. Ibid. 9.482–83, ed. p. 279; trans. p. 240.

136. See n. 57.

137. A. Bouché-Leclercq, *Histoire de la divination dans l'antiquité* (4 vols.; Paris, 1879); Robert Flacelière, *Devins et oracles grecs* (Paris: Presses universitaires de France, 1961).

138. Fontenrose, *The Delphic Oracle: Its Responses and Operations with a Catalogue of Responses* (Berkeley: University of California Press, 1978), pp. 229–32.

139. Georges Roux, *Delphes: Son oracle et ses dieux* (Paris: Belles lettres, 1976), pp. 19–34.

140. H. W. Parke, *A History of the Delphic Oracle* (Oxford: Basil Blackwell, 1939), vol. 1; D. E. W. Wormell, *The Delphic Oracle* (2 vols.; Oxford: Basil Blackwell, 1939–56).

141. Jean Defradas, *Les Thèmes de la propagande delphique* (Paris: C. Klincksieck, 1954), pp. 289, 236–38, 258, 267.

142. Fontenrose, *The Delphic Oracle*, pp. 196–224; Pierre Amandry, *La Mantique apollinienne à Delphes: Essai sur le fonctionnement de l'oracle* (Paris: Boccard, 1950), pp. 41–56, 238–39.

143. See n. 65. But for the distinction between the Dionysian frenzy and the Apolline mediumship, see E. R. Dodds, *The Greeks and the Irrational* (Berkeley: University of California Press, 1951), p. 69.

144. For the essential formulation of the illuminative way see Bonaventure, *De triplici via* 1.10–14.

145. Petrarch, *Ep. fam.* 10.5.8, ed. Rossi, 2: 312; trans. Bernardo, 2: 77.

146. Ibid. 16.14.12–13, ed. 3: 213; trans. 2: 327.

147. Fontenrose, *The Delphic Oracle*, pp. 40–42, 11.

148. Petrarch, *Rerum memorandarum liber* 2.1, ed. Billanovich, p. 43; and for the plan of the work, pp. cxxiv–cxxx. For the Apolline oracles see ibid. 4.15–16, 20–29, ed. pp. 201–2, 204–10. For the oracle on Socrates see 4.22, pp. 204–5, and 3.71, pp. 156–61; and for documentation and discussion of it see Fontenrose, *The Delphic Oracle*, pp. 34, 245–46.

149. See Defradas, *Les thèmes de la propagande delphique*, pp. 276, 284–85.

150. E.g., Xenophon, *Anabasis* 3.1.5; Cicero, *De divinatione* 1.54.122; Plato, *Phaedo* 85b, trans. Benjamin Jowett in *The Dialogues of Plato* (2 vols.; New York: Random House, 1937), 1: 470. See Parke, *A History of the Delphic Oracle*, pp. 412–17.

151. Plato, *Phaedrus* 229d–230a.

152. Defradas, *Les thèmes de la propagande delphique*, pp. 277–80, 286, 284.

153. Plato, *Apologia* 20, 26. For Petrarch on Socrates' death see *Ep. fam.* 2.1.12, ed. Rossi, 1: 56.

154. Petrarch, *Ep. fam.* 2.9.2, ed. Rossi, 1: 91; *De otio religioso* 2, ed. Rotondi, p. 102.

155. Macrobius, *Commentariorum in somnium Scipionis* [libri] 1.9, cited by Fontenrose, *The Delphic Oracle*, p. 294.

156. Bernardo, *Petrarch, Scipio and the "Africa,"* pp. 111–26 and passim.

157. Macrobius, *Commentariorum in somnium Scipionis* [libri] 1.9.2, citing Persius, *Saturae* 1.7; trans. William H. Stahl, *Commentary on the Dream of Scipio* (New York: Columbia University Press, 1952), p. 124.

158. See n. 43.

159. See Pierre Courcelle, *Connais-toi, toi-même, de Socrate à Saint Bernard* (3 vols.; Paris: Etudes augustiniennes, 1974–75); also Martinelli, *Petrarca e il Ventoso*, pp. 198–200.

160. Petrarch, *Ep. fam.* 3.1, esp. 14–15, ed. Rossi, 1: 109; trans. Bernardo, 1: 118–19.

161. Ibid. 2.7.15, ed. 1: 88; trans. 1: 95.
162. Petrarch, *Secretum* 2, ed. Martellotti, p. 72; trans. Draper, p. 51.
163. Petrarch, *Ep. fam.* 4.1.22, ed. Rossi, 1: 158; trans. Bernardo, 1: 177.
164. See n. 24.
165. For Petrarch on medieval culture see Theodor E. Mommsen, "Petrarch's Conception of the 'Dark Ages,'" *Speculum,* 17 (1942), 226–42.
166. For Petrarch's prophesying as established on a knowledge of history consider this avowal: "Mine is not a prophet's inspiration, nor do I foresee future happenings from the course of the stars. Still, to the extent that I foresee the future from past events with the aid of reason . . ." *Ep. fam.* 14.5.21, ed. Rossi, 3: 122; trans. Bernardo, 2: 240.

2. THE SYLVAN CITIZEN

1. Petrarch, *Collatio laureationis,* ed. Godi, 25.
2. J. K. Newman, *The Concept of Vates in Augustan Poetry* (Brussels: Latomus, 1967), pp. 7–42. Petrarch, *Collatio laureationis,* ed. Godi, 13, citing Vergil, *Georgics* 3.291–92. Also, *Georgics* 2.475–77; trans. H. Rushton Fairclough in *Virgil,* rev. ed. (2 vols.; Cambridge, Mass.: Harvard University Press, 1974), 1: 149.
3. Cyril Bailey, *Religion in Virgil* (Oxford: Clarendon, 1935), pp. 163–72.
4. Newman, *The Concept of Vates in Augustan Poetry,* pp. 43–126.
5. Bailey, *Religion in Virgil,* pp. 5–28.
6. Domenico Comparetti, *Vergil in the Middle Ages,* 2d ed., trans. E. F. M. Benecke, (1908; rpt., London: George Allen & Unwin, 1966), pp. 50–238.
7. John W. Spargo, *Virgil the Necromancer: Studies in Virgilian Legends* (Cambridge, Mass.: Harvard University Press, 1934); Comparetti, *Vergil in the Middle Ages,* pp. 239–376.
8. Petrarch, *Ep. fam.* 9.5.15–16, ed. Rossi, 2: 226; trans. Aldo S. Bernardo, *Rerum familiarum libri I–VIII* (Albany: State University of New York Press, 1975), and *Letters on Familiar Matters: Rerum familiarum libri IX–XVI* (Baltimore: Johns Hopkins University Press, 1982), 2: 16. See also Carlo Segrè, "Chi accuso il Petrarca di magia," in his *Studi petrarcheschi* (Florence: Le Monnier, 1903), pp. 199–224. Pierre de Nolhac, *Pétrarque et l'humanisme,* 2d ed. (2 vols.; Paris: Honoré Champion, 1907), 1: 127.
9. Petrarch, *Ep. fam.* 13.6.29, ed. Rossi, 3: 77; trans. Bernardo, 2: 197.
10. For the legends see Cecco d'Ascoli, *Alcabizzo,* before 1327; *Cronica di Partenope,* shortly after 1326; and Cino da Pistoia, *Rime,* 1330. Spargo, *Virgil the Necromancer,* pp. 63–64.
11. Petrarch, *Itinerarium Syriacum,* in "L'itinerarium del Petrarca," ed. Giacomo Lumbroso, Atti della Reale Accademia dei Lincei, 4th ser., *Rendiconti,* 4 (1888), 398. De Nolhac, *Pétrarque et l'humanisme,* 1: 127. For this legend see Spargo, *Virgil the Necromancer,* pp. 292–95.
12. Petrarch, *Itinerarium Syriacum,* ed. Lumbroso, p. 399. For this legend see Spargo, *Virgil the Necromancer,* pp. 87–99. Concerning whether Petrarch

also knew of the talismanic fly see Duane R. Stuart, "The Sources and the Extent of Petrarch's Knowledge of the Life of Vergil," *Classical Philology*, 12 (1917), 403–4.

13. Giovanni Boccaccio, *Genealogiae deorum gentilium* 14.22.

14. Petrarch's note as cited by Achille Ratti, "Ancora del celebre cod. ms. delle opere di Virgilio già di F. Petrarca ed ora della Biblioteca Ambrosiana," in *F. Petrarca e la Lombardia*, ed. Società storica lombarda (Milan: Ulrico Hoepli, 1904), p. 224; my translation. See also *Ep. fam.* 21.10.13, ed. Rossi, 4:64. For this legend see Comparetti, *Vergil in the Middle Ages*, pp. 98, 312; and for the legend of St. Paul's visit to Vergil's burial vault to obtain his books, pp. 312–13, and Spargo, *Virgil the Necromancer*, pp. 20–21 and in general, see J. B. Trapp, "The Grave of Vergil," *Journal of the Warburg and Courtauld Institutes*, 47 (1984), 1–31.

15. Vergil, *Eclogues* 4.6–101; trans. Fairclough 1: 29.

16. Pierre Courcelle, "Les Exégèses chrétiennes de la quatrième églogue," *Revue des études anciennes*, 59 (1957), 294–319.

17. Petrarch, *Rerum memorandarum liber* 4.30, ed. Billanovich, pp. 210–14, esp. p. 213. For the manuscript see de Nolhac, *Pétrarque et l'humanisme*, 1: 205. Petrarch cites from it in *De otio religioso* 1, ed. Rotondi, p. 27.

18. *Ep. fam.* 21.1.7, ed. Rossi, 4: 63; trans. Bernardo, 3: 176.

19. Petrarch, *De otio religioso* 1, ed. Rotondi, p. 29. Cf. *Liber sine nomine* 4, ed. Piur, pp. 178–79.

20. Comparetti, *Vergil in the Middle Ages*, pp. 309–12.

21. For the typology see Arthur Watson, *The Early Iconography of the Tree of Jesse* (Oxford: Oxford University Press, 1934), pp. 1–8.

22. Petrarch, *Ep. fam.* 7.2.3–11,15; ed. Rossi, 2: 98–100.

23. Watson, *The Early Iconography of the Tree of Jesse*, pp. 21–22. Vergil's association with the Virgin may also have been prompted by his epithet "Parthenias." Servius, *In Vergilii Aeneidos commentarius*, praef. 9; Petrarch, *Ep. fam.* 10.4.24, ed. Rossi, 2: 307.

24. Milan, Biblioteca Ambrosiana Ms. S.P. 10, 27; rpt. in facsimile as *Francisci Petrarcae Vergilianus Codex*, ed. Giovanni Galbiati (Milan: Biblioteca Ambrosiana, 1930). For its description see Ratti, "Ancora del celebre cod. ms. delle opere di Virgilio già di F. Petrarca ed ora della Biblioteca Ambrosiana," pp. 217–42; Fredrik Wulff, "L'Ancien Feuillet de garde du *Virgile* de l'Ambrosienne," in his *Deux discours sur Pétrarque en résumé* (Uppsala: Almquist & Wiksell, 1902), pp. 1–16; de Nolhac, *Pétrarque et l'humanisme*, 1: 140–61; and also Giuseppe Billanovich, "Il Virgilio del giovane Petrarca," in *Lectures médiévales de Virgile*, Actes du Colloque organisé par l'Ecole française de Rome, Rome, 15–28 octobre 1982 (Rome: Ecole française de Rome, 1985), pp. 49–64.

25. Milan, Biblioteca Ambrosiana, Ms. S.P. 10, 27, fol. i v. *Simone Martini: The Complete Works*, pl. XV, pls. 113, 114. For this interpretation of it according to the medieval scheme of Vergil's "wheel" see Joel Brink, "Simone Martini, Francesco Petrarca and the Humanistic Program of the Virgil Frontispiece," *Mediaevalia* 3 (1977), 83–117; and Bernhard Degenhart, "Das Marienwunder von Avignon: Simone Martinis Miniaturen für Kardinal Ste-

faneschi und Petrarca," *Pantheon* 33 (1975), 191–203; John Rowlands, "Simone Martini and Petrarch: A Virgilian Episode," *Apollo*, 81 (1965), 264–69.

26. Petrarch, *Epistola posteritati*, in *Prose*, ed. Martellotti, p. 12.

27. Petrarch, *Rerum memorandarum liber* 2.16, ed. Billanovich, pp. 51–52.

28. Brink, "Simone Martini, Francesco Petrarca and the Humanistic Program of the Virgil Frontispiece," 85; Rowlands, "Simone Martini and Petrarch," 266.

29. The proportional theory of root-two construction and a figure illustrating its application to this painting are provided by Brink, "Simone Martini, Francesco Petrarca and the Humanistic Program of the Virgil Frontispiece," 106–9. The interpretation of it, however, is mine. Although Brink acknowledges that the laurel falls on the central axis of the painting and is its central image (97, 98), he does not integrate this observation with his analysis. Again, Vergil's eyes, through which Brink states that the arc passes (107), he interprets as focused on sublime matters (96) rather than on the tree which that arc intersects.

30. Suetonius, "Vita Vergilii" 3, *De viris illustribus*.

31. Watson, *The Early Iconography of the Tree of Jesse*, pp. 83–141, e.g., pl. III.

32. See n. 13.

33. See Jonathan Foster, "Petrarch's *Africa:* Ennian and Vergilian Influences," *Papers of the Liverpool Latin Seminar: Second Volume, 1979*, ed. Francis Cairns (Liverpool: Francis Cairns, 1979), pp. 277–98.

34. The consensus of modern scholars considers Laura to have been an actual woman beloved by Petrarch. Laura de Noves is the favorite candidate. For a survey of the evidence see Emmanuel Davin, "Les Différentes Laure de Pétrarque," *Bulletin de l'association Guillaume Budé*, 15 (1956), 83–104; and further, E. J. Jones, "Further Evidence on the Identity of Petrarch's Laura," *Italian Studies*, 39 (1984), 27–46. For a review of the textual evidence for Laura's existence see Aldo S. Bernardo, *Petrarch, Laura, and the "Triumphs"* (Albany: State University of New York Press, 1974), pp. 64–87, and for modern interpretations of her poetic significance, pp. 1–25.

35. Ernest H. Wilkins, *Life of Petrarch* (Chicago: University of Chicago Press, 1963), p. 77, with my changes to Wilkins's translation as the text reads "laurel," not "Laura," and simply "that light," not "the light of her life." There is no explicit personal reference.

36. Petrarch, *Rime sparse*, ed. Durling, 211.13, pp. 364–65, 336.13, pp. 532–33; *Triunfo mortis* 1.133, in *Francesco Petrarca: Rime, Trionfi e poesie latine*, ed. F. Neri et al., vol. 6 of La letteratura italiana, storia e testi (Milan: F. Ricciardi, 1951), p. 521.

37. Petrarch, *Ep. posteritati*, in *Prose*, ed. Martelloti, p. 12.

38. Petrarch, *Rime sparse*, ed. Durling, 3, pp. 38–39.

39. For an example of this pathetic fallacy in medieval verse see Peter Abelard, Hymn 48, "Ad Sextam."

40. Bortolo Martinelli, "'Feria sexta Aprilis': La data sacra nel *Canzoniere* del Petrarca," in his *Petrarca e il Ventoso* (Rome: Minerva Italica, 1977), pp.

103–48; Carlo Calcaterra, "Feria sexta aprilis," in his *Nella selva del Petrarca* (Bologna: Licino Cappelli, 1942), pp. 209–45.

41. Macrobius, *Saturnalia* 1.12.8–15.

42. Hugo Rahner, *Greek Myths and Christian Mystery,* trans. Brian Battershaw (London: Burns & Oates, 1963), p. 104.

43. The eclipse was astronomically described by Theodore R. von Oppolzer, "Note über eine von Archilochos erwähnte Sonnenfinsterniss," Kaiserliche Akademie der Wissenschaften, Vienna, *Mathematisch-Naturwissenschaftliche Klasse, Sitzungsberichte,* 86 (1882), 790–93; and it appears also so dated by the Julian calendar in his *Canon of Eclipses,* trans. Owen Gingerich (New York: Dover, 1962), No. 1328. The astronomical data were confirmed by J. K. Fotheringham, "A Solution of Ancient Eclipses of the Sun," Royal Astronomical Society of London, *Monthly Notices,* 81 (1920), 107–8. See also Plutarch, *De facie quae in orbe lunae apparet* 19; F. K. Ginzel, *Spezieller Kanon der Sonnen- und Mondfinsternisse für das Landergebiet der klassichen Altertumswissenschaften und den Zeitraum von 900 vor Chr. bis 600 nach Chr.* (Berlin, 1899), p. 169n.

44. Archilochus, fr. 82 (74 Diehl), trans. Richard Lattimore, *Greek Lyrics,* 2d ed., rev. (Chicago: University of Chicago Press, 1960), p. 3.

45. Aristotle, *Rhetorica* 3.16 (1418b28); trans. John H. Freese, *The "Art" of Rhetoric* (New York: G. P. Putnam's Sons, 1926), p. 461.

46. Stobaeus, *Florilegium* 4.46.10 (C.CX).

47. Petrarch, *Bucolicum carmen* 10.125–26, ed. Martellotti, p. 23, and see also his note, p. 55; trans. Thomas G. Bergin, *Petrarch's Bucolicum Carmen* (New Haven: Yale University Press, 1974), p. 153.

48. Ernest Dutoit, *Le Thème de l'adynaton dans la poésie antique* (Paris: Belles lettres, 1936).

49. Oskar Schultz-Gora, "Das Adynaton in der altfranzösischen und provenzalischen Dichtung nebst Dazugehörigem," *Archiv für das Studium der neueren Sprachen,* 161 (1932), 196–209, 199.

50. Petrarch, *Rime sparse,* ed. Durling, 22.37–39, pp. 58–59. For a study of this poem see Marianne Shapiro, "The Petrarchan *Selva* Revisited: Sestina XXII," *Neuphilologische Mitteilungen* 77 (1976), 144–60.

51. Petrarch, *Rime sparse,* ed. Durling, 30.7–10, pp. 86–87.

52. Ibid. 57.5–11, pp. 134–35.

53. Ibid. 237.13–18, pp. 396–97.

54. Ibid. 195.5–14, pp. 340–41. Although these examples are all cited from the *Rime sparse,* consider also that the eleventh eclogue is constructed on the classical adynaton of the cessation of Niobe's tears:

> And, Galatea, your name will live in my heart till the planets
> Fall from the skies, until bees abandon their honey and faithful
> Doves flee their nests and the turtle no longer cleaves to his partner,
> Aye, until wolves leave their prey, he-goats no longer crop frondage,
> Guarded young wives play no tricks and servants cease to be liars.

Petrarch, *Bucolicum carmen* 11.98–102, ed. Avena, p. 159; trans. Bergin, p. 195.

55. See n. 33.

56. Petrarch, *Rime sparse*, ed. Durling, 34, pp. 92–93; see also 188, p. 335, and *Africa* 5.478–87, ed. Festa, p. 120.

57. Yves F.-A. Giraud, *La Fable de Daphné: Essai sur un type de métamorphose végétale dans la littérature et dans les arts jusqu'à la fin du XVII*^{e} *siècle* (Geneva: Droz, 1968), pp. 32–34, 40–59, 89–91. For general studies of this myth in Petrarch's poetry see ibid., pp. 141–49; Sara Sturm-Maddox, *Petrarch's Metamorphoses: Text and Subtext in the Rime Sparse* (Columbia: University of Missouri Press, 1985), pp. 9–38; P. R. J. Hainsworth, "The Myth of Daphne in the *Rerum vulgarium fragmenta*," *Italian Studies*, 34 (1979), 28–44; Marga Cottino-Jones, "The Myth of Apollo and Daphne in Petrarch's *Canzoniere*: The Dynamics and Literary Function of Transformation," in *Francis Petrarch, Six Centuries Later: A Symposium*, ed. Aldo Scaglione (Chapel Hill: Department of Romance Languages, University of North Carolina; Chicago: Newberry Library, 1975), pp. 152–76; Ugo Dotti, "Petrarca: Il mito dafneo," *Convivium*, 37 (1969), 9–23; Calcaterra, "Giovene donna sotto un verde lauro," in his *Nella selva del Petrarca*, pp. 35–87. For studies of the myth in particular poems see Michele Feo "Per l'esegesi della III egloga del Petrarca," *Italia medioevale e umanistica*, 10 (1967), 385–401; Durling, "Petrarch's *Giovene donna sotto un verde lauro*," *Modern Language Notes*, 86 (1971), 1–20; and works cited in nn. 50 and 122.

58. See chapter 4, nn. 15–20.

59. Boccaccio, "De vita et moribus domini Francisci Petracchi de Florentia," in *Opere latine minore*, ed. Aldo F. Massera, p. 243.

60. See Ernst R. Curtius, *European Literature and the Latin Middle Ages*, trans. Willard R. Trask (New York: Pantheon, 1953), pp. 195–200. See also Kenneth E. Cool, "The Petrarchan Landscape as Palimpsest," *Journal of Medieval and Renaissance Studies*, 11 (1981), 83–100; Bernhard König, "Petrarcas Landschaften: Philologische Bemerkungen zu einer neuen Deutung," *Romanische Forschungen*, 92 (1980), 251–82; Karlheinz Siterle, *Petrarcas Landschaften: Zur Geschichte ästhetischer Landschaftserfahrung* (Krefeld: Scherpe, 1978); Terry Comito, *The Idea of the Garden in the Renaissance* (New Brunswick, N.J.: Rutgers University Press, 1978), pp. 57–64; H. M. Richmond, *Renaissance Landscapes: English Lyrics in a European Tradition* (The Hague: Mouton, 1973), pp. 38–55.

61. Petrarch, *De vita solitaria* 1.7, ed. Martellotti, in *Prose*, pp. 366–70.

62. Petrarch, *Rime sparse*, ed. Durling, 60.1, p. 139, 64.9, p. 143, 67.3, p. 147, 5.5, p. 41. 129.70, p. 267, 327.1, p. 515, 337.1–5, p. 535, 228.7, p. 385. 5.13, p. 41, 29.46–47, p. 85, 30.1, p. 87, 107.12, p. 215, 142.8, p. 287, 181.3, p. 327, 195.4, p. 341, 196.1, p. 343, 197.1, p. 343, 228.3–4, p. 385, 246.1, p. 409, 255.10, p. 417, 266.12, p. 435, 269.1, p. 443, 270.65–66, p. 447, 325.32, p. 502, 327.2, p. 515. 23.168–69, p. 69, 34.13–14, p. 93. 337.7–8, p. 535, cf. 30.1, p. 87. 190, p. 337, and for its interpretation see Stefano Carrai, "Il sonetto 'Una candida cerva' del Petrarca: Problemi d'interpretazione e di fonti," *Rivista di letteratura italiana*, 3 (1985), 233–51; B. T. Sozzi, "Per il sonetto: Una candida cerva," *Studi Petrarcheschi*, 8 (1976), 213–17. *Rime sparse*

148.12–14, p. 295. 269.2, p. 443, 327.1–3, p. 515; 60.3–4, p. 139. 142.1–13, p. 287. 24.1–2, p. 71, 29.48–49, p. 85, cf. 113.6, p. 221, 147. 7–11, p. 293. 161.4–6, p. 307, 263.1–2, p. 425, 325.32, p. 509; 28.80–81, p. 79; 24.1–4, p. 71, 119.103–5, p. 233, 363.4, p. 573, 322.9–10, p. 501. See also *Africa* 9.108–23, ed. Festa, pp. 264–65.

63. Petrarch, *Rime sparse,* ed. Durling, 34.7–8, p. 93. See n. 33.

64. Petrarch, *Collatio laureationis,* ed. Godi, 24–25; trans. Wilkins, "Petrarch's Coronation Oration," in his *Studies in the Life and Works of Petrarch* (Cambridge, Mass.: Mediaeval Academy of America, 1955), p. 310.

65. Petrarch, *Rime sparse,* ed. Durling, 5.9–10, pp. 40–41. Isidore of Seville derived *laurus* from *lauda,* as the tree crowned the heads of the victorious. *Etymologiae* 17.7.2.

66. Petrarch, *Rime sparse,* ed. Durling, 228, pp. 384–85. See also 64.6–7, p. 143, 255.9–10, p. 417, 318.7–8, p. 497.

67. E. O. James, *The Tree of Life: An Archaeological Study* (Leiden: E. J. Brill, 1966), pp. 3–4.

68. Gerhart B. Ladner, "Vegetation Symbolism and the Concept of the Renaissance," in *De artibus opuscula XL: Essays in Honor of Erwin Panofsky,* ed. Millard Meiss (2 vols.; New York: New York University Press, 1961), 1: 308.

69. See James, *The Tree of Life,* p. 186; Maarten J. Vermaseren, *Cybele and Attis* (London: Thames & Hudson, 1977).

70. Petrarch, *Rime sparse,* ed. Durling, 30.1, p. 87, 337.7–8, p. 535.

71. Curtius, *European Literature and the Latin Middle Ages,* p. 201.

72. See n. 25.

73. Petrarch, *Africa,* 3.232–41, ed. Festa, p. 61; trans. Thomas G. Bergin and Alice S. Wilson, *Petrarch's Africa* (New Haven: Yale University Press, 1977), pp. 49–50.

74. See Henri Graillot, *Le Culte du Cybèle, mère des dieux, à Rome et dans l'Empire romain* (Paris: Fontemoing, 1912).

75. Petrarch, *Secretum* 3, ed. Martellotti, p. 138.

76. Petrarch, *Ep. fam.* 6.2.5, ed. Rossi, 2: 56.

77. Petrarch, *Africa* 8.866–70, ed. Festa, p. 251; trans. Bergin and Wilson, p. 214. See also Vergil, *Aeneid* 8.333–41.

78. Petrarch, *De otio religioso* 2, ed. Rotondi, p. 105; *Epistolae variae* 22, in *Lettere di Francesco Petrarca,* ed. Giuseppe Fracassetti (5 vols.; Florence, 1863–67), 5: 283. *Ep. fam.* 21.8.5, ed. Rossi, 4: 63.

79. For the metaphor see Curtius, *European Literature and the Latin Middle Ages,* pp. 132–33.

80. Plato, *Symposium* 208e–209a; trans. Benjamin Jowett in *The Dialogues of Plato* (2 vols.; New York: Random House, 1937), 1:333.

81. See n. 56.

82. Petrarch, *De vita solitaria* 1.8, ed. Martellotti, in *Prose,* p. 368; trans. Jacob Zeitlin, *The Life of Solitude* (Urbana: University of Illinois Press, 1924), p. 158.

83. Petrarch, *Rime sparse,* ed. Durling, 193.7, pp. 338–39. The importance of the ecstatic theme in Petrarch's poetry, although interpreted censo-

riously as only illusory contemplation, has also been noted by Kenelm Foster, "Beatrice or Medusa," in *Italian Studies Presented to E. R. Vincent,* ed. C. P. Brand et al. (Cambridge: W. Heffer and Sons, 1962), pp. 42–43, 52.

84. Petrarch, *Rime sparse,* ed. Durling, 169.5–6, pp. 314–15.

85. Ibid. 167, pp. 312–13.

86. Ibid. 6.1–11, pp. 40–41. See also 29.4–14, pp. 82–83. For the image of the bridled soul see Sturm-Maddox, *Petrarch's Metamorphoses,* pp. 80, 82–83; Vincent Moleta, "Guido delle Colonne's 'Amor, che lungiamente m'hai menato': A Source for the Opening Metaphor," *Italica,* 54 (1977), 468–84. A related metaphor of the soul as a charioteer of tame and wild horses in Plato, *Phaedrus* 230b, was preserved in Ambrose, *De virginitate* 15. See Pierre Courcelle, *Recherches sur les Confessions de saint Augustin,* rev. ed. (Paris: E. de Boccard, 1968), pp. 312–19.

87. Petrarch, *Rime sparse,* ed. Durling, 152.1–11, pp. 298–99. For the convention of the alterations of love see John C. Nelson, *Renaissance Theory of Love: The Context of Giordano Bruno's Eroici furori* (New York: Columbia University Press, 1958), pp. 37, 212.

88. Petrarch, *Rime sparse,* ed. Durling, 29.7, p. 83, 50.61, p. 121, 51.12, p. 123, 62.10, p. 141, 79.6, p. 179, 89.10, p. 193, 129.54, p. 267, 197.3, p. 343, 209.7, p. 363, 270.1, p. 443, 355.12, p. 553, 360.38, p. 563. 8.14, p. 43, 76.10, p. 177, 89.10, p. 193, 105.55, p. 211, 266.10, p. 435. 55.15, p. 133, 59.4, p. 137, 69.3, p. 149, 106.5, p. 215, 200.5, p. 347, 214.10, p. 369. 181.1, 12, p. 327, 62.7, p. 141, 263.7, p. 425.

89. Ted-Larry Pebworth, "The Net for the Soul: A Renaissance Conceit and the Song of Songs," *Romance Notes,* 13 (1971), 159–64.

90. Edgar de Bruyne, *Etudes d'esthétique médiévale* (3 vols.; Bruges: De Tempel, 1946), 3: 15.

91. See E. R. Dodds, *The Greeks and the Irrational* (Berkeley: University of California Press, 1951), p. 273, citing Euripides, *Iphigenia Aulidensis* 758. Knots were also believed in Italian religion to impede the working of sacred influences, and thus the hair of women was loosened at funerals. Vergil, *Aeneid* 3.65. Bailey, *Religion in Virgil,* pp. 290–91.

92. Petrarch, *Rime sparse,* ed. Durling, 90, pp. 192–93.

93. Ibid. 197.7–11, pp. 342–43. For "knots" see also 25.4, p. 71, 196.12, p. 343, 198.10, p. 345, 227.4, p. 383, 264.83, p. 431, 59.17, p. 137, 71.51, p. 157, 73.79, p. 173, 119.76, p. 233, 175.2, 14, p. 321, 214.20, p. 369, 256.10, p. 419, 268.65, p. 441, 270.70, 93, pp. 447, 449, 271.1, 13, p. 451, 283.4, p. 463, 296.14, p. 475, 305.1, p. 485, 307.3, p. 487, 330.13, p. 519, 359.56, p. 559.

94. Ibid. 270.59–62, pp. 446–47.

95. *Oxford Classical Dictionary,* 2d ed., s.v. "Gorgo."

96. See Jane Chance Nitzsche, *The Genius Figure in Antiquity and the Middle Ages* (New York: Columbia University Press, 1975), pp. 8–9.

97. Petrarch, *Africa* 4.100–10, ed. Festa, p. 89; trans. Bergin and Wilson, p. 72. See also 7.199–200, ed. Festa, p. 179. Aulis Gellius, *Noctes Atticae* 6.1.3.

98. Petrarch, *Rime sparse,* ed. Durling, 197.5–7, pp. 342–43; cf. 51.13–14,

p. 123. For a survey of this image of petrifaction see Paolo Possiedi, "Petrarca petroso," *Forum italicum*, 8 (1974), 523–45; also Domenico de Robertis, "Petrarca petroso," *Revue des études italiennes*, 29 (1983), 13–37.

99. Petrarch, *Rime sparse*, ed. Durling, 197.12–14, pp. 342–43. 23.80–83, pp. 62–65; cf. 213.9, p. 367. 5.12–14, p. 41.

100. Vergil, *Eclogues* 8.77–78. See also the description in *Aeneid* 1.319.

101. Plato, *Symposium* 196e–197a, 202e; trans. Jowett, 1: 328.

102. Petrarch, *Rime sparse*, ed. Durling, 7.101.5–11, pp. 204–5. 264.91–92, pp. 430–31. 270.79, pp. 448–49. 247.12–14, pp. 408–9. See also 73.1–6, 24, p. 169. 235.1–2, pp. 392–93.

103. Ibid. 134, pp. 272–73.

104. Ibid. 129.1–13, pp. 264–65.

105. Ibid. 142.1–3, 10–12, pp. 286–87.

106. Ibid. v. 13.

107. Ibid. 323.25–30, pp. 502–3.

108. Ibid. 177.3–4, pp. 322–23. 287.9–11, p. 467.

109. Ibid. 193.5–11, pp. 338–39.

110. Ibid. 302, pp. 480–81.

111. Ibid. 295.12–14, pp. 474–75.

112. Ibid. 270.25, pp. 444–45. 32.10, p. 91, 270.25, p. 445, 62.2, p. 141.

113. Ibid. 34.12–14, pp. 92–93.

114. Ibid. 160.1–2, 9–10, pp. 306–7. 309.1–2, pp. 488–89. 94.5, pp. 196–97; 295.9, pp. 474–75.

115. Ibid. 309, pp. 488–89.

116. Ibid. 13.5–8, pp. 48–49.

117. Ibid. 61, pp. 138–39.

118. Ibid. 284.12–14, pp. 462–63; cf. also lines 5–6.

119. Ibid. 188.1–8, pp. 334–35.

120. Ibid. 22.34–36, pp. 58–59.

121. Ibid. 325.31–38, pp. 508–9.

122. Ibid. 23.38–40, pp. 60–61. For studies of this poem of the poet's metamorphosis into the laurel see Thomas M. Greene, *The Light in Troy: Imitation and Discovery in Renaissance Poetry* (New Haven: Yale University Press, 1982), pp. 127–35; Mario Santagata, "La canzone XXIII," in *Lectura Petrarce 1981* (Florence: Leo S. Olschki, 1982), pp. 49–78; Marguerite Waller, *Petrarch's Poetics and Literary History* (Amherst: University of Massachusetts Press, 1980), pp. 84–90; Dennis Dutschke, *Francesco Petrarca Canzone XXIII from First to Final Version* (Ravenna: Longo, n.d.); Alberto J. Rivero, "Petrarch's 'Nel Dolce Tempo de la Prima Etade,'" *Modern Language Notes*, 94 (1979), 92–112; Martinelli, "La canzone delle metamorfosi e la formazione del Canzoniere," in *Petrarca e il Ventoso*, pp. 19–102; John Brenkman, "Writing, Desire, Dialectic in Petrarch's '*Rime 23*,'" *Pacific Coast Philology*, 9 (1974), 12–19.

123. Petrarch, *Rime sparse*, ed. Durling, 237.15, pp. 396–97; cf. 22.17–18, p. 57.

124. Georges Roux, *Delphes: Son oracle et ses dieux* (Paris: Belles lettres,

1976), pp. 123–29; Pierre Amandry, *La Mantique apollinienne à Delphes: Essai sur le fonctionnement de l'oracle* (Paris: Boccard, 1950), pp. 126–34; Joseph Fontenrose, *The Delphic Oracle: Its Responses and Operations with a Catalogue of Responses* (Berkeley: University of California Press, 1978), pp. 224–25; H. W. Parke, *A History of the Delphic Oracle*, vol. 1, and D. E. W. Wormell, *The Delphic Oracle* (2 vols.; Oxford: Basil Blackwell, 1939–56), pp. 25–26.

125. Ibid.

126. Juvenal, *Saturae* 7.19.

127. See the copious examples of this as indexed in *Concordanze del Canzoniere di Francesco Petrarca* (2 vols.; Florence, 1971), 1: 159–60. For the philological tradition in Provençal poetry see Contini, "Préhistoire de l'aura de Pétrarque," in his *Varianti e altra linguistica: Una raccolta di saggi (1938–1968)* (Turin: Einaudi, 1970), pp. 193–99; and for an analysis of Petrarch's usage see Francis Rigolot, "Nature and Function of Paranomasia in the *Canzoniere*," *Italian Quarterly*, 18 (1974), 29–36.

128. Petrarch, *Rime sparse*, ed. Durling, 196.1–5, pp. 342–43. 197.1, pp. 342–43, cf. 286.1–3, p. 465; 109.9–12, pp. 216–17; 356.1, pp. 552–53. 129.65–70, pp. 216–17. 246.1–4, pp. 408–9.

129. Petrarch, *Africa* 9.216–19, 240–45, 252–53, ed. Festa, pp. 269, 270, 271; trans. Bergin and Wilson, p. 231.

130. Ambrose, *Hymni* 7.23–24.

131. For a survey of this topic see W. Meyer, "Die Geschichte des Kreuzholzes vor Christus," *Abhandlungen der philosophisch-philologischen Klasse der Königlich Bayerischen Akademie der Wissenschaften*, 16/2 (1882), 103–66.

132. Petrarch, *Ep. fam.* 22.2.23, ed. Rossi, 4: 108; trans. Bernardo, 3: 214.

133. Petrarch, *Ep. var.* 61, ed. Fracassetti, 5: 472–75.

134. Marjorie Reeves, "The *Arbores* of Joachim of Fiore," in *Studies in Italian Medieval History: Presented to Miss E. M. Jamison*, ed. Philip Crierson and John W. Perkins, *Papers of the British School at Rome*, 24 (1956), 124–36.

135. Ibid., p. 128.

136. Reeves and Beatrice Hirsch-Reich, "The Seven Seals in the Writings of Joachim of Fiore," *Recherches de théologie ancienne et médiévale*, 21 (1954), esp. pp. 218–19, 224–25.

137. Reeves, *The Figurae of Joachim of Fiore* (Oxford: Clarendon, 1972), p. 190.

138. Petrarch, *Rime sparse*, ed. Durling, 105.42–45, pp. 210–11.

3. THE CAPTIVE BABYLONIAN

1. For the description of this domestic Roman neighborhood as based on its earliest document (1331) see Robert Brentano, *Rome before Avignon: A Social History of Thirteenth-Century Rome* (New York: Basic Books, 1974), pp. 39–40.

2. See Franz J. Dölger, *Sol Salutis: Gebet und Gesang im christlichen Altertum* (1925; rpt., Münster: Aschendorff, 1972), pp. 1–20. The description of the basilica is incorporated from Richard Krautheimer, *Early Christian and*

Byzantine Architecture (Harmondsworth, England: Penguin, 1965), pp. 32–36, and E. Baldwin Smith, *Architectural Symbolism of Imperial Rome and the Middle Ages* (Princeton: Princeton University Press, 1956), p. 28.

    3. Petrarch, *Epistolae metricae* 2.1.71–73, ed. Rossetti, 2: 102.

    4. Brentano, *Rome before Avignon*, pp. 60–62.

    5. Ernst H. Wilkins, *Life of Petrarch* (Chicago: University of Chicago Press, 1963), pp. 106–27; *Studies in the Life and Works of Petrarch* (Cambridge, Mass.: Mediaeval Academy of America, 1955), pp. 63–181.

    6. See G. Mollat, *The Popes at Avignon, 1305–1378*, trans. Janet Love (London: Thomas Nelson & Sons, 1963), pp. 44–63.

    7. Petrarch, *Ep. met.* 1.2, ed. Rossetti, 3: 110–34, echoed by the poet's own plea, 1.5, pp. 134–50. *Ep. met.* 2.5, ed. Rossetti, 3: 4–30. For their historical context see Rosa Di Sabatino, "Le epistole metriche a Benedetto XII e Clemente VI," *Studi petrarcheschi*, 6 (1956), 43–54. See also Petrarch, *Rime sparse* 27, ed. Durling, p. 73.

    8. For a description see Delbert R. Hillers, *Lamentations: Introduction, Translation, and Notes* (New York: Doubleday, 1972), pp. 1–29.

    9. Jacopone da Todi, *Laude* 35.

    10. Dante, *Purgatorio* 6.115–17, cf. 27.19; *Epistolae* 8.

    11. See Franz Cumont, "Il sole vindice dei delitti ed il simbolo delle mani alzate," *Atti Pontificia Accademia Romana di Archeologia*, 3d ser., Memorie I/1 (1923), 65–80.

    12. Petrarch, *Epistolae seniles* 7.1, in *Operum*, 2: 899, 903.

    13. Petrarch, *Rime sparse*, ed. Durling, 328.13, pp. 516–17. On a mission of conciliation between Venice and Genoa in 1354 for which Petrarch served as an orator, he also cited this scriptural verse. Wilkins, *Petrarch's Eight Years in Milan* (Cambridge, Mass.: Mediaeval Academy of America, 1958), pp. 329–33.

    14. Pliny, *Naturalis historia* 15.40.133.

    15. Wilkins, *Life of Petrarch*, pp. 63–73; Mario E. Cosenza, *Francesco Petrarca and the Revolution of Cola di Rienzo* (Chicago: University of Chicago Press, 1910); Josef Macek, "Petrarque et Cola di Rienzo," *Historia*, 11 (1965), 5–51; Innocente Toppani, "Petrarca, Cola di Rienzo e il mito di Roma," *Atti dell'Istituto Veneto di Scienze, Lettere ed Arti, Classe di scienze morali, lettere ed arti*, 135 (1977), 155–72.

    16. Petrarch, *Ep. fam.* 11.16.4–5, ed. Rossi, 2: 358; trans. Aldo S. Bernardo, *Rerum familiarum libri I–VIII* (Albany: State University of New York Press, 1975), and *Letters on Familiar Matters: Rerum familiarum libri IX–XVI* (Baltimore: Johns Hopkins University Press, 1982), 2: 121.

    17. Petrarch, *Ep. fam.* 11.16.4, p. 358.

    18. Ibid. 11.16.1–2, p. 357; trans. Bernardo, 2: 120.

    19. Petrarch, *Apologia contra cuiusdam anonymi Galli calumnias*, in *Operum*, 2: 1187. This statement has been considered the best expression of Petrarch's concept of history by Theodor E. Mommsen, "Petrarch's Conception of the 'Dark Ages,'" *Speculum*, 17 (1942), 236–37. For Petrarch's writing of history see Eckhard Kessler, *Petrarca und die Geschichte: Geschichtsschreibung, Rhetorik,*

Philosophie im Übergang vom Mittelalter zur Neuzeit (Munich: Wilhelm Fink, 1978).

20. J. K. Hyde, "Medieval Descriptions of Cities," *Bulletin of the John Rylands Library,* 48 (1965–66), 308–40.

21. Petrarch, *Ep. fam.* 6.2, ed. Rossi, 2: 55–60; cf. 9.13.34–36, pp. 254–55. For previous studies of this letter see Giuseppe Mazzotta, "Antiquity and the New Arts in Petrarch," *Romanic Review,* 79 (1988), 27–32; Thomas M. Greene, *The Light in Troy: Imitation and Discovery in Renaissance Poetry* (New Haven: Yale University Press, 1982), pp. 88–93, and on his peripatetics, "Petrarch *Viator,*" in idem, *The Vulnerable Text: Essays on Renaissance Literature* (New York: Columbia University Press, 1986), pp. 18–45, rpt. from *Yearbook of English Studies* 12 (1982), 35–57; and Angelo Mazzocco, "Petrarca, Poggio, and Biondo: Humanism's Foremost Interpreters of Roman Ruins," in *Francis Petrarch, Six Centuries Later: A Symposium,* ed. Aldo Scaglione (Chapel Hill: Department of Romance Languages, University of North Carolina; Chicago: Newberry Library, 1975), pp. 353–63.

22. Petrarch, *Ep. fam.* 15.8.6, ed. Rossi, 3: 154; trans. Bernardo, 2: 272.

23. Petrarch, *Ep. fam.* 6.2.14, ed. Rossi, 2: 58. For Petrarch's belief that Rome would rise again by knowing itself and thus his effort to make his contemporaries aware of its traditions see Mommsen, "Petrarch's Conception of the 'Dark Ages,'" 240.

24. Petrarch, *Rime sparse,* ed. Durling, 248.3–4, pp. 410–11.

25. Petrarch, *Ep. fam.* 6.2.14, ed. Rossi, 2: 58; trans. Bernardo, 2: 293.

26. Petrarch, *Rime sparse,* ed. Durling, 40.1–8; pp. 106–7.

27. Petrarch, *Epistolae variae* 48, cited Cosenza, *Francesco Petrarca and the Revolution of Cola di Rienzo,* p. 17.

28. Petrarch, *Liber sine nomine* 4, ed. Piur, p. 178; trans. Norman P. Zacour, *Petrarch's Book without a Name* (Toronto: Pontifical Institute of Mediaeval Studies, 1973), p. 48.

29. Ibid., p. 180; trans. Zacour, p. 52.

30. See F. G. Moore, "On Urbs Aeterna and Urbs Sacra," *Transactions of the American Philological Society,* 25 (1894), 34–60.

31. Charles T. Davis, *Dante and the Idea of Rome* (Oxford: Clarendon, 1957).

32. Petrarch, *Liber sine nomine* 7, ed. Piur, pp. 191–93; *Ep. fam.* 11.7, 23.2, ed. Rossi, 2: 337–40; 4: 157–67.

33. Petrarch, *Liber sine nomine* 4, ed. Piur, p. 174; trans. Zacour, p. 46.

34. Petrarch, *Rime sparse* 13.5–8, pp. 48–49.

35. Ibid. 37.37, p. 99, 45.7, p. 111, 80.32, p. 183, 130.13, p. 269, 285.5, p. 465, 331.5, p. 519.

36. Petrarch, *Liber sine nomine* 5, 8, ed. Piur, pp. 185, 193; trans. Zacour, pp. 58, 67. Ibid. 8, 10, ed. pp. 193, 197.

37. See "Babylon," *Realencyclopädie der classischen Altertums Wissenschaft,* ed. A. Pauly and Georg Wissowa (Stuttgart, 1886–1974), 2/2, cols. 2699–700. Strabo, *Rerum Geographicarum libri* 17.1.30.

38. Petrarch, *Liber sine nomine* 10, 17, ed. Piur, pp. 197, 199. For Cambyses see Herodotus, *Historiae* 3.1–38, 61–66; Lucan, *Bellum civile* 10. 279–82.

39. See R. Koldewey, *The Excavations at Babylon,* trans. Agnes S. Jones (London: Macmillan, 1914); Eckhard Unger, *Babylon: Die Heilige Stadt nach der Beschreibung der Babylonier* (Berlin: Walter de Gruyter, 1931); and for more recent, somewhat popular accounts, James G. Macqueen, *Babylon* (London: Robert Hale, 1964); James Wellard, *By the Waters of Babylon* (London: Hutchinson, 1972). Petrarch associated the founding of this Babylon with Semiramis. See Herodotus 1.184, Diodorus Siculus 2.7.2, and Quintus Curtius 5.1.24.

40. Martin Noth, "The Jerusalem Catastrophe of 587 B.C., and Its Significance for Israel," in his *The Laws in the Pentateuch and Other Studies,* trans. D. R. Ap-Thomas (Edinburgh: Oliver & Boyd, 1966), pp. 260–80. For general history see Peter R. Ackroyd, *Israel under Babylon and Persia* (London: Oxford University Press, 1970), pp. 1–161; C. F. Whitley, *The Exilic Age* (Philadelphia: Westminster, 1957).

41. Benjamin ben Jonah, *The Itinerary,* ed. Adler, pp. 42–45.

42. Petrarch associates the new Babylon with its own Nimrod in *Liber sine nomine* 8, 10, ed. Piur, pp. 193, 198–99.

43. For Petrarch's allusion to this etymology in calling Babylon "the city of confusion" see *Liber sine nomine* 10, ed. Piur, p. 198; trans. Zacour, p. 71; *De otio religioso* 2, ed. Rotondi, p. 58; *Ep. fam.* 15.9.16, ed. Rossi, 3: 160.

44. Herodotus, *Historiae* 1.193; Strabo, *Geographia* 16.1.14. See O. E. Ravn, *Herodotus' Description of Babylon,* trans. Margaret Tovborg–Jensen (Copenhagen: Nytl Nordisk, 1942).

45. See J. A. Thompson, "Israel's 'lovers,'" *Vetus Testamentum,* 27 (1977), 475–81; and also Walther Zimmerli, *A Commentary on the Book of the Prophet Ezekiel, Chapters 1–24* (Philadelphia: Fortress, 1979), trans. R. E. Clements, pp. 322–53, 471–92; Walther Eichrodt, *Ezekiel: A Commentary,* trans. Cosslett Quin (London: SCM, 1970), pp. 196–219, 317–33; J. W. Wevers, *Ezekiel* (London: Thomas Nelson & Sons, 1969), pp. 119–33, 178–88; G. A. Cooke, *The Book of Ezekiel* (Edinburgh: T. & T. Clark, 1936), pp. 159–81, 247–64; Moshe Greenberg, *Ezekiel 1–20: A New Translation with Introduction and Commentary* (New York: Doubleday, 1983), pp. 270–306.

46. See also A. Y. Collins, "The Political Perspective of the Revelation to John," *Journal of Biblical Literature,* 96 (1977), 241–56.

47. Paulinus of Nola, *Carmina* 9.

48. Petrarch, *Liber sine nomine* 10, ed. Piur, p. 199.

49. Augustine, *Enarrationes in psalmos* 136. For this work in general see Giuseppe Billanovich, "Nella biblioteca del Petrarca. I. Il Petrarca, il Boccaccio e le 'Enarrationes in Psalmi di Agostino,'" *Italia medioevale e umanistica,* 3 (1960), 1–27.

50. For some examples see Ann H. Hallock, "The Pre-eminent Role of *Babilonia* in Petrarch's Theme of the Two Cities," *Italica,* 54 (1977), 290–97.

51. Petrarch, *Rime sparse,* ed. Durling, 138, pp. 282–83.

52. Petrarch, *Ep. fam.* 15.9, ed. Rossi, 3: 157–63; trans. Bernardo, 2: 277.

53. Petrarch, *Liber sine nomine* 18, ed. Piur, pp. 230–31; trans. Zacour, pp. 111, 112. Petrarch's role as a prophet in *Liber sine nomine* has also been stated by Robert Coogan, "The Nature, Artistry and Influence of Petrarch's 'Epistolae sine nomine,'" in *Acta Coventus Neo-Latini Turonensis,* ed. Jean-Claude Margolin (2 vols.; Paris: J. Vrin, 1980), 1: 109, 110, 113.

54. Gordon Leff, *Heresy in the Later Middle Ages: The Relation of Heterodoxy to Dissent c. 1250–c. 1450* (2 vols.; Manchester: Manchester University Press, 1967), 2: 449, 457, 451; Marjorie Reeves, *The Influence of Prophecy in the Later Middle Ages: A Study of Joachimism* (Oxford: Clarendon, 1969), p. 244.

55. Leff, *Heresy in the Later Middle Ages,* 1: 77; Decima L. Douie, *The Nature and the Effect of the Heresy of the Fraticelli* (Manchester: Manchester University Press, 1932), p. 25.

56. Leff, *Heresy in the Later Middle Ages,* 1: 138, 132–33; Douie, *The Nature and the Effect of the Heresy of the Fraticelli,* p. 114. Edith Pásztor, "Le polemiche sulla 'Lectura super Apocalypsim' di Pietro di Giovanni Olivi fino alla sua condanna," *Bullettino dell'Istituto Storico Italiano per il Medio Evo,* 70 (1958), 365–424.

57. Leff, *Heresy in the Later Middle Ages,* 1: 199; Reeves, *The Influence of Prophecy in the Later Middle Ages,* pp. 205, 7.

58. Douie, *The Nature and the Effect of the Heresy of the Fraticelli,* p. 140.

59. Petrarch, *Liber sine nomine* 2, ed. Piur, p. 169; 11, p. 203; 13, p. 208; 18, pp. 232–35. In addition to the vices of lust, covetousness, pride, and gluttony, which will be discussed shortly, see Petrarch on envy, ibid. 13, p. 208; anger, 1, p. 166; and sloth, 1, p. 166, 5, p. 186, 9, p. 195, 11, p. 202.

60. Petrarch, *Rime sparse,* ed. Durling, 136, pp. 280–81.

61. Quintus Curtius, *Historia Alexandri* 5.1.36–39; Herodotus, *Historiae* 1.196, 199.

62. Petrarch, *Liber sine nomine* 18, ed. Piur, pp. 232–35; trans. Zacour, p. 114. Cf. *Bucolicum carmen* 7, ed. Avena, pp. 127–31. See also Ezio Raimundi, "Una pagina satirica delle *Sine nomine,*" *Studi petrarcheschi,* 6 (1956), 55–61; rpt. as "Un esercizio satirico del Petrarca," in his *Metafora e storia: Studi su Dante e Petrarca* (Turin: Einaudi, 1970), pp. 189–98.

63. Petrarch, *Liber sine nomine* 11, ed. Piur, p. 203; trans. Zacour, p. 75.

64. Ibid. 1, ed. Piur, p. 166; 2, p. 169; 5, pp. 185–86; 9, p. 195; 10, pp. 197–201; 11, pp. 202–3; 13, p. 208; 18, pp. 228, 231. See also *Ep. fam.* 6.1, ed. Rossi, 2: 47–54.

65. Herodotus, *Historiae* 1.193.

66. Petrarch, *Liber sine nomine* 10, ed. Piur, p. 201; trans. Zacour, p. 73. Ibid. 18, p. 231. See Col. 3:5.

67. E.g., *Moralisch-satirische Gedichte Walters von Chatillon,* esp. 1, 2, 5, 10, 11. See also Charles Witke, *Latin Satire: The Structures of Persuasion* (Leiden: E. J. Brill, 1970), pp. 250–51; John A. Yunck, "Economic Conservatism, Papal Finance, and the Medieval Satires on Rome," in *Changes in Medieval Society: Europe North of the Alps,* ed. Sylvia L. Thrupp (New York: Appleton-Century-Crofts, 1964), pp. 72–85.

68. See Mollat, *The Popes at Avignon*, pp. 319–26.
69. Petrarch, *Liber sine nomine* 14, ed. Piur, p. 211; trans. Zacour, p. 86; see also 17, p. 220. Ibid. 18, p. 228; trans. p. 109. Ibid, 2, p. 169; 5, p. 185; 18, p. 232. For the primacy of avarice in medieval lists of the vices see Lester K. Little, "Pride Goes before Avarice: Social Change and the Vices in Latin Christendom," *American Historical Review*, 76 (1971), 16–49.
70. See Mollat, *The Popes at Avignon*, pp. 330–32.
71. Petrarch, *Liber sine nomine* 5, ed. Piur, p. 186; trans. Zacour, p. 59; 18, pp. 228, 232.
72. See n. 45.
73. Petrarch, *Liber sine nomine* 1, ed. Piur, pp. 165–66; trans. Zacour, p. 33; 19, p. 237.
74. See Hugo Gretzmann, "Der Festbecher," in *Sellin-Festschrift: Beiträge zur Religionsgeschichte und Archäologie Palästinas*, ed. U. Jirt (Leipzig: Werner Schoel, 1927), pp. 55–62; W. Lotz, "Das Sinnbild des Bechers," *Neue kirchliche Zeitschrift*, 28 (1917), 396–407.
75. Petrarch, *Liber sine nomine* 1, ed. Piur, p. 166; 2, pp. 168, 169; 6, p. 187; and for stupidity, 2, p. 169.
76. Ibid. 2, p. 168; trans. Zacour, p. 38.
77. See John T. Willis, "The Genre of Isaiah 5:1–7," *Journal of Biblical Literature*, 96 (1977), 337–62: Gale A. Yee, "A Form-Critical Study of Isaiah 5:1–7 as a Song and a Juridical Parable," *Catholic Biblical Quarterly*, 43 (1981), 30–40.
78. Petrarch, *Liber sine nomine* 18, ed. Piur, p. 230. Translation mine. Note Petrarch's ironic use of the Delphic maxim "Know thyself," which is rendered more directly in the text than in Zacour's translation: "Nocisne teipsam, Babilon?"
79. See n. 53.
80. For this episode see Leff, *Heresy in the Later Middle Ages*, 1: 200–201, 224–26.
81. Petrarch, *Ep. fam.* 3.8, ed. Rossi, 1: 118–21; trans. Bernardo, 1: 134.
82. Petrarch, *Rerum memorandarum liber* 4, ed. Billanovich, pp. 191–272.
83. Petrarch, *Ep. fam.* 2.5, ed. Rossi, 1: 81–82.
84. Ibid. 5.7, ed. Rossi, 2: 22–25; trans. Bernardo, 1: 255.
85. See Constance B. Hieatt, *The Realism of Dream-Visions: The Poetic Exploitation of the Dream-Experience in Chaucer and His Contemporaries* (The Hague: Mouton, 1967); Jane Chance Nitzsche, *The Genius Figure in Antiquity and the Middle Ages* (New York: Columbia University Press, 1975), pp. 56–63.
86. Petrarch, *Rime sparse*, ed. Durling, 359, pp. 557–59. See also 282, p. 461, 341, p. 539, 342, p. 539, 343, p. 541, 356, p. 553. For a study of these see Oscar Büdel, "Parusia Redemtricis: Lauras Traumbesuche in Petrarcas Canzoniere," in *Petrarca, 1304–1374: Beiträge zu Werk und Wirkung*, ed. Fritz Schalk (Frankfurt: Vittorio Klostermann, 1975), pp. 33–50. See also *Ep. met.* 1.6.126–28, 140–43, as discussed by Bernardo, *Petrarch, Laura, and the Triumphs* (Albany: State University of New York Press, 1974), pp. 69–72; and consider that Petrarch's *Trionfi* itself was a pageant of dreams.

87. Petrarch, *Africa* 8.462–81, ed. Festa, pp. 236–37; trans. Thomas G. Bergin and Alice S. Wilson, *Petrarch's Africa* (New Haven: Yale University Press, 1977), p. 199. See also Fabius's prophecy of Hannibal's war in *Africa* 7.61–84, ed. Festa, pp. 173–74.

88. Petrarch, *Ep. fam.* 5.5, ed. Rossi, 2: 14–19; trans. Bernardo, I, 244, 245.

89. Ibid. 11.7, pp. 337–40.

90. Ibid. 11.7.2, p. 338; trans. Bernardo, 2: 99.

91. Ibid. 1.1.22, ed. Rossi, 1: 7–8; trans. Bernardo, 1: 8.

92. Petrarch, *Rime sparse*, ed. Durling, 174.1–7; p. 321.

93. Ibid. 328.3–4, pp. 516–17.

94. Ibid. 210.5–6, pp. 364–65.

95. Ibid. 249, pp. 410–11.

96. Ibid. 226.1–2, pp. 382–83.

97. Petrarch, *Liber sine nomine* 9, ed. Piur, p. 196; trans. Zacour, p. 71. Cf. 17, p. 227.

98. For a survey of these as thematic of Petrarch's love of glory see Bernardo, "The Importance of the Non-Love Poems of Petrarch's 'Canzoniere,'" *Italica*, 27 (1950), 302–12; and also Sara Sturm-Maddox, "*Rime sparse* 25–28: The Metaphors of Choice," *Neophilologus*, 69 (1985), 225–35; Marco Santagata, "Sul destinatario della canzone petrarchesca 'O aspectata in ciel beata et bella' (R.V.F. 28)," *Rivista di letteratura italiana*, 3 (1985), 365–80.

99. See Joachim of Fiore, Vat. Lat. 3822, ed. Bignami-Odier, pp. 220–23.

100. Petrarch, *Liber sine nomine* 14, ed. Piur, p. 211; trans. Zacour, p. 86. See also *Ep.* 17, p. 220.

101. Petrarch, *Ep. fam.* 1.8.2–5, ed. Rossi, 1: 39–40; trans. Bernardo, 1: 42.

102. Seneca, *Ad Lucilium* 84.3–4.

103. Charles Trinkaus, *The Poet as Philosopher: Petrarch and the Formation of Renaissance Consciousness* (New Haven: Yale University Press, 1979), p. 9, and see also pp. 23–24. For Petrarch's imitation of classical authors see also Giuseppe Velli, "La memoria poetica del Petrarca," *Italia medioevale e umanistica*, 19 (1976), 171–207; Christian Bec, "De Pétrarque à Machiavel: A propos d'un *topos humaniste* (le dialogue lecteur/livre)," *Rinascimento*, 16 (1976), 3–17; and in general, Greene, *The Light in Troy*, pp. 104–46.

104. Petrarch, *Ep. fam.* 22.2.20–21, ed. Rossi, 4:108; trans. Bernardo, 3: 214.

105. Petrarch, *Rime sparse*, ed. Durling, 43, pp. 108–9. Consider also his statement that the splendor of the ancient philosophers ceases where Christ the sun of righteousness illuminates the mind. *Ep. fam.* 17.1.40, ed. Rossi, 3:229.

106. Seneca, *Ad Lucilium* 84.7–8. Petrarch, *Ep. fam.* 23.19.11–12, ed. Rossi, 4: 206; trans. Bernardo, 3: 301.

107. Fredi Chiapelli, "Petrarch and Innovation: A Note on a Manuscript," *Modern Language Notes*, 96 (1981), 140–42; Anna C. Burgio, "Per lo studio delle varianti petrarchesche: un recente contributo sulla canzone CCCXXIII," *Studi petrarcheschi*, 8 (1976), 257–61; Michele Feo, "Il sogno di Cerere e la

morte del lauro petrarchescho," in *Il Petrarca ad Arquà: Atti del convegno di studi nel VI centario (1370–1374)*, ed. Giuseppe Billanovich and Giuseppe Frasso (Padua: Antenore, 1975), pp. 133–48; Mariarosa Giacon, "Temi e stilemi fra Petrarca e Boccaccio: II. La novella di Nastagio e la canzone delle visioni," *Studi sul Boccaccio*, 8 (1974), 226–49; Chiappelli, *Studi sul linguaggio del Petrarca: La canzone delle visioni* (Florence: Olschki, 1971); idem, "La canzone petrarchesca delle visioni: Costanti e variazioni interstrofiche della struttura metrica," *Yearbook of Italian Studies*, 1 (1971), 235–47; idem, "La canzone delle visioni e il sostrato tematico della 'fabula inexpleta,'" *Giornale storico della letteratura italiana*, 141 (1964), 321–35; Francesco Maggini, "La canzone delle visioni," *Studi petrarcheschi*, 1 (1948), 37–50; and for the fortune of the poem, Julia C. Bondanella, *Petrarch's Visions and Their Renaissance Analogues* (Madrid: José Porrua Turanzas, 1978), and Charles R. Davis, "Petrarch's *Rime* 323 and Its Tradition through Spenser," Ph.D. diss., Princeton University, 1973.

108. For a description of this form see Burke O. Long, "Reports of Visions among the Prophets," *Journal of Biblical Literature*, 95 (1976), 353–65.

109. See Philippe Reymond, *L'Eau, sa vie, et sa signification dans l'ancien testament*, Vetus Testamentum Supplements, 6 (1958), 208.

110. See chapter 1, n. 30.

111. Jean Frappier, "Variations sur le thème du Miroir, de Bernard de Ventadour à Maurice Scève," *Cahiers de l'Association internationale des études françaises*, 11 (1959), 134–58.

112. See D. R. Hillers, "A Convention in Hebrew Literature: The Reaction to Bad News," *Zeitschrift für die alttestamentliche Wissenschaft*, 77 (1965), 86–89.

113. Long, "Reports of Visions among the Prophets."

114. Petrarch, *Ep. fam.* 21.10.25, ed. Rossi, 4: 78–79; trans. Bernardo, 3: 188. See also Dölger, *Die Sonne der Gerechtigkeit und der Schwarze*, pp. 37–48; A. Bouché-Leclercq, *Histoire de la divination dans l'antiquité* (4 vols.; Paris, 1879), 1: 136–38.

115. Vergil, *Aeneid* 2.693, 9. 630–31.

116. See C. Budde, "Das hebräische Klagelied," *Zeitschrift für die alttestamentliche Wissenschaft*, 2 (1882), 1–52; Hedwig Jahnow, *Das hebräische Leichenlied im Rahmen der Völkerdichtung* (Giessen: Alfred Töpelmann, 1923), pp. 197–231.

117. See n. 7.

118. W. H. Brownlee, "Two Elegies on the Fall of Judah (Ezekiel 19)," in *Ex orbe religionum: Studia Geo Widengren*, ed. C. J. Bleeker et al. (2 vols.; Leiden: E. J. Brill, 1972), 1: 93–103; and the commentaries of Zimmerli, Eichrodt, Wevers, Greenberg, and Cooke, ad loc.

119. Phaedrus, *Fabulae Aesopiae* 1.21.8. See also Ben E. Perry's introduction, pp. lxxxiii–iv.

120. See Florence McCulloch, *Mediaeval Latin and French Bestiaries*, 3d rev. ed. (Chapel Hill: University of North Carolina Press, 1962), pp. 137, 139. This figure also symbolized Christ, as Petrarch notes in *Liber sine nomine* 12, ed. Piur, p. 205; cf. Rev. 5:5.

121. For the use of dogs in the medieval hunt and related literature see Marcelle Thiébaux, *The Stag of Love: The Chase in Medieval Literature* (Ithaca, N.Y.: Cornell University Press, 1974), pp. 21–36, 185–86; and for a Petrarchan image see *Africa* 4.345–53, ed. Festa, pp. 97–98.

122. *The Epic of Gilgamesh* 1.109, 136, cited by Cooke's commentary on Ezekiel, p. 207.

123. For Petrarch's *fronte* as meaning visage or appearance and not specifically the face, in analogy with the Latin *frons,* see Phaedrus, *Fabulae Aesopiae* 4.2.6. For the biblical exegesis see H. H. Rowley, *Darius the Mede and the Four World Empires in the Book of Daniel: A Historical Study of Contemporary Theories* (Cardiff: University of Wales Press, 1959), pp. 67–69; Maurice Casey, *Son of Man: The Interpretation and Influence of Daniel* 7 (London: SPCK, 1979), pp. 19–20; André Caquot, "Sur les quatre bêtes de Daniel VII," *Semitica* 5 (1955), 6–13; idem, "Les Quatre Bêtes et le 'fils d'homme' (Daniel 7)," *Semitica,* 17 (1967), 37–71; Louis F. Hartman and Alexander A. Di Lella, *The Book of Daniel* (New York: Doubleday, 1978), pp. 205, 211–12; M. Delcor, *Le Livre de Daniel* (Paris: J. Gabalda, 1971), pp. 143–47. Cf. Rev. 13:1–8, which created a composite beast symbolizing the Roman empire from the lion's mouth and the characteristics of Daniel's three other wild creatures.

124. For the history see "Bianchi," in Paget Toynbee, rev. Charles S. Singleton, *A Dictionary of Proper Names and Notable Matters in the Works of Dante* (Oxford: Clarendon, 1968), pp. 96–98. For Petrarch's use of "black and white" in another sense see *Rime sparse,* ed. Durling, 29.23, p. 83, 72.50, p. 165, 151.7, p. 297.

125. Wilkins, *Life of Petrarch,* pp. 1–3.

126. See H. J. van Dijk, *Ezekiel's Prophecy on Tyre (Ez. 26, 1–28, 19): A New Approach* (Rome: Pontifical Biblical Institute, 1968), pp. 48–91; C. Newsome, "A Maker of Metaphors—Ezekiel's Oracles against Tyre," *Interpretation,* 38 (1984), 151–64; Edwin M. Good, "Ezekiel's Ship: Some Extended Metaphors in the Old Testament," *Semitics,* 1 (1970), 79–103; R. D. Barnett, "Ezekiel and Tyre," *Eretz-Israel,* 9 (1969), 6–7; Frederick L. Moriarty, "The Lament over Tyre (Ez. 27)," *Gregorianum,* 46 (1965), 83–88; Sidney Smith, "The Ship Tyre," *Palestine Exploration Quarterly,* 85 (1953), 97–110; W. Emery Barnes, "Ezekiel's Denunciation of Tyre (Ezek. xxvi–xxviii)," *Journal of Theological Studies,* 35 (1934), 50–52; and the commentaries ad loc. of Eichrodt, Wevers, Cooke, and Zimmerli, *Ezekiel 2: A Commentary on the Book of the Prophet Ezekiel, Chapters 25–48* (Philadelphia: Fortress, 1983), trans. James D. Martin.

127. See Jean Daniélou, *Primitive Christian Symbols,* trans. Donald Atwater (Baltimore: Helicon, 1964), pp. 58–70; Hugo Rahner, *Greek Myths and Christian Mystery,* trans. Brian Battershaw (London: Burns & Oates, 1963), pp. 341–71.

128. Petrarch, *Liber sine nomine* 1, ed. Piur, pp. 165–66.

129. See Herbert G. May, "Some Cosmic Connotations of Mayim Rabbîm, 'Many Waters,'" *Journal of Biblical Literature,* 74 (1955), 9–21, esp. 18.

130. See Lawrence Boadt, *Ezekiel's Oracles against Egypt: A Literary and Philological Study of Ezekiel 29–32* (Rome: Biblical Institute, 1980), pp. 90–123; Fritz Stolz, "Die Bäume des Gottesgartens auf dem Libanon," *Zeitschrift für die alttestamentliche Wissenschaft*, 84 (1972), 141–56; the commentaries of Zimmerli, Eichrodt, Wevers, and Cooke, ad loc.; and for a survey of the image in the history of religions, Mircea Eliade, *Patterns in Comparative Religion*, trans. Rosemary Sheed (London: Sheed & Ward, 1958), pp. 265–330. Cf. the fearful dream of Nebuchadnezzar (Dan. 4:4–33) and his descent to the underworld (Is. 14:4–20), which also employ the symbol of the cosmic tree.

131. See Brownlee, "Two Elegies on the Fall of Judah (Ez. 19)," 93–103; and the commentaries of Zimmerli, Eichrodt, Wevers, Cooke, and Greenberg, ad loc. Cf. Ezekiel 15, for which see Horacio Simian-Yafre, "La Métaphore d'Ezékiel 15," in *Ezekiel and His Book: Textual and Literary Criticism and Their Interrelation*, ed. Johan Lust, Bibliotheca Ephemeridum Theologicarum Lovaniensium, 74 (Louvain: University Press, 1986), pp. 234–47; A. E. Rivlin, "The Parable of the Vine and the Fire: Structure, Rhythm and Diction in Ezekiel's Poetry," *Beth Mikra*, 63 (1974), 562–70 (in Hebrew); Eberhard Baumann, "Die Weinranke im Walde. Hes. 15, 1–8," *Theologische Literaturzeitung*, 80 (1955), 119–20; Robert W. Funk, "The Looking-Glass Tree Is for the Birds," *Interpretation*, 27 (1973), 3–9.

132. Petrarch, *Africa* 3.588–91, 6.254–57, 7.607, ed. Festa, pp. 75–76, 143, 194.

133. Pliny, *Naturalis historia* 2.56.146, 15.40.134–35; Suetonius, *Life of Tiberius* 69; Isidore of Seville, *Etymologiae* 17.7.2.

134. Petrarch, *Collatio laureationis*, ed. Godi, pp. 26–27.

135. See the commentaries of Zimmerli, Eichrodt, Wevers, and Cooke, ad. loc.; and Greenberg, "The Design and Themes of Ezekiel's Program of Restoration," *Interpretation*, 38 (1984), 181–208, Jon D. Levenson, *Theology of the Program of Restoration of Ezekiel 40–48* (Missoula, Mont.: Scholars Press for the Harvard Semitic Museum, 1976).

136. See J. Massyngberde-Ford, *Revelation: Introduction, Translation and Commentary* (New York: Doubleday, 1975), pp. 332–46; G. R. Beasley-Murray, *The Book of Revelation* (London: Oliphants, 1974), pp. 313, 330–32; R. H. Charles, *A Critical and Exegetical Commentary on the Book of Revelation* (2 vols.; Edinburgh: T. & T. Clark, 1920), 2: 443–44; and also Albert Vanhoye, "L'Utilisation du livre d'Ezékiel dans l'Apocalypse," *Biblica*, 43 (1962), 436–76.

137. See Richard Bauckham, "The Eschatological Earthquake in the Apoc. of John," *Novum Testamentum*, 19 (1977), 224–33. *Sib.* 3.401–14, 449, 457, 459; 4.99–100, 107–13, 128–29; 5.128–29, 286–97, and for Babylon, 5.438. See also Lars Hartman, *Prophecy Interpreted: The Formation of Some Jewish Apocalyptic Texts and of the Eschatological Discourse Mark 13 Par.* (Uppsala: Almquist & Wiksells, 1966), pp. 91–94.

138. See the commentaries of Massyngberde-Ford, Beasley-Murray, and Charles, ad loc.

139. Greenberg, "Ezekiel 17 and the Policy of Psammetichus II," *Journal*

of Biblical Literature, 76 (1957), 304–9; Louise P. Smith, "The Eagle(s) of Ezekiel 17," *Journal of Biblical Literature,* 58 (1939), 43–50; and the commentaries of Zimmerli, Eichrodt, Wevers, Cooke, and Greenberg, ad loc.

140. See Herodotus, *Historiae* 2.73.

141. R. van den Broeck, *The Myth of the Phoenix, according to Classical and Early Christian Traditions,* trans. I. Seeger (Leiden: E. J. Brill, 1972), pp. 251–52, 279–80, 172 n. 6, 411 n. 1.

142. Lactantius, *De ave phoenice* 5–14; van den Broeck, *The Myth of the Phoenix,* pp. 25–30.

143. See McCullough, *Mediaeval Latin and French Bestiaries,* pp. 160, 158, 68. For the classical association of the phoenix with Lebanon see van den Broeck, *The Myth of the Phoenix,* pp. 171–72.

144. Van den Broeck, *The Myth of the Phoenix,* pp. 307–9.

145. See McCullough, *Mediaeval Latin and French Bestiaries,* pp. 155–57; and Victor E. Graham, "The Pelican as Image and Symbol," *Revue de littérature comparée,* 36 (1962), 253–43.

146. McCullough, *Mediaeval Latin and French Bestiaries,* pp. 158–59. For ancient sources of the phoenix as building its pyre on a high rock see van den Broeck, *The Myth of the Phoenix,* pp. 178–82.

147. McCullough, *Mediaeval Latin and French Bestiaries,* pp. 114–15.

148. See the commentaries of Zimmerli, Eichrodt, Wevers, and Cooke, ad loc.; and Hans F. Fuhs, "Ez 24—Überlegungen zu Tradition und Redaktion des Ezechielbuchs," in *Ezekiel and His Book,* ed. Lust, pp. 266–82.

149. The use of this classical myth is discussed in other terms in Chiappelli, *Studi sul linguaggio del Petrarca,* pp. 137–83. For general background see Rinaldina Russell, "Studio dei generi medievali italiani: Il compianto per la morte dell'amata," *Italica,* 54 (1977), 449–67.

150. See John Block Friedman, *Orpheus in the Middle Ages* (Cambridge, Mass.: Harvard University Press, 1970), pp. 38–85.

151. See Caquot, "La Parole sur Juda dans le testament lyrique de Jacob (Genèse 49, 8–12)," *Semetica,* 26 (1976), 5–32; E. Testa, "La formazione letteraria della benedizione di Giacobbe (Gen 49, 2–27)," *Studii Biblici Franciscani Liber Annuus,* 23 (1973), 167–205; Calum M. Carmichael, "Some Sayings in Genesis 49," *Journal of Biblical Literature,* 88 (1969), 435–44; E. M. Good, "The 'Blessing' on Judah, Gen 49 8–12," *Journal of Biblical Literature,* 82 (1963), 427–32; W. L. Moran, "Gen 49,10, and Its Use in Ez 21,32," *Biblica,* 39 (1958), 405–25; J. Coppens, "La Bénédiction de Jacob: Son cadre historique à la lumière des parallèles ougaritiques," *Vetus Testamentum Supplements,* 4 (1957), 97–115; Bruce Vawter, "The Canaanite Background of Gen. 49," *Catholic Biblical Quarterly,* 17 (1955), 1–18; Gerhard von Rad, *Genesis: A Commentary,* trans. John H. Marks, rev. ed. (Philadelphia: Westminster, 1972), pp. 419–28; E. A. Speiser, *Genesis* (Garden City: Doubleday, 1981), pp. 361–72.

152. The manuscript indicates corrections dated 13 October and a definitive form dated 31 October 1368. Chiappelli, *Studi sul linguaggio del Petrarca,* pp. 15–19.

153. See C. C. Bayley, "Petrarch, Charles IV, and the 'Renovatio Im-

perii,'" *Speculum,* 17 (1942), 323–41, with citation, 335. Petrarch, *Ep. fam.* 10.1, ed. Rossi, 2: 283–84; trans. Bernardo, 2: 54.

154. Gerald G. Walsh, *The Emperor Charles IV, 1316–1378: A Study in Holy Roman Imperialism* (Oxford: Basil Blackwell, 1924), pp. 75–79; Bede Jarrett, *The Emperor Charles IV* (London: Eyre & Spottiswoode, 1935), pp. 91, 155–56; and for the general background, Mollat, *The Popes at Avignon,* pp. 146–60.

155. See the commentaries of Zimmerli, Eichrodt, Wevers, Cooke, and Greenberg, ad loc.

156. See Bouché-Leclerq, *Histoire de la divination dans l'antiquité,* 1: 127–45, esp. 134.

157. For the phoenix and the Golden Age see van den Broeck, *The Myth of the Phoenix,* pp. 98–116, 229–30; as king of the birds, p. 193; as paradisiacal, pp. 184–85, 309–34.

158. See Bayley, "Petrarch, Charles IV, and the 'Renovatio Imperii,'" 333.

159. Reeves, *Prophecy in the Late Middle Ages,* pp. 267, 326, 367; 306–9, 321–22, and see the index under "Alemani."

160. Reeves and Beatrice Hirsch-Reich, "The Seven Seals in the Writings of Joachim of Fiore," *Recherches de théologie ancienne et médiévale,* 21 (1954), 211–47.

161. Reeves, *The Figurae of Joachim of Fiore* (Oxford: Clarendon, 1972), pp. 85–86.

162. Petrarch, *Liber sine nomine* 15, ed. Piur, p. 216; trans. Zacour, pp. 91–92.

4. WOUNDED LOVERS

1. Petrarch, *Collatio laureationis,* ed. Godi, pp. 25–27. See also *Africa* 9.108–23, ed. Festa, pp. 264–65.

2. Petrarch, *Rime sparse,* ed. Durling, 22.20–22, p. 59. 50.39–42, p. 119; 304.3–4, p. 483. 152.1–2, p. 299. 135.31–45, p. 275. 23.147–60, p. 67. 226.2, p. 383; 287.13–14, pp. 466–67.

3. See Ernst R. Curtius, *European Literature and the Latin Middle Ages,* trans. Willard R. Trask (New York: Pantheon, 1953), pp. 128–30.

4. For a survey of texts see Renée Luciani, "La Barque et le port," in *Actes du Congrès international Francesco Petrarca* (Avignon, 1974), pp. 281–94; and Sara Sturm-Maddox, "Eaux troublés: La Navigation de l'âme dans les *Rimes Sparse* de Pétrarque," in *L'Eau au Moyen Age* (Marseilles: Jeanne Laffitte, 1985), pp. 335–47.

5. See Martin Ninck, *Die Bedeutung des Wassers im Kult und Leben der Alten: Eine symbolgeschichtliche Untersuchung* 2d ed. (Darmstadt: Wissenschaftliche Buchgesellschaft, 1960), pp. 1–99; Philippe Reymond, *L'Eau, sa vie, et sa signification dans l'ancien testament, Vetus Testamentum Supplements,* 6 (1958), pp. 208–22.

6. Pierre Amandry, *La Mantique apollinienne à Delphes: Essai sur le fonc-*

tionnement de l'Oracle (Paris: Boccard, 1950), pp. 134–39; and for the spring Cassotis, which poured from a stone conduit under the temple, Georges Roux, *Delphes: Son oracle et ses dieux* (Paris: Belles lettres, 1976), pp. 136–45. It was characteristic of the Apolline sanctuaries that all were important hydraulic installations, and the inspirational force of the water together with the laurel and the tripod were the sources of the oracle. See René Ginouves, *Balaneutiké: Recherches sur le bain dans l'antiquité grecque* (Paris: E. de Boccard, 1962), pp. 327–44.

 7. R. van den Broeck, *The Myth of the Phoenix, according to Classical and Early Christian Traditions,* trans. I. Seeger (Leiden: E. J. Brill, 1972), pp. 71, 232–304, citing Lactantius, *De ave phoenice* 51–58.

 8. For Petrarch's poetic thought at the summit of the flight of the phoenix see *Rime sparse* 135.1–15, ed. Durling, p. 273; and for Petrarch as a bird, 23.165–66, 165.14 (cf. 163.10–11). For Laura as a phoenix see 185.1, p. 331, 321.1–4, p. 501, and Francesco Zambon, "Sulla fenice del Petrarca," in *Dal medioevo al Petrarca: Miscellanea di studi in onore di Vittore Branca* (2 vols.; Florence: Leo S. Olschki, 1983), 1: 411–25.

 9. Ovid, *Metamorphoses* 10.8–10.

 10. For this rhetorical device, especially in *Rime sparse* 220, see Gordon Poole, "Il topos del' 'effictio' e un sonetto del Petrarca," *Lettere italiane,* 32 (1980), 3–20.

 11. For these traditions see John B. Friedman, *Orpheus in the Middle Ages* (Cambridge, Mass.: Harvard University Press, 1970), pp. 86–145.

 12. Petrarch, *Invective contra medicum* 3, ed. Ricci, p. 62, citing Horace, *Ars poetica* 70–72; trans. H. Rushton Fairclough, *Satires, Epistles and Ars poetica* (New York: G. P. Putnam's Sons, 1929), p. 457.

 13. Jerrold E. Seigel, "Ideals of Eloquence and Silence in Petrarch," *Journal of the History of Ideas,* 26 (1965), 147–54. For the medieval subsumption of poetry to rhetoric, see Curtius, *European Literature and the Latin Middle Ages,* pp. 145–66.

 14. Aristotle, *Ars rhetorica* 3.13; Quintilian, *Institutiones oratoriae* 3.9.1; *Rhetorica ad C. Herennium* 1.3.4; Cicero, *De inventione* 1.14.19; Isidore of Seville, *Etymologiae* 2.7.1.

 15. Petrarch, *Rime sparse,* ed. Durling, 193.13–14, pp. 338–39; cf. 248.1–2, p. 411.

 16. Ibid. 304.7–8, p. 483. 70.1–3, p. 155. 264.79–80, p. 431. 60.1–4, p. 139. 307.7–8, pp. 486–87. 360.113–14, pp. 566–67. 171.9–10, p. 317. 23.141–60, p. 67; see also *Africa* 3.224–31, ed. Festa, pp. 60–61. 23.50–60, pp. 62–63; see Ovid, *Metamorphoses* 1.747–2.380. 221.14, pp. 376–77. 200.6–8, p. 347. 261.11, pp. 422–23. 308.12–14, pp. 486–87.

 17. Petrarch, *Africa* 1.353–54, ed. Festa, p. 18.

 18. Petrarch, *Rime sparse,* ed. Durling, 339, pp. 536–37.

 19. Ibid. 248.13, pp. 410–11.

 20. Ibid. 309.7–14, pp. 488–89.

 21. Ibid. 4, p. 39. 70.41–42, pp. 152–53. 287.14, pp. 466–67. 37.110–11, pp. 102–3; cf. 45.2, p. 111.

 22. Ibid. 23.123–40, p. 67. 70.41–50, pp. 152–53.

23. Ibid. 208.14, p. 363; cf. Matt. 26:41b.
24. Petrarch, *Secretum* 2, ed. Martellotti, p. 76; trans. William S. Draper, *Petrarch's Secret, or, The Soul's Conflict with Passion* (London: Chatto & Windus, 1911), p. 54.
25. Petrarch, *Ep. fam.* 12.5.2–3, ed. Rossi, 3: 24; trans. Aldo S. Bernardo *Rerum familiarum libri I–VIII*, (Albany: State University of New York Press, 1975); *Letters on Familiar Matters: Rerum familiarum libri IX–XVI* (Baltimore: Johns Hopkins University Press, 1982), 2: 147.
26. *Ep. Fam.* 16.3.9, ed. Rossi, 3: 181; 6.1.4, ed. 2: 48. 1.8.8–9, 1: 40–41; 3.20.11, 1: 147; 3.7.4, 1: 117; Petrarch, *Rime sparse*, ed. Durling, 105.35–36, pp. 35–36. *Ep. fam.* 3.18.1–2, ed. Rossi, 1: 138–39; trans. Bernardo, 1: 157. 1.8.12, ed. Rossi, 1: 41; trans. Bernardo, 1: 43. 1.3.6, ed. Rossi, 1: 22; trans. Bernardo, 1: 23; see also 1.18, 1: 5. *Rime sparse*, ed. Durling, 247.9–14, pp. 408–9.
27. Petrarch, *Rime sparse*, ed. Durling, 37.65–69, pp. 100–101. 292.13, pp. 470–71, 271.13–14, pp. 450–51. 186.13–14, pp. 332–33. 354.1–5, p. 551.
28. Ibid. 157.1–4, pp. 302–3. 100.10–11, pp. 202–3. 30.28, p. 89; 50.55, p. 119; 62.9, p. 141; 79.2, p. 179 and 101.13, p. 205; 107.7, p. 215 and 145.14, p. 291; 118.1, p. 227; 122.1, p. 237; 212.12, p. 367 and 221.8, p. 377; 364.1–4, p. 573 and 271.2, p. 451; 278.14, p. 457.
29. Ibid. 144.1–7, pp. 290–91.
30. Ibid. 20, pp. 54–55.
31. Ibid. 23.167–69, pp. 68–69. 142.19–22, pp. 286–87.
32. Ibid. 337.12–14, pp. 534–35.
33. Ibid. 344.5–6, pp. 540–41. 345.5–14, pp. 542–43. 348.10, p. 545. 327.10–11, pp. 514–15. 346.1–8, pp. 542–43.
34. Ibid. 354.12–14, pp. 550–51.
35. Ibid. 354.4, 7–8, p. 551. 346.9–14, pp. 542–43.
36. Ibid. 347, pp. 544–45.
37. Ibid. 225.9–11, pp. 380–81.
38. For Petrarch on the papal debate concerning this question see *Ep. fam.* 2.12.9, ed. Rossi, 1: 101; and for background, Decima L. Douie, "John XXII and the Beatific Vision," *Dominican Studies*, 3 (1950), 154–74. See also Mario M. Rossi, "Laura morta e la concezione petrarchesca dell'aldilà," *Studi petrarcheschi*, 7 (1957), 301–21.
39. Petrarch, *Rime sparse*, ed. Durling, 206.55–59, pp. 354–55. For serving Rachel rather than Leah see Augustine, *Contra Faustum Manichaeum* 12.52.
40. See Cuthbert Butler, *Western Mysticism*, 2d ed. (London: Constable, 1927), pp. 227–87; Daniel Csanyi, "*Optima pars*: Die Auslegungsgeschichte von Lk 10, 36–42 bei den Kirchenvätern der ersten vier Jahrhunderte," *Studia Monastica*, 2 (1960), 5–78.
41. Petrarch also applies the allegory in *De vita solitaria* 2.10, ed. Martellotti, pp. 503–4.
42. Petrarch, *Rime sparse*, ed. Durling, 313.9–11, pp. 492–93.
43. Petrarch, *De vita solitaria* 2.3, ed. Martellotti, pp. 424–26; see also 2.13, p. 552.
44. For the history of Elijah's chariot see Jean Daniélou, *Primitive Chris-*

tian Symbols, trans. Donald Attwater (Baltimore: Helicon, 1964), pp. 71–88. He cites Eunapius, fr. 26 in *Fragmenta historicorum graecorum,* 4: 24–25; and Sedulius 1.186.

45. See chapter 2, n. 2.
46. See chapter 1, nn. 32, 36, 37.
47. Dante, *Paradiso* 11.49–50; trans. Charles S. Singleton in *The Divine Comedy* (Princeton: Princeton University Press, 1975), p. 121.
48. Petrarch, *Rime sparse,* ed. Durling, 4.12–14, pp. 38–39. This imitation of Dante's verses has been stated by Nicola Scarano, "L'invidia del Petrarca," *Giornale storico della letteratura italiana,* 29 (1897), 23; Ezio Chiorboli in his commentary to *Le "Rime sparse"* (Milan: Trevisini, 1924), p. 7; Mario Santagata, "Presenza di Dante comico nel *Canzoniere del Petrarca,*" *Giornale storico della letteratura italiana,* 146 (1969), 196; Paolo Trovato, *Dante in Petrarca: Per un inventario dei Dantismi nei "Rerum vulgarium fragmenta"* (Florence: Leo S. Olschki, 1979), p. 46.
49. For extensive documentation see Stanislao da Campagnola, *L'angelo del sesto sigillo e l' "Alter Christus": genesi e sviluppo di due temi francescani nei secoli XIII–XIV* (Rome: Laurentianum, 1971), pp. 127–29, citing *Mira circa nos* in *Bullarium Franciscanum Romanorum Pontificium,* 1: 98–99; Celano, *Vita I S. Francisci* 36; *Analecta franciscana,* 10:377. Bonaventure, *Legenda maior S. Francisci,* prol. 1; trans. Ewert Cousins, *The Soul's Journey into God, The Tree of Life, The Life of St. Francis* (New York: Paulist, 1978), p. 180.
50. Campagnola, *L'angelo del sesto sigillo, e l' "Alter Christus",* p. 187, citing Matthew of Acquasparta, *Sermones de sancto Francisco* 74, pp. 190–91.
51. Bonaventure, *Legenda maior S. Francisci* 4.4; trans. Cousins, p. 209.
52. Campagnola, *L'angelo del sesto sigillo e l' "Alter Christus,"* citing Ubertino da Casale, *Arbor vitae crucifixae Jesu* 5.3. Bonaventure, *Legenda maior S. Francisci,* prol. 1; trans. Cousins, pp. 180–81.
53. Campagnola, *L'angelo del sesto sigillo e l' "Alter Christus",* pp. 173–97, 240–41, 255.
54. See Celano, *Vita II S. Franciscani* 1.3.
55. Dante, *Paradiso* 11.76–78; trans. Singleton, p. 173.
56. Petrarch, *De otio religioso* 2, ed. Rotondi, pp. 74, 80. On the Franciscans see also Anna Maria Voci, *Petrarca e la vita religiosa: Il mito umanista della vita eremitica* (Rome: Istituto Storico Italiana per l'Età Moderna e Contemporanea, 1983), pp. 67–81.
57. Petrarch, *De vita solitaria* 2.6, ed. Martellotti, pp. 454–56; trans. Jacob Zeitlin, *The Life of Solitude* (Urbana: University of Illinois Press, 1924), p. 220.
58. Petrarch, *Ep. fam.* 14.1.40–41, ed. Rossi, 3:104–5. Ibid. 13.4.20, 23, 25, ed. Rossi, 3: 63, 64, 65; trans. Bernardo 2:185. See also 13.5.6–7, ed. Rossi, 3:67.
59. Petrarch, *Rime sparse,* ed. Durling, 7.10, pp. 42–43.
60. Petrarch, *Invective contra medicum* 2, ed. Ricci, p. 54. See also *Ep. fam.* 7.10.10, ed. Rossi, 2:116; 8.4.27, p. 167; 17.8, ed. 3:254–56.
61. Petrarch, *Ep. fam.* 7.3, with the citation at 7.10, ed. Rossi, 2:103–5;

trans. Bernardo, 1:342. For another discourse on avarice as the most fatal of the vices see *Ep. fam.* 6.1, ed. Rossi, 2:47–54; cf. 11.16.21–23, ed. Rossi, 2: 362–63; and on the virtue of poverty, 6.3.38–51, pp. 68–72.

62. Petrarch, *Ep. var.* 55, ed. *Operum*, 2:1140. See also *Ep. fam.* 19.5.2–3, ed. Rossi, 3:321; 19.17.1–8, p. 347.

63. Petrarch, *Rime sparse*, ed. Durling, 270.6, p. 443. Ibid. 207.22, p. 357.

64. Ibid. 125.79, pp. 242–43.

65. Ibid. 308.1–2, pp. 486–87.

66. See Plato, *Symposium* 203b–d.

67. See especially Bonaventure, *Legenda maior* 5 and *Itinerarium mentis in Deum*.

68. Petrarch, *Rime sparse*, ed. Durling, 4, pp. 38–39.

69. For an introductory survey see John Moorman, *A History of the Franciscan Order: From Its Origins to the Year 1517* (Oxford: Clarendon, 1968), pp. 123–39, 240–55, 365–68.

70. For this literature see ibid., pp. 266–72, 399–401; F. J. E. Raby, *A History of Christian-Latin Poetry from the Beginnings to the Close of the Middle Ages*, 2d ed. (Oxford: Clarendon, 1953), pp. 415–53.

71. Celano, *Vita II S. Franciscani* 2.90.127; trans. in *St. Francis of Assisi, Writings and Early Biographies: English Omnibus of the Sources for the Life of St. Francis*, ed. Marion A. Habig, 3d rev. ed. (Chicago: Franciscan Herald, 1973), p. 467.

72. *Legend of Perugia* 43; trans. ibid. 1021–22.

73. Petrarch, *Rime sparse*, ed. Durling, 141.5–6, p. 285. 325.99–100, pp. 512–13. 212.5–9, p. 367; 165.14, pp. 310–11.

74. Ibid. 48.11–13, pp. 114–15.

75. Ibid. 338.1, p. 535; 363.1, p. 573. 268.17, p. 437; 327.5–6, pp. 514–15. For this metaphor see also Fredi Chiappelli, "Le Thème de la Defectio solis dans le Canzoniere: *vario intus*," *Travaux de linguistique et de littérature*, 16 (1978), 75–84. 352.12–13, p. 549. 254.9, p. 417; 275.1–2, p. 455. 306.1–3, p. 484–85. 326.9–10, p. 515, 328.9–11, pp. 516–17. 24.9–11, p. 71.

76. Ibid. 334.3–4, p. 531. 327.12–14, pp. 514–15.

77. Petrarch, *Secretum* 2, ed. Martellotti, pp. 72–76.

78. Cicero, *Orator* 8–10.

79. Petrarch, *Secretum* 3, ed. Martellotti, p. 164; trans. Draper, p. 141. The citation is Vergil, *Aeneid* 4.69–73; trans. H. Rushton Fairclough in *Virgil*, rev. ed. (2 vols.; Cambridge, Mass.: Harvard University Press, 1974), 1:401.

80. Petrarch, *Rime sparse*, ed. Durling, 61.4–8, p. 139; 75.1–2, p. 175; 87.5–8, p. 191; 95.5–6, p. 199; 126.11, p. 245; 133.5, p. 271; 144.9–12, p. 291; 151.5–14, p. 297; 174.5–8, p. 321. For this conceit see John C. Nelson, *Renaissance Theory of Love: The Context of Giordano Bruno's Eroici furori* (New York: Columbia University Press, 1958), pp. 18, 25.

81. Petrarch, *Rime sparse*, ed. Durling, 270.76–79, pp. 448–49.

82. Ibid. 297.10–11, p. 477. 29.17, p. 83; 75.1–4, p. 175; 174.5–8, p. 321, 105.87, p. 213; 14.7, p. 49; 127.42, p. 251; 159.12, p. 305; 164.11, p. 311; 221.12–13, p. 377; 363.9, p. 573. 97.3–4, p. 201; 90.14, p. 193.

83. Ibid. 195.12–14, pp. 340–41.
84. Ibid. 2.5–8, p. 37; 73.86, p. 173; 87.5–8, p. 191; 61.8, p. 139, 126.11, p. 245; 195.8, p. 341. 195.7–8, p. 341; 199.6, p. 345, 342.4, p. 539; 196.4, p. 343, 296.13–14, p. 475; 296.3–4, p. 475. 87.5–8, p. 191. 29.34–35, p. 85.
85. Pliny, *Naturalis historia* 23.43.86; 23.80.152, 155, 157.
86. Petrarch, *Rime sparse,* ed. Durling, 6.12–14, pp. 40–41.
87. Ibid. 1.12–14, p. 37. 214.22–30, pp. 368–69; cf. 46.1–4, p. 113.
88. Petrarch, *Ep. fam.* 6.3.54, ed. Rossi, 2:73; trans. Bernardo, 1:308. For background see Gervais Dumeige, "Le Christ médecin dans la littérature chrétienne des premiers siècles," *Rivista di archeologia cristiana,* 48 (1972), 115–42.
89. See Henri Gregoire, *Asklèpios, Apollon Smintheus et Rudra: Etudes sur le dieu à la taupe et le dieu du rat dans la Grèce dans l'Inde* (Brussels: Bureau de la société, 1950).
90. Petrarch, *Rime sparse,* ed. Durling, 29.30–31, p. 85; 209.12, p. 363; 228.1–2, p. 385; cf. 88.6, p. 191.
91. Ibid. 241, pp. 402–3.
92. See Cyril Bailey, *Religion in Virgil* (Oxford: Clarendon, 1935), pp. 79–87.
93. Petrarch, *Ep. fam.* 11.17, ed. Rossi, 2: 366–67.
94. Petrarch, *Liber sine nomine* 17, ed. Piur, p. 226; trans. Norman P. Zacour, *Petrarch's Book Without a Name* (Toronto: Pontifical Institute of Mediaeval Studies, 1973), p. 106.
95. Ibid. 12, ed. Piur, p. 204; trans. Zacour, p. 78.
96. Petrarch, *Ep. met.* 1.2, 2.5, ed. Rossetti, 3:110–40.
97. Petrarch, *Rime sparse,* ed. Durling, 53.63–65, pp. 128–29. For a recent study see Anna Maria Voci, "Per l'interpretazione della canzone *Spirto gentil* di Francesco Petrarca," *Romanische Forschungen,* 91 (1979), 281–88.
98. Petrarch, *Rime sparse,* ed. Durling, 128, pp. 256–57.
99. For Scipio's father see the full citations n. 100. For the wounds of the slain Romans see Petrarch, *Africa* 1.368, 382, 556; 3.20–21; ed. Festa, pp. 19, 20, 26, 52; and the wounds of the enemy, 1.572, p. 27. For Lucretia: 3.732, 736, 741, 755, p. 81; 8.919–20, p. 253; for Massinissa: 5.120–21, p. 106; 5.470–71, p. 121. For the wounds inflicted by Hannibal's army see 4.183, p. 92; the massacre of Croton, 6.477–80, p. 152; Hannibal's memory of the slaughters, 6.532–46, pp. 154–55, 6.670–76, pp. 159–60; Mago's death, 6.886, p. 168; Hannibal's prediction that Scipio will vanquish without a wound, 7.237, p. 180; Juno beholding the forthcoming battle, 7.626, p. 195; Carthage's wounds, 7.526, p. 192, 7.1054, p. 212, 8.737, p. 247. Cf. also related imagery, 6.638–43, p. 158; 7.449, p. 188; 8.173, p. 224. For crucifixion see 8.793, p. 249; 8.1025–26, p. 257.
100. Ibid. 1.161–229, pp. 9–12; trans. Thomas G. Bergin and Alice S. Wilson, *Petrarch's Africa* (New Haven: Yale University Press, 1977), pp. 6–8.
101. Ibid. 1.10, p. 3; trans. Begin and Wilson, p. 1.
102. See chapter 1, nn. 97–99.
103. Petrarch, *Africa* 3. 20–21, ed. Festa, p. 52; trans. Bergin and Wilson, p. 42.

104. This particular parallel has also been noted by Bernardo, *Petrarch, Scipio and the "Africa": The Birth of Humanism's Dream* (Baltimore: Johns Hopkins University Press, 1962), p. 249 nn. 26–27.
105. Petrarch, *Rime sparse*, ed. Durling, 62, pp. 140–41. See chapter 1, p. 31.
106. Petrarch, *Africa* 3.87–264, ed. Festa, pp. 54–62. For studies of this description see Enrico Fenzi, "Di alcuni palazzi, cupole e planetari nella letteratura classica e medioevale e nell' 'Africa' del Petrarca," *Giornale storico della letteratura italiana*, 153 (1976), 12–59, 186–229; Ernest H. Wilkins, "Descriptions of Pagan Divinities from Petrarch to Chaucer," *Speculum*, 32 (1957), 511–19; Eberhard Leube, "Petrarca und die alten Götter: Zum Bild der antiken Mythologie in der *Africa* und im übrigen lateinischen Werk des Dichters," *Romanistisches Jahrbuch*, 11 (1960), 89–107; Festa, *Saggio sul "Africa" del Petrarca* (Palermo: Remo Sandrone, 1926), pp. 94–109; Jean Seznec, *The Survival of the Pagan Gods*, trans. Barbara F. Sessions (New York: Pantheon, 1953), pp. 17–79.
107. Petrarch, *Africa* 3.90–110, citing 101–5, ed. Festa, p. 55; trans. Bergin and Wilson, p. 45. Apollo himself is depicted with the conventional iconography of the solar steed, sacred lyre, bow and arrows, and the laurel, ibid. 3.156–73, ed. Festa, pp. 57–58.
108. See Léopold Pannier, *Les Lapidaires français du moyen âge des XIIe, XIIIe, et XIVe siècles* (Paris, 1882), pp. 52, 95–96, 134, and for its location in Africa, pp. 135, 163; *Le Lapidaire du quatorzieme siècle*, ed. Is. del Sotto (Vienna, 1862), pp. 3–4; Paul Studer and Joan Evans, *Anglo-Norman Lapidaries* (Paris: E. Champion, 1924), pp. 49, 175.
109. Jean de Meun, *Roman de la Rose* 19931–20026.
110. See George Ferguson, *Signs and Symbols in Christian Art* (Oxford: Oxford University Press, 1959), p. 22.
111. Petrarch, *Rime sparse*, ed. Durling, 3.1–3, 7–8, pp. 38–39.
112. Ibid. 16, pp. 50–51.
113. Dante, *Paradiso* 31.103–111; trans. Singleton, pp. 353–54.
114. Petrarch, *Ep. fam.* 9.13.34, ed. Rossi, 2:254. For the veil see Sixten Ringbom, *Icon to Narrative: The Rise of the Dramatic Close-Up in Fifteenth-Century Devotional Painting* (Turku, Finland: Åbo Akademi, 1965), pp. 23–24.
115. Petrarch, *Rime sparse*, ed. Durling, 264.1–14, pp. 426–27.
116. Ibid. 357.9–11, pp. 554–55.
117. Ibid. 358.5–7, pp. 554–55.
118. Petrarch, *Ep. fam.* 6.3.54, ed. Rossi, 2:73; trans. Bernardo, 1:308.
119. Cited in translation by Wilkins, *Life of Petrarch* (Chicago: University of Chicago Press, 1963), p. 77; but this translation is mine.
120. The most recent major study, which emphasizes the ecological basis, is Robert Gottfried, *The Black Death: Natural and Human Disaster in Medieval Europe* (New York: Free Press, 1983).
121. Francis A. Gasquet, *The Great Pestilence* (London, 1893), p. 37.
122. Anne-Marie Hayez, "Avignon au temps de Pétrarque," in *Actes du Congrès international Francesco Petrarca* [Avignon, 1974], p. 261.
123. Gasquet, *The Great Pestilence*, pp. 38–40.

124. Ibid., p. 28.

125. Petrarch, *Ep. met.* 1.14.7–10, ed. Rossetti, 2: 80; trans. Bergin, *Petrarch's Bucolicum Carmen* (New Haven: Yale University Press, 1974), p. 235. See also *Ep. fam.* 8.7, ed. Rossi, 2: 174–79; and for a survey, Renée Neu Watkins, "Petrarch and the Black Death: From Fear to Monuments," *Studies in the Renaissance*, 19 (1972), 196–223.

126. See Douie, *The Nature and the Effect of the Heresy of the Fraticelli* (Manchester: Manchester University Press, 1932), p. 172, noting the treatise of Jean d'Anneux, a Parisian doctor of theology who was in Avignon as chaplain to the cardinal of San Lorenzo.

127. See Moorman, *A History of the Franciscan Order*, p. 355.

128. See Gasquet, *The Great Pestilence*, pp. 40–41.

129. See Douie, *The Nature and the Effect of the Heresy of the Fraticelli*, pp. 19, 129.

130. See Moorman, *A History of the Franciscan Order*, pp. 205–15, 406–16.

131. *Regula Sanctae Clarae* 11–12, citation 11.7; trans. Regis J. Armstrong and Ignatius C. Brady in *Francis and Clare: The Complete Works* (New York: Paulist, 1982), p. 223.

132. Ibid. 5.11.

133. For these parishes see Hayez, "Avignon au temps de Pétrarque," pp. 259–62. Hayez, who is city archivist, accepts the common literal interpretation of Petrarch's reference as the "soeurs de Sainte-Claire dans l'église desquelles le poète vit Laure pour la première fois" (p. 262).

134. Celano, *Legenda Sanctae Clarae Virginis* 1.2; trans. Brady in *The Legend and Writings of Saint Clare of Assisi* (St. Bonaventure, N.Y.; Franciscan Institute, 1953), pp. 19–20.

135. Alexander IV, *Clara claris praeclara;* trans. Armstrong and Brady in *Francis and Clare: The Complete Works*, p. 169.

136. Karl Buresch, *Klaros: Untersuchungen zum Orakelwesen des späteren Altertums* (Leipzig, 1899; rpt., Aalen: Scientia, 1973); Louis Robert, "L'Oracle de Claros," in *La Civilisation grecque de l'antiquité à nos jours*, ed. Charles Delvoye and Georges Roux (2 vols.; Brussels: La Renaissance du livre, 1967), 1:305–12.

137. Bonaventure, *Legenda maior S. Francisci* 1.5–6; Celano, *Vita I S. Francisci* 94–95; Bonaventure, *Legenda maior* 13.3, 15.2; *Legenda minor S. Francisci* 6.2–3; *Itinerarium mentis in Deum* 7.3. For a biography that focuses on this theme see Stéphane-Joseph Piat, *Saint François d'Assise et la découverte du Christ pauvre et crucifié* (Paris: Editions franciscaines, 1968). For a collection of primary sources see *Le stimmate di santo Francesco dagli scritti del XIII e XIV secolo*, ed. Marino B. Barfucci (Arezzo: La Verna, 1975).

138. Petrarch, *De vita solitaria* 2.10, ed. Martellotti, p. 454; trans. Zeitlin, p. 219.

139. Bonaventure, *Legenda minor* 1.4; Celano, *Vita II* 10–11; Henri d'Avranches, *Legenda versificata* 12.53–55; Umberto da Casale, *Arbor vitae crucifixae Jesu* 5.3.

140. See Richard J. Kieckhefer, *Unquiet Souls: Fourteenth-Century Saints and*

Their Religious Milieu (Chicago: University of Chicago Press, 1984), pp. 89–121.

141. See Williell R. Thomson, "The Earliest Cardinal-Protectors of the Franciscan Order: A Study in Administrative History, 1210–1261," *Studies in Medieval and Renaissance History*, 9 (1972), 27–39; Robert Brentano, *Rome before Avignon: A Social History of Thirteenth-Century Rome* (New York: Basic, 1974), p. 180.

142. Livario Oliger, "B. Margherita Colonna," *Lateranum*, n.s., 1/2 (1935); Brentano, *Rome before Avignon*, pp. 174–79.

143. Bonaventure, *De perfectione vitae ad sorores* 6.2, cited in translation by Moorman, *A History of the Franciscan Order*, pp. 260–61. Cf. also Catherine of Siena: "Make his wounds your home," cited by Kieckhefer, *Unquiet Souls*, p. 109.

144. Celano, *Legenda Sanctae Clarae* 20–22; trans. Brady in *The Legend and Writings of Saint Clare of Assisi*, pp. 39–40, 41.

145. E.g., "Legenda versificata," "Gaudia S. Clarae Assisiensis seu vita eius versificata," in Celano, *Legenda Sanctae Clarae*.

146. Among the *cinque santi* in the transept of the lower church and also in the lower church in the Capella di San Martino. *Simone Martini: The Complete Works*, pl. 26.

147. Petrarch, *Liber sine nomine* 1, ed. Piur, pp. 165–66; 8, p. 193, 10, pp. 200–201, 11, p. 203, 16, p. 217, 19, p. 235; see also Gaetano Cipolla, "Labyrinthine Imagery in Petrarch," *Italica*, 54 (1977), 263–89; 8, p. 193, 15, p. 216; and Jacomino of Verona, "De Babilonia civitate infernali."

148. Petrarch, *Liber sine nomine* 17, ed. Piur, p. 221; trans. Zacour, pp. 99–100. See also *Ep. fam.* 6.1.21–22, ed. Rossi, 2:52.

149. Petrarch, *Liber sine nomine* 7, ed. Piur, pp. 191–93; trans. Zacour, pp. 64–66. For the addressee see Wilkins, "Petrarch and Cardinal Niccola Capocci," in *Studies in the Life and Works of Petrarch* (Cambridge, Mass.: Mediaeval Academy of America, 1955), pp. 186–92.

150. Petrarch, *Liber sine nomine* 12, ed. Piur, pp. 195–208; trans. Zacour, p. 78.

151. Ibid. 17, pp. 222–23; trans. p. 101.

152. See William H. Brownlee, "Ezekiel's Poetic Indictment of the Shepherds," *Harvard Theological Review*, 51 (1958), 191–203; and the commentaries of Zimmerli, Eichrodt, Wevers, and Cooke, ad loc.

153. See Lorenz Dürr, *Ursprung und Ausbau der israelitisch-jüdischen Heilandserwartung* (Berlin: C. A. Schwetschke, 1925), pp. 116–24.

154. Petrarch, *Bucolicum carmen* 6, 7, ed. Avena, pp. 119–31.

155. Petrarch, *Ep. fam.* 8.7.12–15, ed. Rossi, 2:176–77; trans. Bernardo, 1:417.

156. See G. Mollat, *The Popes at Avignon, 1305–1378*, trans. Janet Love (Edinburgh: Thomas Nelson & Sons, 1963), pp. 182–83; J. B. Christophe, *Histoire de la papauté pendant le XIV siècle* (3 vols.; Paris, 1853), 2:138–39, 141–43.

157. Gasquet, *The Great Pestilence*, p. 42.

158. Petrarch, *Ep. fam.* 7.18.7, ed. Rossi, 2:138; trans. Bernardo, 1: 385. 8.3.11, ed. 2:160; trans. 1: 399. 12.7.5–6, ed. 3:28–29; trans. 2:152–53.

159. Ibid. 13.7.4, ed. Rossi, 3: 80; trans. Bernardo, 2: 199. 13.12.5–7, ed. 3: 94; trans. 2: 214.

160. Petrarch, *Collatio laureationis,* ed. Godi, pp. 13–17.

161. See John E. Wrigley, "Réhabilitation de Clément VI: Sine nomine 13 et le Royaume de Naples," *Archives de l'histoire des papes,* 3 (1965), 127–38. See also Petrarch's biography of Semiramis in *De viris illustribus,* ed. Pierre de Nolhac, "Le 'De viris illustribus' de Pétrarque: Notice sur les manuscrits originaux suivie de fragments inédits," *Notes et extraits des manuscrits de la Bibliothèque Nationale,* 34/1 (1895), 119–21; her foundation of Babylon, *Ep. fam.* 21.8.11–12, ed. Rossi, 4: 64, and incestuous lust, 9.9.4, ed. 2:218.

162. Petrarch, *Liber sine nomine* 8, ed. Piur, p. 193. 10, ed. p. 199; trans. Zacour, pp. 67, 72; see also 10, ed. p. 197, 17, ed. p. 220. 13, ed. p. 209; trans. p. 83.

163. See Mollat, *The Popes at Avignon,* pp. 175–83.

164. Petrarch, *Ep. fam.* 5.1.2–3, ed. Rossi, 2:3; trans. Bernardo, 1:228.

165. Ibid. 5.3.8–16, ed. pp. 7–9; trans. p. 234.

166. Ibid. 6.5, ed. pp. 81–85; trans. pp. 318–23.

167. For a history of the interpretation of this pericope see Pierre Prigent, *Apocalypse 12: Histoire de l'exégèse* (Tübingen: J. C. B. Mohr, 1959), and for the woman, A. Y. Collins, *The Combat Myth in the Book of Revelation* (Missoula, Mont.: Scholars, 1976), pp. 101–16.

168. Petrarch, *Rime sparse,* ed. Durling, 366.1–6, 29, 31, 43–44, pp. 573–74, 575–76, 577–78. The imagery of light as dominating the first six stanzas has also been noted by Edward Williamson, "A Consideration of 'Vergine Bella,'" *Italica,* 29 (1952), 227, although he does not acknowledge its citation of Rev. 12:1. For other studies of this poem see Georg Rabuse, "Petrarcas Marienkanzone im Lichte der 'Santa Orazione' Dantes," in *Petrarca 1304–1374: Beiträge zu Werk und Wirkung,* ed. Fritz Schalk (Frankfurt: Vittorio Klostermann, 1975), pp. 243–54; Luigi Pietrobono, "'Vergine bella che di sol vestita,'" *Annali della cattedra petrarchesca,* 2 (1931), 135–62; Alfonso Bertoldi, "La canzone alla Vergine," in *Esempi di analisi letteraria,* ed. Ciro Trabalza et al. (2 vols.; Turin: G. B. Paravia, 1926), 1: 348–62, rpt. from *Rivista d'Italia,* 13 (1910), 521–38.

169. For the type see Millard Meiss, "The Madonna of Humility," *Art Bulletin,* 18 (1936), 435–64; H. W. van Os, *Marias Demut und Verherrlichung in der sienesischen Malerei 1300–1450* (The Hague: Staatsuitgeverij, 1969), pp. 75–142. For the fresco see *Simone Martini: Complete Edition,* pp. 47–48 and pl. 102, with *sinopia* drawings, pls. 104, 105; and François Enaud, "Les fresques de Simone Martini a Avignon et leurs restaurations," in *Simone Martini: Atti del convegno* (Siena, 27, 28, 29 marzo 1985), ed. Luciano Bellosi (Florence: Centro Di, 1988), pp. 217–20, and figs. 2 and 3 of before and after restoration, and also figs. 6–21. Restoration of the very badly damaged fresco was done in 1979–80, and it was moved to Avignon, Musée du Palais des Papes.

170. *Rime sparse* 30.1, p. 87, 34.12–14, p. 93, 160.9–10, p. 307, 337.7–8, p. 535.

171. *Africa* 7.23–24, ed. Festa, p. 199.

172. Ibid. 3.232–41, ed. Festa, p. 61.

173. See M. J. Vermaseren, *Corpus Cultus Cybelae Attidisque (CCCA)* (7 vols.; Leiden: E. J. Brill, 1977–89), vol. 5, pl. CXIX, no. 344. Cf. vol. 3, pl. CCXXXV, no. 378; pl. CCXXXIX, no. 384; pl. CCXLIV for examples from Italia-Latium.

174. Chapter 2, pp. 50–53.

175. For the tradition of a Martini portrait of Laura see Alessandro Bevilacqua, "Simone Martini, Petrarca e i ritratti de Laura e del poeta," *Bollettino del Museo Civico di Padova*, 68 (1979), 107–50. The relevant poems are in *Rime sparse*, ed. Durling, 77, p. 177, and 78, p. 179. On these see also Giuseppe Mazzotta, "Antiquity and the New Arts in Petrarch," *Romanic Review*, 79 (1988), 36–40; Willi Hirdt, "Sul Sonetto del Petrarca *Per mirar Policleto a prova fiso*," in *Dal medioevo al Petrarca: Miscellanea di studi in onore di Vittore Branca* (2 vols.; Florence: Leo S. Olschki, 1983), 1: 435–47.

176. See chapter 1, n. 107. For an artistic example in which the Madonna's body merges with the laurel see the painting by Giovanni Agostino da Lodi (pseudo-Boccaccino), Madonna and Child with Donors, Naples, Muzeo Nazionale. Reproduced in Mirella Levi d'Ancona, *The Garden of the Renaissance: Botanical Symbolism in Italian Painting* (Florence: L. S. Olschki, 1977), p. 202 fig. 76.

177. For numerous examples of this attribution see the concordance to *Rime sparse*, s.v.

178. *Rime sparse*, ed. Durling, 363–65, pp. 573–75. For his literature of personal repentance see Marino Sasali, "Petrarca 'penitenziale': Dai *Salmi* alle *Rime*," *Lettere italiane*, 20 (1968), 366–82.

179. Petrarch, *Ep. fam.* 16.5.2, ed. Rossi, 3:187; trans. Bernardo, 2:302.

180. Petrarch, *Rime sparse*, ed. Durling, 80, pp. 181–83.

181. Ibid. 81, pp. 184–85.

182. Ibid. 366.46–52, pp. 578–79.

183. For a theological critique of the inadequacies of Augustine's aesthetics with which this author is in essential agreement see Robert J. O'Connell, *Art and the Christian Intelligence in St. Augustine* (Cambridge, Mass.: Harvard University Press, 1978).

184. Consider also the ascription to Petrarch of a "humanistic mind intent on showing that Mount Parnassus and Mount Calvary are not *necessarily* contradictory. At the summit of each is something too beautifully human and too beautifully divine to be mutually exclusive. And this something is the power of creativity for which Man is crowned with a crown of laurel and God with a crown of thorns. This explains Petrarch's near-obsession with Good Friday and Christ's Passion which remain so inextricably bound with his very existence." Bernardo, *Petrarch, Laura, and the Triumphs* (Albany: State University of New York Press, 1974), p. 194.

185. See chapter 2, nn. 76–79.

EPILOGUE

1. Letter of Luigi Marsili to Guido del Pelagio, cited by Marjorie Reeves, *The Influence of Prophecy in the Later Middle Ages: A Study of Joachimism* (Oxford: Clarendon, 1969), pp. 253–54.

2. Petrarch, *Rime sparse*, ed. Durling, 166.1–2, pp. 312–13. See Lucan, *Bellum civile* 5.82–85. It should be noted that Petrarch's "Letter to the Florentines expressing gratitude for the restitution, or better, the gift of his estate," in response to the redemption of his ancestral land at public expense and a summons for the poet to return to that city is dated "the sixth of April." *Ep. fam.* 11.5, ed. Rossi, 2: 331–35. *Rime sparse* 166 implies that Florence did not have its poet or its prophet in Dante, although Dante did anticipate certain aspects of his role and poetics. For this issue see Robert E. Lerner, "Petrarch's Coolness toward Dante: A Conflict of Humanisms," in *Intellectuals and Writers in Fourteenth-Century Europe, The J. A. W. Bennett Memorial Lectures, Perugia, 1984*, ed. Piero Boitano and Anna Torti (Tübingen: Gunter Narr; Cambridge: D. S. Brewer, 1986), pp. 204–25; Giuliano Tanturli, "Il desprezzo per Dante dal Petrarca al Bruni," *Rinascimento*, 25 (1985), 199–219; Nancy J. Vickers, "Re-membering Dante: Petrarch's 'Chiare, fresche et dolci acque,'" *Modern Language Notes*, 96 (1981), 1–11; Aldo S. Bernardo, "Petrarch's Attitude toward Dante," *Publications of the Modern Language Association*, 70 (1955), 488–517.

3. Johannes Wolf, *Lectionum memorabilium et reconditarum centenarii XVI* (Laving, 1600), 2:889ff., cited by Reeves, *The Influence of Prophecy*, pp. 488–89 n. 11. In his own lifetime Petrarch acknowledged the title of "theologian," as applied to him by Francesco Bruni in *Ep. sen.* 1.6, in *Operum*, 1:745. Cited by Paul Oskar Kristeller, "Petrarcas Stellung in der Geschichte der Gelehrsamkeit," in *Italien und die Romania in Humanismus und Renaissance*, ed. Klaus W. Hempfer and Enrico Straub (Wiesbaden: Franz Steiner, 1983), p. 105.

4. For absolute certitude as the epistemological basis of Luther's rejection of allegorical method in theology see Boyle "The Chimera and the Spirit: Luther's Grammar of the Will," in *The Martin Luther Quincentennial*, ed. Gerhard Dünnhaupt (Detroit: Wayne State University Press for *Michigan Germanic Studies*, 1985), pp. 17–31, and my *Rhetoric and Reform: Erasmus' Civil Dispute with Luther* (Cambridge, Mass.; Harvard University Press, 1983), pp. 47–56. For Luther's criticism of the moralizers of Ovid see his *Enarratio in Genesin* 30:9, in *Werke*, 43, 668.

5. Jacob Burckhardt, *The Civilization of the Renaissance in Italy* (New York: Modern Library, 1954), p. 219; cf. Georg Voigt, *Die Wiederbelebung des classischen Alterthums* (Berlin, 1859). See Werner Handschin, *Francisco Petrarca als Gestalt der Historiographie* (Basel: Helbing & Lichtenhang, 1964), pp. 170–71.

6. Thus Ronald Witt, "Coluccio Salutati and the Conception of the *Poeta Theologus* in the Fourteenth Century," *Renaissance Quarterly*, 30 (1977), 539, 542–43, 544. His notion of theology as expressing "truths accessible to natural reason" (539) is contrary to Christian tradition; that is the function of philosophy, not theology.

7. Petrarch, *Ep. sen.* 14.7, in *Operum,* 2:1038–39.

8. For studies emphasizing the influence of Augustine on Petrarch see especially Evelyne Luciani, *Les Confessions de saint Augustin dans les lettres de Pétrarque* (Paris: Etudes augustiniennes, 1982); Nicolae Iliescu, Il canzoniere petrarchesco e sant'Agostino (Rome: Società accademica romana, 1962); Pietro P. Gerosa, *Umanesimo cristiano del Petrarca: Influenza agostiniana, attinenza medievali* (Turin: Bottega d'Erasmo, 1966).

9. Ernest H. Wilkins, "Petrarch's Ecclesiastical Career," in *Studies in the Life and Works of Petrarch* (Cambridge, Mass.: Mediaeval Academy of America, 1955), pp. 3–32.

10. For a contrary argument that Petrarch's literature exhibits strong monastic elements see Giles Constable, "Petrarch and Monasticism," in *Francesco Petrarca: Citizen of the World* (Washington, D.C.; n.p., 1980), pp. 53–99. To the texts discussed there should be added a consideration of the "Collatio" attributed to St. Francis of Assisi, *Archivum Franciscanum Historicum,* 7 (1904), 527–29. It has since been "probably" attributed to Petrarch by Cajetan Esser in his critical edition of Francis of Assisi, *Opuscula,* p. 37. See also Giuseppe Mazzotta, "Humanism and Monastic Spirituality in Petrarch," *Stanford Literary Review,* 5 (1988), 57–74.

11. Erasmus, *Epistolae* 2771.78–84. *Paraclesis,* ed. Holborn, pp. 145, 142. Cf. *Epistolae* 858.559–61. See my *Erasmus on Language and Method in Theology* (Toronto: University of Toronto Press, 1977), pp. 129–30.

12. See chapter 3, n. 96.

13. Petrarch, *Ep. fam.* 13.6, 13.7, ed. Rossi, 3:71–79, 79–84; *De remediis utriusque fortune* 1.44, in *Operum,* 1: 55–57, and see also the annotated edition of this dialogue by Conrad Rawski, *Petrarch: Four Dialogues for Scholars* (Cleveland: Western Reserve University Press, 1967), pp. 46–54, 145–59.

14. Petrarch, *Ep. fam.* 5.17.8, ed. Rossi, 2:39–40.

15. Petrarch, *Liber sine nomine* 4, ed. Piur, p. 183; trans. Norman P. Zacour, *Petrarch's Book without a Name* (Toronto: Pontifical Institute of Mediaeval Studies, 1973), p. 56.

16. Petrarch, *Rime sparse,* ed. Durling, 239.29–30, pp. 400–401.

17. Ibid. 325.108, pp. 512–13.

18. Petrarch, *Ep. fam.* 3.22.1, ed. Rossi, 1: 149.

19. Ibid. 11.8.10, ed. Rossi, 2: 342; trans. Bernardo, *Rerum familiarum libri I–VIII* (Albany: State University of New York Press, 1975); *Letters on Familiar Matters: Rerum familiarum libri IX–XVI* (Baltimore: Johns Hopkins University Press, 1982), 2: 103.

20. Ibid. 14.2.6, ed. Rossi, 3:107; trans. 2:227.

21. Petrarch, *Rime sparse,* ed. Durling, 7.5–11, p. 43.

22. Ibid. 1.9–10, pp. 36–37. See also 292.14, p. 471; cf. Job 30:31.

23. Ibid. 105.1–4, 16–17, 46–48, pp. 208–9, 210–11. See also F. J. Jones, "An Analysis of Petrarch's Eleventh *Canzone:* 'Mai non vo' più cantar com'io soleva,'" *Italian Studies,* 41 (1986), 24–44. He interprets this of Laura, not the Church, although he argues her birth date as the feast of the Chair of St. Peter (February 22). The Chair was Rome!

24. *Rime sparse,* ed. Durling, "Poems Excluded from the *Rime sparse,*" 8.11, pp. 592–93; cf. 14.14, p. 49.

25. See my *Erasmus on Language and Method in Theology* and *Christening Pagan Mysteries: Erasmus in Pursuit of Wisdom* (Toronto: University of Toronto Press, 1981), pp. 15–25.

26. See chapter 1, n. 57; chapter 2, n. 135.

27. Petrarch, *Ep. fam.* 21.10.8–15, ed. Rossi, 4:75–77. For this argument see Gerosa, *Umanesimo cristiano del Petrarca,* pp. 278–316.

28. Petrarch, *Ep. sen.* 1.5, in *Operum,* 2: 818–19.

29. See n. 23.

Primary Sources

PETRARCH'S WORKS

Operum. Basel, 1554. 3 vols. Rpt. Ridgewood, N.J.: Gregg, 1965.
Africa. Ed. Nicola Festa. Edizione nazionale, vol. 1. Florence: G. C. Sansoni, 1926.
Il Bucolicum carmen e i suoi commenti inediti. Ed. Antonio Avena. Padua: Società cooperativa tipografica, 1906.
[Bucolicum carmen]. *Laurea occidens: Bucolicum carmen X.* Ed. Guido Martellotti. Rome: Storia e letteratura, 1968.
Il Codice Vaticano Lat. 3196: Autografo del Petrarca. Vatican City: Biblioteca Apostolica Vaticana, 1941.
"La 'Collatio laureationis' del Petrarca." Ed. Carlo Godi. *Italia medioevale e umanistica,* 13 (1970), 1–27.
Il "De otio religioso" di Francesco Petrarca. Ed. Giuseppe Rotondi. Vatican City: Biblioteca Apostolica Vaticana, 1958.
De secreto conflictu mearum curarum [*Secretum*]. In *Prose,* pp. 22–214.
De sui ipsius et multorum ignorantia liber. In *Prose,* pp. 710–66.
"Le 'De viris illustribus' de Pétrarque: Notice sur les manuscrits originaux suivie de fragments inédits." Ed. Pierre de Nolhac. *Notes et extraits des manuscrits de la Bibliothèque Nationale,* 34/1 (1895), 61–148.
De vita solitaria. In *Prose,* pp. 286–590.
Epistolae familiares: Le familiari. Ed. V. Rossi and U. Bosco. Edizione nazionale, vols. 10–13. Florence: Sansoni, 1933–42.
Epistolae metricae. In *Poesie minori del Petrarca.* Ed. Domenico Rossetti. 3 vols. Milan, 1829–34. Vols. 2–3.
Epistolae variae. In *Lettere di Francesco Petrarca.* Ed. Guiseppe Fracassetti. 5 vols. Florence, 1863–67. Vol. 5, 203–490.
Invective contra medicum. Ed. Pier Giorgio Ricci. Rome: Storia e letteratura, 1950.
"L'Itinerarium del Petrarca." Ed. Giacomo Lumbroso. *Atti della Reale Accademia dei Lincei,* 4th ser. *Rendiconti,* 4 (1888), 390–403. = Lumbroso, *Memorie italiane del buon tempo antico,* pp. 16–49. Turin, 1889.
Liber sine nomine. Petrarcas "Buche ohne Namen" und die papstliche Kurie: Ein Beitrag zur Geistesgeschichte der Frührenaissance. Ed. Paul Piur. Halle: Max Niemeyer, 1925.
Posteritati. In *Prose,* pp. 2–18.

Prose. Ed. G. Martellotti et al. Milan: Ricciardi, 1955.
Rerum memorandarum liber. Ed. Giuseppe Billanovich. Edizione nazionale, vol. 5. Florence: G. C. Sansoni, 1945.
[*Rime sparse*]. *Petrarch's Lyric Poems: The Rime sparse and Other Lyrics.* Ed. Robert M. Durling. Cambridge, Mass.: Harvard University Press, 1976.
[*Rime sparse*]. *Canzoniere.* Ed. Gianfranco Contini. Turin: Einaudi, 1964.
[*Trionfi*]. In *Rime, trionfi e poesie latine.* Ed. F. Neri et al., pp. 481–578. Milan: R. Ricciardi, 1951.

OTHER WORKS

Abelard, Peter. *Hymnarius Paraclitensis.* Ed. Joseph Szövérffy. 2 vols. Albany, N.Y.: Classical Folia, 1975.
Alain de Lille. *De planctu naturae.* Ed. Nicolaus M. Häring. *Studi Medievali,* 3d ser., 19/2 (1978), 797–879.
Ambrose. *Hymni.* In *Early Latin Hymns.* Ed. A. S. Walpole, pp. 16–114. Cambridge: Cambridge University Press, 1922.
Archilochus. *Fragments.* Ed. François Lasserre. Paris: Belles lettres, 1958.
Aristides. *Opera.* Ed. William Dinsdorff. 3 vols. Leipzig, 1829. Rpt. Hildesheim: Georg Olms, 1964.
Aristotle. *Ars rhetorica.* Ed. W. D. Ross. Oxford: Clarendon, 1959.
———. *Metaphysica.* Ed. Werner Jaeger. Oxford: Clarendon, 1957.
———. *Poetica.* Ed. D. W. Lucas. Rev. ed. Oxford: Clarendon, 1972.
———. *Problemata.* In *Opera.* Ed. Immanuel Bekker. 11 vols. Oxford, 1837.
Arnulf of Orleans. *Allegoriae super Ovidii Metamorphosin.* In "Arnolfo d'Orleans: Un cultore di Ovidio nel secolo XII." Ed. Fausto Ghisalberti. *Memorie del Reale Istituto Lombardo di Scienze et Lettere, classe di lettere, scienze morali e storiche,* 24 (1932), 157–234.
Athenagoras. *Legatio and De resurrectione.* Ed. William R. Schoedel. Oxford: Clarendon, 1972.
Augustine. *Confessionum libri XIII.* Ed. Lucas Verheijen. Turnholt: Brepols, 1981.
———. *Contra Faustum Manichaeum.* In *Patrologia latina* 42, 209–518.
———. *De civitate Dei.* Ed. Bernard Dombart and Alphonse Kalb. 2 vols. Turnholt: Brepols, 1955.
———. *De doctrina christiana.* Ed. Joseph Martin. Turnholt: Brepols, 1962.
———. *Enarrationes in psalmos.* Ed. Eligius Dekkers and Iohannes Fraipont. 3 vols. Turnholt: Brepols, 1956.
———. *Retractationum libri II.* Ed. Almut Mutzenbecher. Turnholt: Brepols, 1984.
Avranches, Henri d'. *Legenda versificata.* In *Legendae S. Franciscani Assisiensis. Analecta Franciscana,* 10 (1941), 405–521.
Benjamin ben Jonah. *The Itinerary of Benjamin of Tudela.* [Hebrew text]. Ed. Marcus Adler. New York: Philipp Feldheim, 1907.

Bernardus Silvestris. *Cosmographia.* Ed. Peter Dronke. Leiden: E. J. Brill, 1978.
Bersuire, Pierre. *Opera omnia.* 3 vols. Moguntiae, 1609.
Boccaccio, Giovanni. *Genealogiae deorum gentilium liber XIV.* Ed. Jeremiah Reedy. Toronto: Pontifical Institute of Mediaeval Studies, 1978.
———. *Opere latine minore.* Ed. Aldo F. Massera. Bari: G. Laterza, 1928.
Bonaventure. *Opera omnia.* 11 vols. Quaracchi: Collegium S. Bonaventurae, 1882–1902.
———. *Legenda maior S. Francisci.* In *Legendae S. Francisci Assisiensis. Analecta Franciscana,* 10 (1941), 555–678.
Casale, Umberto da. *Arbor vitae crucifixae Jesu.* Venice, 1485. Rpt. Turin: Bottega d'Erasmo, 1961.
Celano, Thomas de. *Legenda Sanctae Clarae Virginis.* Ed. Francesco Pennachi. Assisi: Metastasio, 1910.
———. *Vita I S. Francisci. Vita II S. Francisci.* In *Legendae S. Francisci Assisiensis. Analecta Franciscana,* 10 (1941), 1–260.
Cicero. *Academica.* Ed. James S. Reid. Rev. ed. London, 1885.
———. *De divinatione.* In *De divinatione, De fato, Timaeus.* Ed. Remo Giomini. Leipzig: B. G. Teubner, 1975.
———. *De inventione.* In *De inventione, De optimo genere oratorum, Topica.* Ed. H. M. Hubbell. Cambridge, Mass.: Harvard University Press, 1949.
———. *De oratore.* Ed. Augustus S. Wilkins. In his *Rhetorica,* vol. 1. Oxford: Clarendon, 1902.
———. *Pro A. Licinio Archia poeta.* In *Ausgewaehlte Werke.* Ed. Karl Halm. 2 vols. Berlin, 1856. Vol. 1, 179–206.
Clara claris praeclara. In *Bullarium Franciscanum Romanorum Pontificum.* Ed. J. H. Sbarabeae et al. 7 vols. Rome, 1759–1914. Vol. 2, 81–84.
Clement of Alexandria. *Protrepticus and Paedagogus.* Ed. Otto Stählin. Berlin: Akademie, 1972.
Curtius Rufus, Quintus. *Historiarum Alexandri Magni Macedonis libri quae supersunt.* Ed. Theodore Vogel. Leipzig, 1893.
Dante Alighieri. *La Commedia secondo l'antica vulgata.* Ed. Giorgio Petrocchi. 4 vols. Milan: Mondadori, 1966–68.
———. *Epistolae.* In *Opere minore.* Vol. 2, pp. 323–469. Ed. Angelo Jacomuzzi. Turin: Unione Tipografico, 1962–.
Diodorus Siculus. *Bibliotheca historica.* Ed. Immanuel Bekker et al. 5 vols. Stuttgart: B. G. Teubner, 1964.
Ennius. *The Tragedies of Ennius: The Fragments.* Ed. H. D. Jocelyn. Cambridge: Cambridge University Press, 1969.
Erasmus, Desiderius. *Ausgewählte Werke.* Ed. Hajo Holborn with Annemarie Holborn. Munich: C. H. Beck, 1964.
———. *Epistolae.* Ed. P. S. Allen et al. 12 vols. Oxford: Clarendon, 1906–58.
Euripides. *Tragoediae.* Ed. August Nauck. 3 vols. 3d ed. Leipzig, 1869–81.
Francis of Assisi. *Opuscula.* Ed. Cajetan Esser. Rome: Collegium S. Bonaventurae ad Claras Aquas, 1978.

Gaudia S. Clarae Assisiensis seu vita eius versificata. Ed. Livario Oliger. In Archivum Franciscanum Historicum, 12 (1919), 110–31.
Gellius, Aulus. Noctes Atticae. Ed. P. K. Marshall. 2 vols. Oxford: Clarendon, 1968.
Gower, John. Confessio Amantis. Ed. G. C. Macaulay. 2 vols. Oxford: Oxford University Press, 1900–1901.
Gregory the Great. Dialogorum libri quatuor de miraculis patrum italicorum. Ed. Adalbert de Vogue. 3 vols. Paris: Cerf, 1978–80.
Herodotus. Historiae. Ed. Carolus Hude. Oxford: Clarendon, 1908.
Homer. Opera. Ed. David B. Monro and Thomas W. Allen. 4 vols. 2d and 3d eds. Oxford: Clarendon, 1919–20.
Horace. Horace on Poetry: The Ars Poetica. Ed. C. O. Brink. Cambridge: Cambridge University Press, 1971.
———. Opera. Ed. Edward C. Wickham and H. W. Garrod. 2d ed. Oxford: Clarendon, 1912.
———. Carmina. Ed. Lucianus Mueller. Leipzig, 1881.
Isidore of Seville. Etymologiarum [libri]. Ed. W. M. Lindsay. 2 vols. Oxford: Clarendon, 1911.
Jacomino of Verona. "De Babilonia civitate infernali." In Documents inédits pour servir à l'histoire littéraire de l'Italie. Ed. F. A. Ozanam. Paris, 1850.
Jacopone di Benedetti da Todi. Laude. Ed. Franco Mancini. Rome: Guis. Laterza, 1974.
Jerome. Commentariorum in Amos prophetam libri tres. In Opera, Pars exegetica, vol. 1/6. Ed. M. Adriaen. Turnholt: Brepols, 1969.
Joachim of Fiore. Concordia Novi ac Veteris Testamenti. Venice, 1519. Rpt. Frankfurt: Minerva, 1964.
———. De septem sigillis. Ed. Marjorie Reeves and Beatrice Hirsch-Reich. In "The Seven Seals in the Writings of Joachim of Fiore." Recherches de théologie ancienne et médiévale, 21 (1954), 231–47.
———. Vat. Lat. 3822. Ed. Jeanne Bignami-Odier. In "Notes sur deux manuscrits de la Bibliothèque du Vatican, contenant des traités inédits de Joachim de Fiore." Mélanges d'archéologie et de la histoire, 54 (1937), 211–41.
John Chrysostom. In epistolam ad Corinthos 1, homiliae. In Patrologiae, cursus completus, series graeca. Ed. J.-P. Migne. 164 vols. Paris, 1857–1912. Vol. 61, 9–610.
John of Garland. Integumenta Ovidii: Poematto inedito del secolo XIII. Ed. Fausto Ghisalberti. Messina: Giuseppe Principato, 1933.
Juvenal. Saturae. Ed. J. D. Duff. Cambridge: Cambridge University Press, 1925.
Lactantius. De ave phoenice. In Emanuele Rapisarda, Studii paleocristiani, pp. 91–103. Catania: Centro studi sull'antico cristianesmo, università, 1970.
———. De ira Dei. Ed. Christiane Ingremeau. Paris: Cerf, 1982.
———. Divinarum institutionum libri. In Patrologiae, cursus completus, series latina. Ed. J.-P. Migne. 221 vols. Paris, 1879–90. Vol. 6, 111–822.
Legenda versificata [sanctae Clarae]. Ed. Benvenuto Bughetti. Archivum Franciscanum Historicum, 5 (1912), 237–60, 459–81, 621–31.

Lucan. *Belli civilis libri decem.* Ed. A. E. Housman. Oxford: Basil Blackwell, 1927.
Luther, Martin. *Werke.* 58 vols. Weimar: H. Böhlau. Rpt. Graz: Akademische, 1964–.
Macrobius. *Opera.* Ed. Francis Eyssenhardt. Leipzig, 1893.
Martini, Simone. *Simone Martini: Complete Edition.* Ed. Andrew Martindale. Oxford: Phaidon, 1988.
Meun, Jean de, and Guillaume de Lorris. *Roman de la rose.* Ed. Ernest Langlois. 5 vols. Paris: Firmin-Didot, 1914–24.
Milton, John. *The Works of John Milton.* Ed. Frank A. Patterson et al. 18 vols. New York: Columbia University Press, 1931–38. Vol. 1/1: *The Minor Poems.*
Mussato, Albertino. *Opera.* Venice, 1630. Rpt. in Jo. Georg. Graevius, *Thesaurus Antiquitarum et Historiarum Italiae,* vol. 6/2, cols. 34–62. Leiden, 1722.
Origen. *Contra Celsum.* Ed. Marcel Borret. 5 vols. Paris: Cerf, 1967–76.
Ovid. *Metamorphoses.* Ed. O. Korn and H. J. Muller. 2 vols. in 1. Berlin: Weidmann, 1915–16.
Ovide moralisé. Ed. C. de Boer. 5 vols. Amsterdam: J. Muller, 1915–38.
Paulinus of Nola. *Carmina.* Ed. Wilhelm A. Hartel. Vienna, 1894.
Persius. *The Satires of A. Persius Flaccus.* Ed. John Conington. 3d ed. rev. Oxford, 1893.
Phaedrus. *Fabularum Aesopiarum* [libri]. In *Babrius and Phaedrus.* Ed. Ben E. Perry. Cambridge, Mass.: Harvard University Press, 1965.
Pico della Mirandola, Giovanni. *Opera omnia.* Ed. Eugenio Garin. 2 vols. Turin: Bottega d'Erasmo, 1970.
Plato. *Opera.* Ed. Ioannes Burnet. 5 vols. Oxford: Clarendon, 1900–1907.
Pliny. *Naturalis historia.* Ed. H. Rackham et al. 10 vols. Cambridge, Mass.: Harvard University Press, 1938–42.
Prudentius. *Carmina.* Ed. Maurice P. Cunningham. Turnholt: Brepols, 1966.
Quintilian. *Institutiones oratoriae.* Ed. M. Winterbottom. 4 vols. Oxford: Clarendon, 1970.
Regulae Sanctae Clarae. In *Seraphicae legislationis testus originales,* pp. 49–75. Quaracchi, 1897.
Rhetorica ad C. Herennium. Ed. Gualterio Calboli. Bologna: Ricardo Pàtron, 1969.
Sedulius. *Opera.* Ed. Johannes Huemer. Vienna, 1885.
Seneca. *Opera quae supersunt.* Ed. Friedrich Haase. 3 vols. in 2. Leipzig, 1852–53.
Servius. *In Vergilii carmina commentarii.* Ed. George Thilo and Hermann Hagen. Leipzig, 1881–87. Rpt. Hildesheim: G. Olms, 1961.
Speculum perfectionis. Ed. Paul Sabatier. Manchester: Manchester University Press, 1928.
Stobaeus. *Florilegium.* Ed. Curtius Wachsmuth and Otto Hense. 3 vols. Berlin, 1884–94.
Strabo. *Rerum geographicarum, libri XVII.* 2 vols. Oxford, 1807.

Suetonius. *De viris illustribus* and *De vita Caesarum*. In *Suetonius*. Ed. J. C. Rolfe. 2 vols. Cambridge, Mass.: Harvard University Press, 1913–14.
Suger, Abbot. *Abbot Suger on the Abbey Church of St.-Denis and Its Art Treasures*. Ed. and trans. Erwin Panofsky. 2d ed. by Gerda Panofsky-Soergel. Princeton: Princeton University Press, 1979.
Tatian. *Oratio ad Graecos*. Ed. Ioann. Carol. Theod. Otto. Wiesbaden, 1851. Rpt. Wiesbaden: Martin Sandig, 1969.
Theophilus of Antioch. *Ad Autolycum*. Ed. Robert M. Grant. Oxford: Clarendon, 1970.
Vergil. *Opera*. Ed. R. A. B. Mynors. Rev. ed. Oxford: Clarendon, 1972.
Walter of Chatillon. *Moralisch-satirische Gedichte Walters von Chatillon*. Ed. Karl Strecker. Heidelberg: Carl Winter, 1929.
Xenophon. *Opera omnia*. Ed. E. C. Marchant. 5 vols. Oxford: Clarendon, 1961–63.

Index of Petrarch's Works

Africa, 11–12, 22–23, 24, 25, 30–31, 32, 37, 38, 40, 58, 61, 62, 65, 71, 90, 101, 116, 131–34, 145–46, 150
Apologia contra calumnias, 78
Bucolicum carmen, 13–14, 26, 29, 57, 144
Collatio, 10
Collatio laureationis, 12–13, 23–24, 44, 51, 60, 101, 113, 146
De ignorantia, 33
De otio religioso, 40, 49, 62, 125
De remediis, 7, 154
De vita solitaria, 23, 34, 59, 63, 121, 125, 140
Epistola posteritati, 11–12, 51, 54
Epistolae familiares, 2, 11–12, 19–20, 27, 33, 34, 40, 41–42, 43, 48, 49, 50, 62, 71, 78–79, 84, 89, 90–91, 92, 95, 110, 118, 121, 125–26, 130, 131, 134, 137, 145, 146, 147, 151, 154, 155, 156
Epistolae metricae, 74, 77, 90, 131, 137
Epistolae seniles, 15, 18, 77, 154, 156
Epistolae variae, 71, 79, 126
Invective contra medicum, 33, 115, 126
Itinerarium Syriacum, 48
Liber sine nomine, 13, 79–80, 81, 82, 83, 84–85, 86–88, 92, 98, 131, 142–44, 146–47, 154–55
Rerum memorandarum liber, 39–40, 49, 51, 89
Rime sparse, 1–3, 5, 8–9, 17–18, 23, 31–32, 36–37, 54, 56–57, 58, 59–60, 61, 63–70, 71, 73, 77, 79, 80, 84, 85–86, 90, 91–93, 93–109, 113–18, 119–21, 122–23, 126, 127, 128, 129–30, 131, 133, 134, 135, 149–52, 153, 155–56
Secretum, 3, 15–17, 18–19, 24, 25, 39, 42, 62, 118, 129
Trionfi, 54, 90

Index of Names

Actaeon, 113, 116
Actium, 35
Aeneas, 31, 45, 47
Aesop, 96
Alain de Lille, 21, 22
Alberti, Leon Battista, 7
Ambrose, 13, 36, 71
Amos, 94, 95
Andrew of Hungary, 147, 148
Apollo, 23, 24, 25, 26–43, 44–46, 56, 58–59, 60, 61, 64, 65–66, 68, 69, 70, 74, 89, 90, 93, 111, 113, 114, 117, 121, 122, 129, 130, 133, 139–40, 150, 153, 155
Arator, 29
Archilochus, 55, 57
Aristotle, 5–6, 13, 14, 18, 55
Arnulf of Orleans, 32
Attis, 150
Augustine, 3–5, 10, 13, 14–15, 19, 25, 28, 33, 41, 49, 83, 84, 154
Augustinus, 3–5, 9–10, 15–17, 18–19, 23, 24, 25, 34, 39, 42, 66, 117, 118, 126, 129, 152, 154
Ausonius, 27
Avignon, 1, 11, 48, 54, 62, 75–77, 80–89, 92, 96–97, 108, 110, 131, 136–38, 139, 142–45, 147, 149, 150

Babel, 82, 99, 115
Babylon, 73, 74, 80, 81, 82, 83, 84–88, 92, 95, 103, 108, 125, 147, 152
Bacchus, 25
Balaam, 91
Beguins, 85, 88
Benedict, Saint, 27
Benedict XII (pope), 81–82
Bernard of Clairvaux, 135
Bersuire, Pierre, 33
Boccaccio, Giovanni, 48, 59
Bonaventure, 123–25, 141

Caesar Augustus, 25, 35, 45, 49, 80, 90, 122

Cambyses, 81
Capitoline, 11, 12, 18, 23, 42, 44, 60, 74, 113, 146
Carmenta, 62, 63
Cassandra, 24, 64
Charles IV (emperor), 78, 109–10, 111–12, 145
Cicero, 12, 20, 24, 39, 59, 90, 118, 129, 156
Cino da Pistoia, 67
Clare of Assisi, 126, 138–40, 141–42
Claros, 140
Clement VI (pope), 76, 77, 144, 145
Cola di Rienzo, 77–78, 79, 80, 110
Colonna, Giovanni, 136, 141
Colonna, Margherita, 141
Constantine, 35, 74
Cumae, 45, 46
Cybele, 61–62, 63, 150

Daniel, 94, 97
Dante, 2, 9, 20, 29–30, 47, 67, 80, 123, 135, 139, 153
Daphne, 27, 32, 33, 37, 56, 58–59, 60, 62, 93, 115, 117, 150, 155
Delos, 31, 45, 46
Delphi, 26, 27, 38–39, 40, 41, 70, 72, 114
Demosthenes, 118
Dido, 129
Dionigi da Borgo San Sepolcro, 33

Elijah, 121–22, 123–24, 127
Elisha, 123
Elysian Fields, 106, 111
Ennius, 22–23, 24, 71, 156
Erasmus, 156
Eurydice, 109, 111, 115
Evander, 62

Franceschino degli Alblizi, 67
Francis of Assisi, 36, 122–25, 126, 127–28, 140, 142, 154

Index of Names   215

Franciscans, 88, 118, 124, 127, 138–39, 154
Franciscus, 3, 15–17, 23, 24, 25, 34, 39, 71, 129

Gaea, 70
Gauthier (Gossouin) de Metz, 106
Gellius, Aulus, 65
Gherardo. *See* Petrarca, Gherardo
Ghibellines, 97
Giovannino of Mantua, 14
Gorgo, 65
Gower, John, 21, 22
Gregory XI (pope), 76–77
Gregory the Great, 27
Guelphs, 97

Hildegard of Bingen, 153
Homer, 23, 38, 71, 118, 156
Horace, 14, 17, 20, 21, 34, 35, 44, 45, 115

Innocent VI (pope), 76
Isaiah, 87
Isles of the Blessed, 106, 111
Italy, 75, 76, 77, 90, 131, 145

Jacopone da Todi, 77
Jean de Meun, 21, 22, 134
Jeremiah, 77, 81, 87, 88, 95
Jerome, 13, 36
Jerusalem, 102–3, 104
Jews, 8, 137
Joachim of Fiore, 72–73, 85, 92, 112, 153
Joanna of Naples (queen), 110, 145, 146–47, 149
John XXII (pope), 75, 138
John of Garland, 32
John of Salisbury, 47
Jupiter, 11, 21, 23, 25–26, 34, 45, 60, 69, 95, 101, 116
Juvenal, 13, 71

Lactantius, 27, 106, 114
Laura, 1, 53, 59, 61, 62, 63, 64, 65, 93, 94, 115, 122–23, 127, 128, 129, 137, 139, 145, 150, 151
Leah, 121
Lebanon, 106–7, 108, 115
Leonardo da Vinci, 6
Ludwig, 138
Luther, Martin, 5, 153

Macrobius, 31, 41, 54
Magna Mater. *See* Cybele

Mars, 8, 69, 155
Marsili, Luigi, 154
Martini, Simone, 51–53, 54, 72, 142, 149–50
Medusa, 65
Milton, John, 30
Monicus, 26
Monte Cassino, 27
Montrieux, 2
Moslems, 7, 81
Muses, 15, 23, 27–29, 31, 44, 70, 114, 122
Museus, 45
Mussato, Albertino, 14

Naples, 47, 48, 90–91, 147–49
Nebuchadnezzar, 81, 96, 97, 99, 100, 105, 108, 112
Nicholas of Cusa, 153
Nostradamus, 153

Olivi, Peter John, 85, 88
Origen, 26
Orpheus, 22, 109, 111, 114
Ovid, 9, 32, 46, 56, 58

Pacificus, Brother, 128
Parma, 76, 137
Parnassus, 12, 18, 23, 24, 25, 31, 42, 44
Paul, Saint, 48–49, 67, 71
Paulinus of Nola, 27–28, 32, 83
Peneus, 58, 59
Persius, 23, 41
Peter, Saint, 103, 104, 144, 155
Petrarca, Gherardo, 2, 13, 23, 26
Phaedrus, 96
Pico della Mirandola, Giovanni, 30
Pierre de Bauvais, 106
Plato, 20, 39, 40, 62–63, 66, 129, 156
Plautus, 20, 56
Plutarch, 40
Posidonius, 44
Propertius, 45
Prosper, 13
Prudentius, 13, 28–29
Pythagoras, 40
Pythia, 26, 38–39, 40, 70, 114
Python, 31, 32

Rachel, 121
Robert, Friar, 147
Robert of Naples (king), 11–12, 24, 42, 48, 53, 78, 110, 147, 148
Rome, 73, 74–75, 77–80, 83, 84, 86, 90, 91, 95, 104, 109–10, 111, 131–33, 135, 145

Index of Names

Scipio Africanus, 7, 11, 12, 37, 44, 65, 131–33, 138, 155
Sedulius, 13, 29, 122
Semiramis, 146–47
Seneca, 20, 93
Servius, 51–52, 53
Sibyls, 45, 49–50, 70, 90, 103
Silvestris, Bernardus, 21
Silvius, 26
Socrates, 40, 41, 66
Sophonisba, 37, 131
Suger, Abbot, 7
Syphax, 61, 133, 155

Tatian, 27
Tempe, 59, 70
Templars, 8, 75
Theodosius (emperor), 21, 38
Tibullus, 45
Tommaso da Messina, 41
Tyre, 97–98, 109, 111

Ubertino da Casale, 85, 138
Urban V (pope), 76, 77

Valla, Lorenzo, 6
Varro, 25, 46
Vatican, 35, 74–75, 134
Vaucluse, 76
Ventoux, Mont, 19–20, 41, 42
Venus, 21, 54, 65, 86
Vergil, 12, 25, 31, 44–53, 58, 59, 61, 72, 89, 95, 118, 122, 129, 131, 136, 150, 154, 156
Veronica, 134–35
Virgin Mary, 32, 33, 50, 149–50, 151–52
Visconti, 110, 111

Wolf, Johannes, 153

Zeus, 32, 35, 38, 137

Compositor:	Braun-Brumfield, Inc.
Text:	10/13 Bembo
Display:	Bembo
Printer:	Braun-Brumfield, Inc.
Binder:	Braun-Brumfield, Inc.